Raising Additional Resources in the States

R. K. BANSAL

ATLANTIC PUBLISHERS & DISTRIBUTORS
B-2, Vishal Enclave, Najafgarh Road,
New Delhi-110027

Published by

Atlantic Publishers & Distributors
B-2, Vishal Enclave, Najafgarh Road
New Delhi-110027
Phone : 5413460

Printed at : M.D.R. Printing Press through Chawla Composers
Hari Nagar, New Delhi

PREFACE

In developing countries where augmentation of domestic savings is a pre-requisite for rapid economic development, the fiscal policy in general and the tax policy in particular play a pivotal role. Mobilisation of domestic resources for economic progress implies the two-fold task of reinforcing the total supply of savings and channelling it into the desired form of investment. One of the fundamentals of planning in a developing economy is to devise a fiscal policy for the provision of infrastructure, public savings and investment. The extent to which such a policy can fulfil the growing needs of a developing economy depends basically on the ability of the government to impose taxes and the capacity of the tax structure to generate revenue with or without additional tax effort. A question often arises whether there is any scope for an increase in the level of taxation in the country or not. If not, what could be alternative sources for additional resource mobilisation. Further, how does the tax effort of a State compare with that of any other State in a federal country like India.

In the present study an attempt has been made to examine the scope of additional resource mobilisation in Punjab both from tax and non-tax sources. In particular, State lotteries as a source of non-tax revenue and their economic implication have been examined. The book has been divided into eight chapters. Chapter 1 briefly introduces the problem and unfolds the methodology. This chapter also presents a review of the main studies conducted in India and abroad in our chosen field. While inter-State tax effort on aggregate account is given in chapter 2, chapter 3 deals with an analysis of individual taxes. Chapter 4 examines the non-tax efforts of different States. Evolution and economic significance of State lotteries have been presented in chapter 5. Chapter 6 probes the economic impact of State lotteries. The characteristics and views of persons participating in

State lotteries are recorded in chapter 7. The concluding chapter 8 epitomises the study and enumerates the main findings.

Punjabi University
Patiala
1988

R.K. BANSAL

ACKNOWLEDGEMENTS

This book is a somewhat revised version of my doctoral dissertation entitled "Some Aspects of Raising Additional Resources in Punjab" accepted by the Punjabi University in 1987.

The research work was carried out under the supervision of Dr. H.K. Manmohan Singh, Professor Emeritus, Punjabi University, and Dr. J.R. Gupta, Reader, Department of Economics, Punjabi University, to whom I owe an overwhelming debt of gratitude. Without their guidance and constant encouragement, perhaps it would not have taken the form of a book so soon after its completion.

The production of this book has been subsidised out of the funds made available to the Department by the University Grants Commission under the Special Assistance Programme. I am naturally indebted to the Commission and to the Head of the Department, Professor Rajbans Kaur. Thanks are also due to my publishers, Atlantic Publishers and Distributors, for publishing this book in a record time.

I shall be failing in my duty if I do not express my hearty thanks to my wife, Rekha, whose supports and sacrifice meant a great deal to the successful completion of this book.

Punjabi University
Patiala

R.K. BANSAL

ACKNOWLEDGEMENTS

The book is essentially a revised version of my doctoral dissertation entitled "Some Aspects of Raising Additional Resources in Punjab", accepted by the Panjabi University in [illegible].

The research work was carried out under the supervision of Dr. [illegible] Mohan Lal Singh, Professor Emeritus, Panjabi University, and Dr. [illegible] Gupta, Reader, Department of Economics, Panjabi University, to whom I owe an overwhelming debt of gratitude. But for their guidance and constant encouragement [illegible] could not have taken the form of a book [illegible].

The publication of this book has been subsidised out of the funds made available to the Department by the University Grants Commission under the Special Assistance Programme. I am grateful to the Commission and to the Head of the Department, Professor [illegible]. Thanks are also due to my publishers, Ajanta Publishers and Distributors, for publishing this book in a nice volume.

Last but not the least, my duty [illegible] to express [illegible] whose encouragement and sacrifice [illegible] the successful completion of this book.

CONTENTS

1

INTRODUCTION

India being a federal country, the State governments have an exclusive Constitutional right over several sources of public revenue. In addition, the States receive funds from the Union Government as grants and also share some taxes levied by the latter. The financial dependence of the States on the Union Government has been on the increase in recent years. It is felt that the resources available to the States under present dispensation are not adequate for meeting their requirements. However, it is also felt that to a large extent, the financial problems of the States arise owing to lack of effort on their own part to raise additional resources.

In a federal setup, devolution of resources from the federal government to the States has become an issue of increasingly controversial nature at both academic and political levels. This necessarily means an increasing tendency for centralisation of resources. As fiscal autonomy of the federal units is of vital importance for harmonious growth of the federal economy, the criteria determining the overall resource devolution to the States become matters of great concern. On this account, the need for comparing the tax efforts of different States has been felt for quite some time.

It may not be out of context to mention here that the public expenditure has been soaring day by day. In the recent past, it has been suggested that public expenditure must be restrained and unproductive expenditure eliminated. Several economy measures were explored in order to cut down public expenditure. But they turned out to be politically infeasible. Hence, it becomes obvious that additional finances must be raised to cope with the mounting expenditure.

In such circumstances, taxes provide the best alternative. It appears that taxation in developing countries is low as compared to that in the developed countries. Not only the percentage of tax to national income is comparatively low in these countries but the yield of such taxes is also low. Therefore, governments do not get adequate revenue for carrying out bold programmes of development. The low tax yield of developing countries is to be ascribed largely to the very low level of income in these countries. The majority of the populalion is living at the subsistence level which can hardly be brought within the purview of direct taxes. The levels of consumption and expenditure are very low; consequently, the scope for indirect taxes is also very limited. Another reason for the low percentage of tax revenue is the presence of non-monetized sector. To levy taxes is easier in an economy with monetary or market transactions than in a barter economy. In the latter economy a large proportion of national income originates in the agriculture sector and the major portion of it is consumed by the producers themselves; and this limits the scope of commodity taxes.

Borrowings are another source for strengthening resources for economic development. But with the rising cost of living, the general public is left with little margin to save for lending to government. In any event, unless prices show a sign of stability, people would be loath to contribute to public borrowing because they apprehend that by the time the loan matures after 10 or 15 years, the value of the rupee might be greatly reduced. Moreover, those who have money and are the main beneficiaries of development cannot be taxed any more because directly or indirectly they influence the government administration. They can save and lend to government but do not do so because they need their savings for ploughing them back into their own industry and business.

In short, it seems that the government cannot raise any more resources through taxation or borrowing. At the same time, they cannot reduce even a part of their unproductive administrative expenditure. How should then the finances be raised for meeting the rising and unrestrainable public expenditure ? And, how can this be done without inconveniencing the people ? To the extent that the non-tax receipts can be augmented, the need for placing an additional burden of tax on the people can be obviated. In this regard, State lotteries provide a novel source to replenish the State coffers.

In the 1960's, faced with the problem of raising additional revenue for the Fourth Five Year Plan and for fulfilling the ever-growing normal expenditure needs, the State governments started running their own lotteries. The government of Kerala was the first to introduce lottery scheme in January 1968, followed by Punjab (July 1968) and Madras (August 1968).

In the present study an attempt has been made to examine the scope of additional resource mobilisation in Punjab both from tax and non-tax sources. In particular, State lotteries as a source of non-tax revenue and their economic implications have been examined. However, the specific objectives of the study are :

(i) to work out the untapped potential for mobilising additional resources in Punjab through the existing tax and non-tax structure;

(ii) to study the scope of imposing additional tax and non-tax levies;

(iii) to examine the role of State lotteries as a source of revenue;

(iv) to analyse the socio-economic background of persons participating in State lotteries; and

(v) to work out the incidence of State lotteries among different income groups.

REVIEW OF STUDIES

Problems of resource mobilisation in developing countries have received a great deal of attention in recent years in the context of world concern for accelerating the pace of their economic growth under conditions of stability. Much of the theoretical as well as applied work has been related to the task of constructing productive and equitable tax systems suited to the peculiar economic and social conditions prevailing in various developing countries. In working out a development plan or a stabilisation programme, a major question that always arises is—how much tax and non-tax revenues can a country reasonably expect to raise and what sources should be tapped ? Systematic inter-country or intra-country (*i.e.* inter-State) comparisons may be illuminating and a number of recent empirical studies may be helpful in identifying the ideal tax and non-tax structures. Some of these studies conducted in India and abroad have attempted to discover the underlying economic and other factors that may be said to account for differences in tax ratios and tax structures among developing countries. A second type of empirical studies carried out in India relates to analysis of tax effort of the Union Government *vis-a-vis* State Governments or of inter-State performance in this direction. Further, some researchers have also examined the possibility of exploiting new channels of resource mobilisation, neglected so far, like the State lotteries. In what follows an attempt is made to summarize the main findings of some of these studies.

STUDIES RELATING TO INTER-COUNTRY COMPARISON OF TAX EFFORT

In developing countries where augmentation of domestic savings is a pre-requisite for rapid economic development, fiscal policy in general and tax policy in particular play a very significant role. Mobilisation of domestic resources for economic development implies the twofold task of increasing the total supply of savings and directing it into the desired form of investment. One of the essential requirements for increasing the incremental savings ratio is to reduce the rate of growth of private consumption and this can be achieved by an appropriate tax structure and suitable tax rates. Thus, an increase in tax effort can greatly assist the development process and permit the government to avail itself of a rise in personal savings. The tax effort may be measured in terms of the ratio of tax revenue to the gross domestic product. It is to be noted that tax effort is only one of several factors that should be considered in making tax policy decisions.[1]

C.R. Thiagaraja Varma's study (1972) for the period 1960-68 covering 16 developing countries including India showed that, in spite of the increase in tax effort, the ratio of the government savings to current revenues declined in many countries, while in many others it remained stationary. He attributed this phenomenon to the fact that the government's current expenditure rose just as fast as current revenue.

Varma's study further revealed that, during the period

1960-68, the average tax effort of selected developing countries increased slightly from 16 per cent of gross domestic product to 18 per cent. Considering their own requirements as well as the high ratio of tax effort (25 to 35 per cent of GDP) in developed countries, this ratio was considered rather low.[2]

R.L. Srivastava's (1964) analysis for the year 1962-63, covering 14 countries (7 developed and 7 underdeveloped), indicated that the percentage share of taxes to national income was 25.3 for developed and 14.0 for underdeveloped countries. He attributed the low level of taxation in underdeveloped countries to the poor tax yields, largely due to low level of incomes. The majority of the population is living at the subsistence level which can hardly be brought within the purview of direct taxes. The scope for indirect taxes is also very limited because of the low level of consumption standards. Another reason which has been pointed out for the low percentage of tax yield in these countries is the presence of a larger non-monetized sector there than that in developed countries. It is easier to levy taxes in an economy with monetary or market transactions than in a barter economy, where it is difficult to assess the real income. In underdeveloped countries a large proportion of national income originates in the agriculture sector and the major portion of it is consumed by the producers themselves and does not pass through the market mechanism. It is naturally difficult to impose indirect tax on this part of consumption.[3]

J.R. Lotz and E.R. Morss (1967) discussed certain criteria by which tax effort could be measured and on the basis of these criteria, the authors ranked 72 selected countries (developed and developing and including India) taking 1963-65 average. They measured tax effort in terms of the ratio of tax revenue to gross national product. France had the highest tax ratio (37.7 per cent) while Afghanistan (5.9 per cent) was at the bottom. India, with a tax ratio of 12.5 per cent, occupied the 57th position. However, the authors cautioned about the limitations of this method which did not take into account certain economic and non-economic factors which might be especially important in evaluating the tax effort of particular countries.[4]

Lotz and Morss also attempted a linear regression analysis in order to estimate the relationship between tax/income ratio and per capita income—

$$\frac{T}{Y}=a_1+b_1\,Y_{p1}$$

where T=tax revenue,

Y=gross national product,

and Y_p=per capita income.

They compared the actual tax ratios with the estimated ones. The country whose actual tax ratio exceeded the estimated one by the largest percentage was given the highest tax effort rank and *vice versa.* This method placed Democratic Republic of Congo at the top while France was pushed to the sixth place. India got the 48th place. They further compared the performance of low income countries (whose per capita GNP was below US $800) with that of high income countries (whose per capita GNP was above US $800) during the study period (1963).[5]

However, the above method *i.e.* to judge the tax effort in terms of tax revenue as a proportion of GNP, has many limitations. Raja J. Chelliah has pointed out that the tax/GNP ratio does not indicate anything about the proportion of national output generated in the public sector *i.e.* the role of government as a producer. So it would be necessary to employ the ratio of value added in the public sector to total value added. Secondly, the tax/GNP ratio also does not take into consideration the role of the public sector as a final purchaser of goods and services. Further, while on the one hand, some part of the revenue is returned to the private sector in the form of transfer payments; on the other hand, real expenditure is often partly financed through borrowing. So the best measure is the ratio of net revenue (*i.e.* total revenue minus all government transfer payments) to GNP.[6]

Nevertheless, in order to study the trends in taxation, Chelliah too used the tax/GNP ratio. He compared the three years' averages of 1953-55 and 1966-68 for 27 developing countries India included. The tax ratio was found to have increased between the two periods in more than two-thirds of the countries in the sample while in some countries (like Ghana) the ratio actually declined. For the group as a whole, the average tax ratio increased from 11.3 per cent to 13.8 per cent and in India it mounted from 6.3 per cent to 15.1 per cent.[7]

Considering that the marginal tax rate gives a better idea of the proportion of additional national product that the government has been able to divert to the public sector, Chelliah found that whereas this ratio was as high as 25.6 per cent in Tunisia, it was as low as 7.5 per cent in Indonesia. For the entire sample, the average rate was 14.9 per cent and for India, 15.1 per cent. This means that the developing countries with a tax ratio of about 11 per cent in the early 1950's on an average, had taxed away about 15 per cent of the additional income.[8]

A simple comparison of marginal tax rates in different countries, however, is also not a very meaningful measure of the relative efforts made by different developing countries as no allowance is made for differences in the average rates in the base period. For this purpose income elasticity of tax revenue is a relatively satisfactory index. Income elasticity, on the one hand, shows the percentage change in taxes associated with a 1.0 per cent change in income; on the other hand, it expresses the ratio between the marginal tax rate and the tax ratio of the earlier period. Hence, a comparison of income elasticities shows both the variation in tax changes in relation to income changes, and the extent of difference between the marginal tax rate and the tax ratio in the base period. The average income elasticity of total taxes for a group as a whole was 1.4. There were five countries (*viz.* India, Korea, Morocco, Honduras and Paraguay) with income elasticity coefficient equal to or greater than 2. These were the countries where the marginal tax rates in relation to the average had been the highest for the base period. In other words, these were the countries which had done well to raise the tax ratios.[9]

In spite of the general rise in tax levels in developing countries, the average levels of taxation continue to be much below the developed, high-income countries. The average tax/GNP ratio in a group of 16 developed countries of Europe and North America amounted to 25 per cent whereas in developing countries it was 15 per cent of GNP.[10]

Roy, W. Bahl (1971) explained that the inter-country variance in the tax ratio (σ_t^2) may be partitioned into variations attributable to taxable capacity (σ_c^2) and to tax effort (σ_e^2) such that

$$\sigma_t^2 = \sigma_c^2 + \sigma_e^2$$

The above equation suggests two possible approaches to identifying the determinants of the inter-country tax variance. If the objective is to explain the variation in the tax ratio, a stochastic model, such as $T/Y=f(x_1, x_2, x_3 \ldots x_N, U)$ may be used. Here T/Y is the tax ratio, the x's are independent variables that are proxies for the determinants of taxable capacity and tax effort, and U is an error term. This may be termed as tax ratio approach. On the other hand, if the objective is to identify inter-country differences in tax effort, the x's in the above equation are to be defined to reflect only, and all, the variance in taxable capacity, and since

$$\sigma_t^2-\sigma_c^2=\sigma_e^2,$$

some expression of the residual (U) becomes a comparative measure of effort. This may be termed as 'tax effort approach'.[11]

Bahl revealed that if the specification of the model is correct, both approaches can be used for inter-country comparison. The tax effort approach, by permitting the calculation of a tax effort index *i.e.* the ratio of actual tax collections to estimated tax collections, makes explicitly inter-country comparisons possible. But it only states that a country's tax effort is comparatively high or low, and not whether it ought to be raised or lowered.[12]

The tax ratio approach could be addressed to the question as to why the level of taxation in a given country is relatively high or low. Significant regression coefficients would suggest that countries having a given set of economic and social characteristics are more likely to have a higher level of taxation than countries without these characteristics. Further, whereas the tax ratio treats tax yield simply as a function of income, tax effort may be defined as the extent to which a country makes use of its taxable capacity. In other words, tax effort is the ratio of actual tax collections to taxable capacity. In order to rank countries on the basis of tax effort, the tax ratio is assumed to be a function of two general factors, taxable capacity ($\bar{T}/Y$) and tax effort (E) *i.e.*

$$T/Y=f(\bar{T}/Y, E).$$

Since $\bar{T}/Y$ is the taxable capacity term and since the tax effort is defined as the extent to which taxable capacity is being used, the effort ratio in any given country may be defined as

$$E=(T/Y)/(\overline{T}/Y),$$

or $E_i=T_i/\overline{T}_i$.

Hence, the effort ratio for the ith country is the ratio of actual tax yield to the tax yield that is expected, given the tax base proxies of the ith country and the average practice of countries in the sample. Therefore, the first step in the statistical analysis is to estimate the taxable capacity of a country.[13]

The hypothesis tested by Bahl was that taxable capacity was a function of three major factors : (i) the stage of development, (ii) the sectoral composition of the income produced, and (iii) the size of the foreign trade sector. These factors were measured respectively by the agricultural share of income, the mining share of income and the export share of income. The simple correlation matrix showed that each of the three proxy variables, taken separately, was significantly related to the level of tax ratios. Further, while formulating a consolidated estimate of taxable capacity, Bahl combined these three factors into a single multiple regression equation for 49 developing countries, inclusive of India, taking the three years' average for the period 1966-68.

The statistical results were found to be consistent with the hypothesis developed above. Taxable capacity responded positively to higher mining share of income (and implicitly to higher export ratios) and negatively to higher agricultural shares. Bahl also ranked the countries on the basis of estimated taxable capacity and tax effort. Four countries (Zambia, Guyana, Zaire and Tunisia) which had relatively high levels of tax effort as well as taxable capacities had in common a heavy reliance on the mining sector. By comparison, certain countries, *viz.*, Trinidad, Tobago and Bolivia which had high taxable capacity and a relatively important mining share, chose to use this capacity at a much lower level than the international average. India was found to have a comparatively low taxable capacity but high tax effort.[14]

However, the stochastic approach, too, has a number of methodological problems that cannot be overcome completely. In general, this approach does not allow a desirable examination of the kinds of explicit relationships between particular taxes and particular economic structure variables, that would seem useful for purposes of making inter-country comparison of taxable capacity and tax effort.[15]

In view of the above limitations, Bahl developed the representative tax system approach, in which the taxable capacity is defined as the total tax amount that would be collected if each country applied an identical set of effective rates to the selected tax bases. This may be termed 'the yield of a representative tax system'. The first step in estimating taxable capacity with a representative tax system approach involves identification of the magnitude of actual tax bases. However, data limitations prohibit the use of actual tax bases. Therefore, an attempt may be made to use measures that reflect inter-country variations in the true bases. Necessarily, the choice of these proxies reflects some amount of subjective judgement. Naturally, the derived tax effort indices will vary, depending on the proxy bases chosen.[16]

Bahl explained that the second step in estimating taxable capacity with a representative tax system approach would require a set of representative rates. There are two possible ways of deriving a set of representative rates. The first is to hypothesize a rate structure strictly on *a priori* basis. Such an approach would require a decision as to how intensively each proxy base ought to be used. Bahl rejected this method because he intended to retain the positive content of this analysis. The other possibility for estimating a set of representative rates which Bahl adopted was simply to calculate the arithmetic mean for the countries in the sample. Specifically for each tax he computed the following ratio :[17]

$$r_i = \frac{\sum_{j=1}^{m} T_{ij}/B_{ij}}{m} \qquad i = 1, 2, \ldots\ldots$$

where r_i = representative tax rate for ith tax.

T_{ij} = actual collections of the ith tax in the jth country,

B_{ij} = value of the assumed base of the ith tax in the jth country, m = number of countries for which data on revenues for the ith tax are available.

Bahl calculated a set of representative rates simply by averaging the actual effective rates in the developing countries in the sample. This set of average rates was then applied to the corresponding tax base in each country, thereby generating estimates of the yield of a representative tax structure, *i.e.*, estimates of taxable capacity. The ratio of actual tax collection to this measure of taxable capacity is the corresponding measure of tax effort. Bahl calculated the representative tax rates for (a) personal income taxes, (b) corporate income taxes, (c) property taxes (including poll and personal taxes), (d) internal indirect taxes (sales, excise and other internal indirect taxes), (e) import taxes, and (f) export taxes. He estimated the tax effort for a set of 49 developing countries taking the three years' average for 1966-68.[18]

Bahl found that, on an average, developing countries extracted 2.35 per cent in personal income taxes and 6.34 per cent in internal indirect taxes from their non-agricultural income. In respect of these taxes, the countries like Brazil, Chad, Chile, India, Tunisia, Turkey, Upper Volta, Kenya and Korea were found to have a higher tax effort rate than the average. The average effective rate in the case of property tax comes out to be 1.32 per cent of the total income and the countries like Chad, Malaysia, Mali, Mexico, Singapore, and Tanzania were found to have a higher tax effort than the average. In terms of ranking, Mali had the highest tax effort index (1.4906) and Nepal the lowest (0.4455). India attained the fourth place and Brazil and Chad, the second and third places respectively.[19]

STUDIES RELATING TO TAX EFFORT IN INDIA

Before we come to the studies undertaken in India, it should be borne in mind that India has adopted a federal setup. There is a comprehensive enumeration of taxes in the Union and the State lists which are appended to the Constitution of India. Broadly speaking, taxes with an inter-State base are under the legislative jurisdiction of the Union Government while those with a restricted base are under the legislative jurisdiction of the State Governments. The residuary powers, if any, are vested in the Union Government. Thus, both the Union and the State Governments levy taxes and, consequently, the total tax revenue for India from direct as well as indirect taxes includes the yield from both the Union and the State taxes.

Moreover, in a developed economy, the governmental revenue is expected to increase automatically owing to buoyancy built into the tax structure by providing the requisite flexibility. Under normal circumstances, the increase in revenue thus attained should be reasonably sufficient to meet the expanding requirements of the government. Buoyancy can be built into the tax structure only when the economy reaches a certain stage of maturity. In the context of a developing country like India, particularly in its early stage of growth, the base and composition of the various sectors in the economy undergo both qualitative and quantitative changes, necessitating radical alterations in the scheme of taxation. New taxes have to be imposed and the coverage and rates of the existing ones altered. But, the process of change need not be carried on for ever.[20]

K.B.K. Rao (1972) observed that in the fifties and the early sixties the rationale for the changes in taxes had two aspects : one, to meet the changes of a growing and diversifying economy; two, and more importantly, to provide additional revenue to the government for financing plans and also for achieving other policy objectives. The innumerable tax changes that have been made, year after year, should be judged by the extent to which (a) they have helped to rationalise the system of taxation to make it revenue-elastic, and (b) the revenues so mobilised have been used to create productive, and socially beneficial public assets.[21]

Rao's findings revealed that governments' performance on these accounts was unfortunately not quite satisfactory. In spite of the numerous changes, the Indian tax structure did not acquire the requisite stability with revenue-elasticity. Rao cautioned that this did not imply that the tax system was not income-elastic. What he wanted to emphasize was the fact that while all manner of changes had been experimented with, the tax system had not been made as elastic as it could have been. This can be established even on *a priori* basis. If the income-tax were to be comprehensive so as to include incomes originating from all sectors, including agriculture, and if the excise taxation were based on the amount of all production or value added instead of being confined to specified commodities, the elasticities of the overall tax structure would have indeed been significantly greater.[22]

As regards the second objective of proper utilization of the additional resources mobilised, the situation is somewhat more disquieting. It is true that usually in the year of the additional levy the revenue goes into investment but in the following and subsequent years, the inexorably rising non-plan spending usurps a lion's share of it.[23]

With reference to the comparative reliance on tax and non-tax revenue, Varma observed that tax revenues formed a major part of the total revenue of the Union Government. In 1950-51, the percentage of tax revenue to the total revenue was 91.19. There was a change in the position in the subsequent years. The percentage of tax revenue to the total revenue was 79.79 in 1960-61 and 78.20 in 1971-72. Taking into account the revenues of both the Union and the State Governments, the percentage of total revenue to gross national product showed generally an upward trend. In 1950-51, the percentage of total tax revenue to the gross national product was 6.9, in 1960-61 it was 10.4, and in 1965-66 it rose to 14.0 per cent, However, in 1970-71, it fell to 11.8 per cent.[24]

Srivastava's analysis also showed that the total tax revenue of the Union and the States for the year 1961-62 was 10.5 per cent of the GNP, compared with 7.4 per cent in 1951-52. Thus, the tax revenue as a proportion of GNP grew at the rate of 0.35 per cent per annum during this period. On the other hand, the rates of annual increase in the per capita income and per capita taxation were 6.64 per cent and 1.61 per cent respectively. The above trend of tax revenue indicates the low degree of elasticity of Indian tax system. The elasticity of the taxes of the Union and the States taken together was found to be 0.833, *i.e.* 1 per cent rise in GNP brought about only 0.833 per cent increase in the Union and the State taxes as a whole. An efficient tax system ought to give a better result and with a view to achieving self-sustained growth and a progressive tax structure, this elasticity must be greater than unity.[25]

Srivastava further pointed out that the low percentage of tax revenue to GNP and also the low degree of elasticity were due to the existence of a large non-monetized sector, a considerable share of agriculture in the GNP, low per capita level of taxation, inefficient and corrupt administration, etc.[26]

M.M. Ansari's study (1984) showed that the ratio of tax revenue to GNP reached 18.5 per cent in 1980-81 and the overall tax revenue swelled at the annual average rate of 12.0 per cent over the period 1950-51 through 1980-81. The breakup of the growth rates over the different decades showed that the compound rate of increase in revenue was 15.0 per cent per annum during 1970-80 as against 12.7 per cent and 8.5 per cent during 1960-70 and 1950-60 respectively. Compared with this the GNP (at current prices) grew at the rate of 4.3 per cent, 10.0 per cent and 10.1 per cent in the respective periods. Thus, the increase in overall revenue displayed quite an impressive record of resource mobilisation efforts. A further decomposition of the revenue showed that the tax revenue increased at a marginally higher rate than the non-tax revenue. Moreover, within the tax source, the rate of growth of indirect taxes was much above the rate of direct taxes. A further split-up brought out that the overall revenue of the States grew at a higher rate than that of the Union.[27]

Although there is no doubt that the tax revenue mobilisation efforts have been commendable as compared to the rise in the GNP, yet the growth rates hide some significant characteristics of tax performance. First, the growth rates indicate nothing about the relative weights *i.e.* the extent of contribution of an individual tax in the aggregate tax revenue. Secondly, neither these results give an idea about the nature of tax bases that have been exploited up to the desirable extent nor they indicate the potential tax sources that may be utilized further for augmenting revenues, without unduly burdening the taxpayers.

It has often been said that the States are at a disadvantage *vis-a-vis* the Union in the distribution of tax powers. In support of this view, it is pointed out that the tax sources assigned to the States are inelastic whereas those assigned to the Union are elastic. But the analysis presented by Rao has revealed that Union taxes are no more elastic in relation to income than State taxes. But the Union Government has been able to improve its revenues to a much greater extent than the State Governments on account of its willingness to utilise its tax sources more intensively.[28]

K.B.K. Rao (1969) estimated the coefficient of elasticity between the net tax yield and GNP for the ten-year period

1956-57 to 1965-66. The coefficient for all the States worked out to 0.9127 and for the Union Government 0.9741. As both the coefficients were less than unity, tax revenues for the Union, as well as the States were, strictly speaking, income inelastic. Though the coefficient for the Union was a little higher, the difference was so small that it had no quantitative significance.[29]

While the responsiveness of Union and State tax sources to income changes was about the same, there might be a difference in the willingness of the Union and that of the States to exploit intensively all the tax sources available to them. Intensity of exploitation has been measured by estimating the 'buoyancy' of tax system. For the period 1950-51 to 1964-65, Rao found the coefficient of buoyancy for the Union to be 2.309 and for the States, 1.548. Clearly, the difference here is very marked. Thus, whatever the reasons, the States did not exploit their sources for tax revenues as diligently as the Union Government did.[30]

M.M. Jain (1969) also estimated the income elasticity of the Union and the State taxes for the period 1955-56 to 1965-66. His results confirmed the findings of Rao. However, he found that indirect taxes were more buoyant than direct ones.[31] It means that our additional tax efforts have mostly been confined to indirect taxes.

Tax-wise analysis showed that at the Union level, corporation tax was the most 'buoyant' (coefficient of buoyancy being 3.224), followed by Union excises and import duty with coefficients of 2.951 and 2.263 respectively. At the State level, the general sales tax with a buoyancy coefficient of 1.871 occupied a coveted place in fiscal armoury. Motor vehicles tax (2.047) and entertainment tax (1.977), though highly buoyant, contributed very insignificat amount to the State exchequer. Land revenue (0.552), agriculture income-tax (0.407) and State excises (0.719), though important in the fiscal system, were income inelastic in terms of buoyancy.[32]

Jain further tried to gauge the automatic increase in tax yields which might arise as a result of the interaction between built-in tax structure and changes in GNP. That is, he found out the response of tax revenues, at constant tax formulae (constant rate and coverage) to changes in GNP. His analysis for the period under review revealed a high degree of built-in flexibility, which, measured in terms of overall elasticity of the tax system, was 1.461, for the Union taxes 1.584 and for the State taxes 1.228.[33]

A tax-wise analysis done by Jain brought to light that the revenue from two important Union direct taxes, *viz.*, corporation tax and income-tax, when regressed with GNP, had coefficients of 2.721 and 0.792 respectively. But at the State level, the two important direct taxes, *viz.*, land revenue and agricultural income-tax, when related to agricultural income, had a considerably low elasticity. Among the Union direct taxes, Union excises (2.620) were the most elastic, followed by import duties (1.388). At the State level, the general sales tax was the most elastic (1.837) indirect tax.[34]

Ansari's study for the period 1960-61 to 1980-81 revealed that the overall revenue of the States rose at a higher rate than that of the Union. While for all the Union taxes, the elasticity coefficients were below unity, for the States' taxes these were mostly above unity. In other words, the regression coefficient exhibited that the States' taxes were duly elastic with respect to income.[35]

With a view to examining the impact of the Union taxes on the base for States' own tax collections, J.F. Patil estimated (a) the total amount of overall Union taxes (shareable as well as non-shareable) collected in a State, expressed as a percentage of the State's income, (b) the amount of shareable Union taxes collected in the State, expressed as a percentage of the State's income, and (c) the amount of shareable Union taxes actually received by the State, expressed as a percentage of the State's income. The first ratio shows the share of the Union taxes in the State's income reducing to that extent the base for the State's own taxation. The second ratio, that is, the level of shareable Union taxes, shows the maximum level to which the Union Government can share its tax revenue with the States, if Constitutional provisions remain unchanged. The third ratio shows how little is actually shared finally with the States. The third ratio also shows to what extent the States are actually compensated for the reduction in the base for their own taxation.[36]

J.F. Patil's analysis (1983), pertaining to the period 1961-62 through 1975-76 revealed that the growth rate of overall Union taxes (14.8 per cent) was less than the growth rates of shareable (15.37 per cent) and actually shared (16.37 per cent) Union taxes. The total tax revenue transferred to the States expressed as per cent of total collection of shareable Union taxation indicated a slowly rising tendency. In 1961-62, the Union Government transferred only 27.16 per cent of the total revenue from shareable taxes; the percentage having increased to 36.14 in 1971-72 showed a gradual decline thereafter.[37]

Per capita burden of shareable Union taxes for all the States was Rs. 14.83 in 1961-62 which rose to Rs. 80.77 in 1975-76. But the per capita share received from Union taxes by the States was Rs. 4.03 in 1961-62 which rose to Rs. 24.69 in 1975-76. Patil's analysis showed that the States contributed a large amount to the Union pool of shareable taxes but received back very little; so, there was a further scope to raise the share of the States.[38]

Lately, a controversy has been developing with regard to the fact whether India is one of the highest taxed countries or not. An answer to this question may throw some light on the prospects of resource mobilisation through additional taxes. Srivastava's analysis reflects that India compares well with the underdeveloped countries in respect of direct taxes. The average percentage of direct tax revenue to the total tax revenue in many other underdeveloped countries is slightly lower than that in India. However, this percentage is much lower here than in the case of any developed country where more than half of the tax revenue is obtained from direct taxes. One reason which seems quite pertinent for the low percentage of direct tax revenue is that a number of tax concessions and incentives have to be provided for capital formation in countries like India.[39]

Another related question that is often asked is whether the taxable capacity of the people has already been exceeded. N. Nagaraja's study (1965) explained that the yield in the case of some taxes was not showing any appreciable increase. But this trend could be well attributed to tax evasion and avoidance rather than to the fact that the limit of taxable capacity has been reached. One should not be afraid of reaching the limit of 25 per cent fixed by Colin Clark because taxable capacity is not a constant phenomenon. It must increase along with development. The attitude of the people is also a very important determinant of the taxable capacity. Efforts should be directed towards developing the right outlook and a sentiment of patriotism, which would certainly lead to lesser evasion on the part of tax-payers.[40]

Suresh Chandra Srivastava made a comparative study (1970)

of tax structures of different countries of the world and found that the rate of direct taxes in India was the highest. It is an oft-repeated public statement that India is not the highest taxed country. The argument which is generally advanced in support of this statement is that the tax effort in this country is only 12.5 per cent of GNP. According to Srivastava, this argument was misleading because about half of the population in India lived below the poverty line and as such they were outside the purview of direct taxes. Therefore, when the direct taxes were worked out on per capita basis, the figure got diluted. Further, because of political reasons, the agricultural income was not taxed and, therefore, the percentage of tax revenue to GNP got distorted. Srivastava also highlighted the phenomenon of large-scale tax evasion and tax avoidance. He asserted that India was the highest taxed country, particularly in respect of direct taxes.[41]

There is another aspect of the resource mobilisation problem *i.e.* the Union *versus* the States. The States argue that the heads of taxation left to them are hardly adequate to meet the expenditure responsibilities cast on them and so they want the Union Government to transfer more resources to them. The Union Government, on the other hand, feels that such an easy access to resources would tend to induce profligacy on the part of the States. It is generally said that States' tax powers were growth inelastic or less buoyant than the Union Government's, but, it is not true. There is a comprehensive enumeration of taxes in the Union and the State lists, appended to the Constitution. Functions allotted to the States are significant and call for massive investment because they constitute the basic infrastructure on which the general pace of development depends. Different States are at different levels of development. As a result, the individual problems of the States like resource mobilisation, resources needed for development, Union's transfer of resources to the States, differ. In a federal system of government, proper evaluation of the tax performance of the different federating units should be a useful fiscal exercise, especially for formulating suitable rational criteria for the transfer of resources from the Union to the States. A few studies have been conducted to compare the tax effort or tax performance of different States in India.

S. Chandrashekhar (1968) measured the inter-State disparities of tax burden in India for the period 1960-61 to 1965-66. He examined the tax burden both in per capita terms and in proportion to State income. Further, he grouped the States as agricultural and less agricultural on the basis of their income composition. During 1960-61, the per capita burden of State taxes was the highest in Bombay (Rs. 14.48) and the lowest (Rs. 4.91) in Orissa. It was also high in the States of West Bengal (Rs. 14.39), Punjab (Rs. 13.03) and Kerala (Rs. 12.22). In 1965-66, the per capita burden of State taxes was of the order of Rs. 25.77 in Bombay, the highest of all the States. Punjab and West Bengal, with a burden of Rs. 23.68 and Rs. 22.58, occupied the second and third positions respectively. The lowest burden again was in Orissa (Rs. 10.53). For agricultural States, he worked out the burden of land revenue and found that while in 1960-61 it was the highest in Rajasthan (Rs. 3.65), in 1965-66 Assam (Rs. 3.68) held the first place. However, in the most agricultural States, *viz.* Rajasthan, Uttar Pradesh and Punjab, the per capita burden diminished over the period. The increase was notable only in the case of Kerala, while in the other States it was nominal.[42]

S. Chandrasekhar's study (1968) also revealed that in 1960-61 per capita sales tax in Bombay was the highest. In West Bengal, Kerala, Madras, Andhra Pradesh and Punjab, too, it was considerably high. In 1965-66, again, Bombay topped with the per capita sales tax at Rs. 13.57. It is worthwhile to mention that per capita sales tax did not fall in any of the States. Madras, West Bengal, and Punjab continued to carry comparatively high tax burden.[43]

Chandrasekhar also found out the burden of State taxation in terms of the State incomes so as to examine the impact of growing incomes on taxation. State taxation as a proportion to State income was low in West Bengal, Punjab, Madhya Pradesh, Uttar Pradesh and Orissa both in 1960-61 and 1965-66. Further, where agriculture accounted for 50 per cent or more of the State income, the land revenue burden was generally rather high. Punjab and Orissa were, however, exceptions. Thus, in both these States there was a scope to enhance the land revenue burden. In the States, where commercial income amounted to 50 per cent or more of the State income, the sales tax burden was comparatively high, barring West Bengal.[44]

Chandrasekhar in another study (1968) analysed the composition of the State Governments revenue with a view to identifying the important sources. The study covered the period 1957-58 to 1963-64. He observed that while revenue from direct taxes, which virtually meant land revenue and agricultural income-tax, was on the decline in a majority of the States, grants-in-aid and other contributions made by the Union Government constituted the major part of non-tax revenue, and in most of the States it was on the rise as compared to the falling character of receipts from administrative and public enterprises.[45]

Although we generally appraise the tax performance of a government on the basis of tax-income ratio, yet such an approach is not a satisfactory index of the tax effort as it does not take into account other factors like distribution of income, sectoral composition of national output, patterns of governmental outlay, extent of urbanisation, degree of monetization, etc. which have a close bearing on taxable capacity. While it would be difficult to make statistical quantification of all the variables affecting the tax performance of governments, some of the major relevant variables, other than national and per capita income, such as degree of urbanisation, extent of incomes originating in the industrial sector, degree of openness of the economy, etc. are capable of quantification direct or through indirect methods. The choice of the relevant sets of variables would depend on whether one is doing inter-country or inter-State comparisons, subject, of course, to the general constraints of data availability.

K.V. Nambiar and M. Govinda Rao (1972) employed three methods, *viz.* regression analysis (simple and multiple), income elasticity and incremental rates, in order to study the tax effort of different states for the period 1961-62 through 1967-68. In the regression analysis, the dependent variable was the ratio of the States' own tax revenue to their Net State Domestic Product (NSDP). The per capita income, degree of urbanisation (as measured by the ratio of urban population to total population), share of non-agricultural income in NSDP, per capita developmental expenditure, were taken as the independent variables. Since the regression analysis did not give a full idea about the individual performance of the States over a period of time, income elasticity of State taxes and their incremental rates were also estimated.[46]

Elasticity was measured using the equation,

$$E=\frac{\Delta T}{T}\Big/\frac{\Delta Y}{Y}=\frac{\Delta T}{T}\ \frac{Y}{\Delta Y}$$

Where E stands for elasticity, ΔT and ΔY for changes in tax revenue and NSDP respectively and, T and Y for tax revenue and NSDP in the base period respectively. The term 'income elasticity', as used by them, was not in the sense of elasticity of a static function but as the ratio of the percentage change in revenue to the percentage change in NSDP over the period. Thus, it took into account the effects of both the changes in the rate structure and in the base structure on the productivity of taxes. The incremental rate is a more simple measure and relates change in tax revenue to change in NSDP $\left(\frac{\Delta T}{\Delta Y}\right)$.[47]

Nambiar and Rao then proceeded to rank the different States on the basis of elasticity and incremental ratios. The ranking on the basis of regression analysis indicated the gap between tax effort and the estimated tax potential. Thus, a high ranking in the regression analysis indicated that the particular State had been taxing very near to its potential. The States falling in this category were Kerala, Assam, Tamil Nadu, Andhra Pradesh, Rajasthan and Maharashtra. However, their ranking on the basis of elasticity and incremental ratios happened to differ. While Kerala, Tamil Nadu and Maharashtra maintained their high positions, which showed that their performance was of a high order. The States of Punjab, Mysore, Uttar Pradesh and Bihar on the basis of regression occupied the medium ranks. This implied that compared with the former group of States, there was much untaxed potential in these States. However, the rates of exploitation in Mysore and Punjab (as revealed by the elasticity and incremental ratios) were much higher than those of Uttar Pradesh and Bihar which obtained low rankings in terms of elasticity and incremental ratios.[48]

The Fifth Finance Commission took the initiative and attempted for the first time a measurement of the inter-State tax effort. To do so, the Commission related per capita tax collection to per capita income of a State. This measure, however, was rejected by K.N. Reddy (1975) for three reasons. First, this measure ignored the inter-State disparities in income distribution which would naturally affect the capacity of a State to raise taxes. Secondly, the structure of income (*i.e.* its inter-sectoral distribution) might differ from State to State and this, too, might affect the relative capacities of the States to raise taxes. Thirdly, there was implicit in this measure a normative judgement requiring the States to maintain a proportionate tax burden within their respective boundaries. Even when two States had similar income distribution as well as income structures, the State with higher per capita income should ordinarily be able to raise a higher proportionate tax than the State with lower per capita income.[49]

Reddy further stressed that apart from taxes there was a need to take into account non-tax revenue for the purpose of assessing a State's effort in raising additional revenues. To concentrate only on tax revenue, was not only to disregard the role of non-tax revenue in covering the expenditure of the State Governments but also to overlook the existence of wide variations among the States in regard to the importance of non-tax revenues. Non-tax revenues of the States taken together comprised as much as 29.69 per cent of their own resources for three years' average (1970-72). As between the States, the proportion varied from 17.25 per cent for West Bengal to 55.75 per cent for Jammu and Kashmir. Some of the underdeveloped States like Uttar Pradesh, Orissa, Madhya Pradesh and Jammu and Kashmir raised a higher proportion of revenues through non-tax sources than some of the relatively developed States like West Bengal, Gujarat, Andhra Pradesh and Punjab.[50]

Reddy applied the following indices of tax performance for three years' average (1970-72) :

(i) State's own tax revenue as per cent of the State's income (T/Y);

(ii) State's own tax and non-tax revenue as per cent of the State's income (R/Y);

(iii) State's own tax and non-tax revenue as per cent of the State's income net of direct taxes paid to the Union (R/Y_N).

He found that per capita tax as per cent of per capita income (T/Y) was the highest (6.23) for Tamil Nadu and the lowest (2.65) for Orissa. In this respect, Maharashtra (6.16) was at number two and Punjab (6.03) at number three. But, according to the second criterion *i.e.* per capita tax and non-tax revenue as per cent of per capita income, Karnataka (8.82) was at the top and Bihar (4.11) at the bottom. Tamil Nadu, Jammu and Kashmir, Maharashtra and Punjab with percentage shares of 8.62, 8.35, 8.17 and 8.09, occupied the second, third, fourth and fifth positions respectively. Ranking by the third criterion also yielded the same results.[51]

Reddy also calculated income elasticity of tax revenues and marginal tax rates to make an inter-State comparison of tax performance. Income elasticity of tax revenues referred to the ratio of percentage change in per capita total tax revenue to percentage change in per capita income. But marginal tax rates referred to the absolute change in total tax revenue divided by the absolute change in total income. The income elasticity of tax revenues between the periods 1962 through 1964 and 1970 through 1972 was the highest (2.75) in the case of Jammu and Kashmir and the lowest (0.72) in the case of West Bengal. Tamil Nadu with income elasticity of 2.53 stood at number two and Gujarat with elasticity of 2.10 occupied the third place. The marginal tax rate for the same period was the highest (11.12) for Tamil Nadu and the lowest (2.40) for Orissa.[52]

Reddy also used the multiple regression model to study the relative tax effort of States and applied the following least square model to estimate the regression coefficients:

$$Y_1 = a_1 + b_1X_1 + b_2X_2 + b_3X_3 + b_4X_4 + b_5X_5 + b_6X_6,$$

where Y is some variant of the tax performance mentioned earlier and X_1 is agricultural income, X_2 is share of non-agricultural income, X_3 is percentage of the people above subsistence level, X_4 is percentage of urban population, X_5 is per capita development expenditure and X_6 is degree of literacy. Comparing the estimated tax ratios with the actual tax ratios, he obtained the performance of the States. The State whose actual tax ratio was more than the estimated tax ratio was considered to be taxing rather near to its capacity.[53]

The statistical results of Reddy revealed that the above mentioned six factors together explained about 79 per cent of the variations in the tax effort of the States measured by T/Y, and

84 per cent of variations in the tax performance measured by R/Y and R/Y_N) The coefficient of multiple determination (R^2) was statistically significant. Urbanisation and level of services (developmental expenditure) were the two factors affecting the tax ratio. But Reddy cautioned that it should not be inferred from this that per capita income and the structure and distribution of income had very little influence on the tax effort. In fact, per capita income was the major factor influencing per capita tax revenue. The regression coefficient of income per capita was low because it was the same factor as entered into the dependent variable (as a denominator in the ratio).[54]

After comparing the actual tax ratios with the expected tax ratios, Reddy ranked the States and obtained startling results. Bihar, which all along had been considered a State with a large untapped tax potential and a State making the least tax effort emerged as one of the States raising more than the capacity. Some of the States which were otherwise raising more revenue than expected, had lower rankings when all the three criteria were taken together. These States were Karnataka, Gujarat and Andhra Pradesh. But Maharashtra, Punjab, Haryana and Kerala continued to rank high in tax effort. Rather interesting was the case of West Bengal. In spite of its industrialisation and high level of development, it ranked low insofar as the tax effort was concerned.[55]

Changes over time in tax revenues depend on factors affecting the taxable capacities and tax efforts of the States. M. Govinda Rao (1975) made an attempt to segregate the effect of these two forces, specifically, he tried to examine and quantify :[56]

(i) the effect of various economic factors—relating to both capacity and effort—on the changes in individual tax revenues as well as aggregate tax revenues of the States;
(ii) the effect of political factors, particularly the influence of ideological leanings of the parties in power and the impact of political stability considerations on the States' fiscal outcomes; and
(iii) the behaviour of the additional tax efforts put in by the States over various developmental plans.

Rao's study covered four States, *viz.*, Kerala, Mysore, Orissa and West Bengal. The choice of the States depended on the available and comparable data for a fairly long period; besides, the political history of these States made them suitable for a systematic study. While for Orissa and West Bengal the period covered was from 1951-52 to 1971-72, for Kerala and Mysore the period covered was from 1957-58 to 1971-72. As changes in per capita tax revenues of the States depended on changes in taxable capacity and/or efforts of the States, Rao experimented with a number of plausible capacity and effort variables. Since many of the explanatory variables generally follow a time trend, the problem of multicollinearity forced him to confine his analysis only to three capacity factors *i.e.* per cent of income from the primary sector, per capita income at constant (1961) prices, and working class consumer price indices in the States' capitals.[57]

While the explanatory variables mentioned above were expected to affect tax revenues of the States through their effect on the taxable capacities, there existed a host of other factors, which might plausibly affect the tax revenues through their effect on the tax efforts of the States. Rao considered the following factors falling in this category :

(i) per cent of previous years' budgetary deficit/surplus to States' expenditure in the previous year;
(ii) changes of the parties in power; and
(iii) developmental plans.

The effects of various developmental plans and changes of political parties in power were quantified by the dummy variable technique. The previous years' deficit/surplus as a percentage of the previous years' expenditure reflected the budgetary position of the States, depending on which the States were supposed to change their tax efforts in raising revenues. As ideological leanings of the parties in power determine the extent and nature of the States' activities and hence the tax revenue, a State should raise tax revenue from its own resources. The party with 'leftist' orientation is likely to raise higher tax revenues, and the parties oriented relatively towards the play of market forces are likely to put in comparatively low tax effort. The strategy of economic development through Five Year Plans and the consequent large public investments in various services place a direct demand for high tax efforts to be made by the States. Existence of matching provisions in the plan grants to the States induce them to increase tax efforts.[58]

The effect of various explanatory variables mentioned above was estimated by the multivariate least squares regression method. To determine the parameters, Reddy employed the double log regression model of the form—

$$\text{Log } Y = \text{Log } a + b_1 \text{ Log } X_1 + b_2 \text{ Log } X_2 + b_3 \text{ Log } X_3 + b_4 D + c_1 w_1 \ldots + c_j w_j + d_1 z_1 + \ldots + d_t z_t + U,$$

where Y = per capita tax revenue,

X_1 = per cent of primary sectoral income,

X_2 = per capita income at 1960-61 prices,

X_3 = consumer price index for the working class,

D = deficit variable,

w_1 to w_j = dummy variables representing the political parties in power; taking value one for observation in the 'j'th form of government and zero in others,

z_1 to z_t = dummy variables representing the plan period, taking value one for observation in 't'th plan and zero in others,

Log a, b_1 to b_4, c_1 to c_j, d_i to d_t = parameters to be estimated, and

'U' = stochastic error term.[59]

Rao's results showed that the increase in the tax revenues of the States seemed to have been caused mostly by increasing prices rather than expansion of the real tax base, expressed either through changes in per capita real incomes or through declining percentage share of primary sectors' income. The only exception was West Bengal where the elasticity of tax revenue with respect to per capita real income was found to have been greater than unity.[60]

Raja J. Chelliah and Narain Sinha (1983) also measured tax effort of the different States for the period 1973-76. The tax effort of a State was expressed as a relationship (ratio) between the actual amount of its tax collection and some measure of taxable capacity. Realising that taxable capacity and tax effort in absolute terms did not carry much sense, they converted their results into relative terms. Chelliah and Sinha cautioned that although many a time the ratio of the tax revenue to the total income of a State (tax ratio) is taken as an indicator of the relative tax effort, yet its use involved the implicit assumption that total income, irrespective of other circumstances, was the appropriate indicator of relative taxable capacity. However, the capacity to pay as well as to collect taxes is affected by the size of the population in relation to income, the capability of 'tax handles', the degree of monetization, etc. Therefore, actual tax ratios must be adjusted either for variations in these tax capacity factors or by estimating the amount of taxes that could be collected through the use of the potential bases available to the States. While in the former approach, the regression analysis is used to estimate or measure the influence of capacity factors on the tax ratio; in the latter approach, a model or a representative tax system is applied to potential bases to estimate the relative taxable capacity. Chelliah and Sinha applied the representative tax system to measure the tax efforts of different States for the period 1973 through 1976.[61]

The representative tax system method involves three major steps :

(i) For each tax, an appropriate base has to be identified; this should not be the actual base as recorded in the official tax statistics, but rather the potential base which may be taken to represent the relative taxable capacity;

(ii) A representative set of tax rates, which may be said to constitute the representative tax system, has to be generated. Chelliah and Sinha derived the representative rate for a tax as the average of the effective rates of that tax in different States, the effective rate in a State being computed as the ratio of the actual tax collections to the potential tax base; and

(iii) The average effective rate and the potential base of a tax are then multiplied to indicate the revenue which the concerned State could raise from that source if its potential was used to the average extent. The average effective rate of a tax can be derived in two ways. One way is to regress the revenue series on the chosen bases, the regression coefficient of the base being taken to represent the average effective rate. Alternatively, an arithmetic average—weighted or unweighted—of the effective rates of that tax in the several States may be worked out. Chelliah and Sinha adopted the second alternative.* Then they applied the set of average effective rates to the corresponding tax bases in a State so as to derive the yield of the representative tax structure in that State. This yield was then divided by the actual tax revenue and the resulting ratio was called 'index of tax effort.'[62]

Their results showed that only three States, *viz.* Punjab, Kerala and Haryana, had indices distinctly above the overall average and four States, *viz.* Tamil Nadu, Maharashtra, Gujarat and Andhra Pradesh, had indices just above the average. The tax performance of the rest of the seven States under study was below the average. The range of variation between the highest (Punjab) and the lowest (Bihar) indices was 24.0 per cent to −52.0 per cent. The results further revealed that the States with high indices of tax effort were those which had high indices of the use of potential for the general sales tax, state excise duty, stamp duty and registration fees, and the tax on passengers and goods. Thus, these taxes might enable the State Governments to exploit their taxable capacity adequately. They cautioned, however, that it did not mean that land revenue or agricultural taxation had no role to play in this direction. But, as the yield of the land revenue and agricultural income-tax was very low in comparison with that of the commercial taxes, a substantial rise in the rate

*In the prssent study, we, too, have applied this technique.

of land revenue would be required before it could make a significant contribution to the tax effort in a State.[63]

Autar S. Dhesi and B.S. Ghuman (1984) also used three methods *i.e.* income elasticity of tax revenue, marginal tax rate, and regression analysis to determine the tax performance of the Punjab State.[64] They used the following three ratios as indicators of the performance of Punjab in relation to other States:

(i) The State's own per capita tax revenue as per cent of States' own per capita income (T/Y).

(ii) The State's own total revenue (tax revenue plus non-tax revenue) as per cent of the State's income (R/Y).

(iii) The State's own total revenue as per cent of the State's per capita income net of taxes paid to the Union *i.e.* income-tax, corporation tax, union excise duty, estate duty, wealth and gift tax, etc. (R/Y_N).

They have taken per capita income, percentage share of non-agricultural sector in State income, percentage of urbanisation and percentage of literacy as the independent variables for regression analysis. The following linear regression equations were used to estimate the parameters :

$$Y_i = \alpha_{1i} + \beta_{1i} X_1 + \beta_{2i} X_2 + \beta_{3i} X_4 + U_i,$$

where $i = 1,2,3,$

$Y_1 =$ State tax as per cent of State income,

$Y_2 =$ total revenue of the State as per cent of State income,

$Y_3 =$ total revenue of the State as per cent of State income net of taxes paid to the Union,

$X_1 =$ per capita income,

$X_2 =$ percentage share of non-agriculture sectors in State income,

$X_3 =$ percentage of urbanisation,

$X_4 =$ percentage of literacy,

$U_i =$ error term.

Dhesi and Ghuman's results for the period 1967-69 to 1974-76 brought out that the independent variables (as mentioned above) taken together explained 58 per cent of the variations in the tax effort of the State measured by T/Y. Measured by R/Y, these variables showed 56 per cent of variations and measured by R/Y_N, 60 per cent. The degree of urbanisation, share of the non-agricultural sector in State's income, literacy and per capita income emerged as factors affecting taxable capacity in that order. To evaluate the performance of tax efforts of Punjab *vis-a-vis* other States, the ratios of actual tax-income ratio to estimated tax-income ratio were calculated. The State for which these ratios were the highest were regarded as taxing nearest to capacity. The respective positions of Punjab were 7th, 9th and 12th, corresponding to the three tax performance indices T/Y, R/Y, and R/Y_N.[65]

STUDIES RELATING TO STATE LOTTERIES

Hitherto, we have been discussing the various studies relating to tax efforts to raise additional resources. However, in view of the ever-increasing expenditure on development programmes, efforts are being made to exploit new channels of resource mobilisation. One such source is public borrowing which, in the opinion of V.M. Dandekar, has already reached the limit-point, so is taxation. As far as public expenditure is concerned, according to Dandekar (1970), it is not possible to reduce even a part of unproductive expenditure. How should then the finances be raised for meeting the mounting and unrestrainable public expenditure ? And, how could this be done without inconveniencing the people ? After much thought, the source of State lotteries, unexploited so far, became apparent.[66]

Kerala was the first State in India to use lottery for resource mobilisation in January 1968. Punjab became the second State to introduce State lottery in July 1968 followed by Tamil Nadu in August 1968.

In this country, the lottery scheme has assumed economic importance mainly for two reasons : first, it enables State Government to raise additional funds without introducing new taxes and secondly, it provides employment to many persons. In order to judge the merits and demerits of the lottery scheme,

Rukhan Singh, conducted an attitude survey in 1970 which revealed that the scheme was opposed by some sections of the people on two economic grounds. One, the scheme did not distinguish between the haves and the have-nots. It, thus, widened the gap between them, leading to an unequal distribution of income and wealth, which is against the spirit of our Constitution. Two, it amounted to voluntary taxation which was regressive in character because the proportion of low income group ticket-purchasers was very high compared with the high income group.[67]

The study conducted by G. Joag Shreekant and Subhash C. Mehta (1981) also brought to light that the lower income segments constituted most of the buyers of lottery while the middle, the high income and the affluent classes remained relatively secluded from it. The reasons why this was so could be found in the unsatisfied basic needs of the financially lower segments of the society. The economic situation and prospects in India being as they are, the lower income classes really have no hope of raising their standard of living substantially through savings or augmented income. Invariably, the members of these segments blindly believe in God and luck.[68]

A. Dutta's analysis (1972) also showed that State lotteries attracted the poor to a greater extent than the rich. Dazzled by the prospect of easy and sudden gains, the poor devoted their meagre savings and often a major portion of their income, with curtailment of daily necessities, to the purchase of lottery tickets.[69]

L.G. Bapat's study (1972) pointed out that the State Governments had actually failed to secure a large revenue from lotteries. In 1969-70, 12 States obtained Rs. 24.66 crores from lotteries and they spent Rs. 15.29 crores to obtain this gross revenue. Thus, out of every Rs. 100 paid by the people, only a sum of Rs. 38 was available to the States for utilisation. The cost of obtaining a net income of Rs. 38 was as high as Rs. 62. But in 1971-72, 15 States expected their gross receipts from the lotteries to be Rs. 36.18 crores and they intended to spend Rs. 31.76 crores for getting that revenue. It meant that in order to get a net revenue of Rs. 12, the States were spending more than seven times *i.e.* Rs. 88. While the people lost Rs. 100, the States got only Rs. 12.[70]

To study the degree of response of the public to the lottery scheme of Tamil Nadu Government, A.V. Rangachari conducted a survey in and around Chidambaram town in Tamil Nadu during 1972. His results brought out that out of the 221 respondents, 215 were males and 6 females. Two-thirds of them were married and one-third unmarried. When classified according to different age groups, it was observed that every third person was in the age group of 25 years to 55 years. One in three was in the age group of 15 years to 25 years and one in fourteen, in the age group of 55 years and above. This clearly indicated that aged people were not interested in the purchase of lottery tickets and that lottery was popular only among the middle age group.[71]

Rangachari tried to find out whether a large family was interested in making 'quick money'. His results revealed that nearly one-half of the respondents were from the medium households and a fourth from the large households. This confirmed the hypothesis that nearly eight out of every ten of the medium and large families were purchasing lottery tickets, while only a fifth of the smaller households were doing so. Response to lottery seemed to be positively correlated with levels of education. He found that 45 per cent of the purchasers had high/higher secondary school education and 33 per cent higher education. The results further showed that service class, professions and students constituted nearly 50 per cent of the purchasers.[72]

Rangachari's results further showed that the propensity to purchase a lottery ticket was high with the low income groups. The respondents belonging to low-income groups generally purchased a number of tickets in the hope of becoming rich. The number of lottery-tickets purchased decreased with increase in monthly income.[73]

Rangachari stressed that lottery was not a sound fiscal tool for raising revenue. It did not fulfil any sound maxim of taxation, *viz.* equity, economy and certainty. It was also regressive in nature. The lottery scheme, being voluntary, could not serve as a permanent source of revenue in spite of the initial rush for lottery tickets. Moreover, the lottery scheme could not be used to achieve social objective of reducing inequalities of income and wealth in the long run. The scheme involved the participation of poor people and poverty was pooled to make a few rich overnight while the rich continued to be rich. Even if a State Government utilised the net revenue from lotteries for providing welfare amenities in a planned way to the poor and the needy, it was still an inefficient fiscal tool to achieve this social objective.[74]

A study was conducted in 1976 by the Institute for Social and Economic Change, Bangalore, to assess the socio-economic implications of State lottery in Karnataka. The results showed that of the total number of individuals participating in the State lotteries, 55.2 per cent were in the per capita income group of below Rs. 1000 per annum. Another 26.4 per cent were in the income group of Rs. 1000-1500 and 13 per cent, in that of Rs. 1500-3000. Thus, 81.6 per cent of the households participating in State lotteries had an annual per capita income of Rs. 1500 or lower. Further, 73 per cent of them were illiterate or had not completed their high school education. Lottery to such people offered a one-time opportunity to change the life-style altogether. In spite of the small probability of winning, the value of the prize was so luring to this class that they bought lottery tickets even by cutting down their already minimal consumption needs.[75]

In terms of occupational groups, the results showed that the non-agricultural manual labourers and non-manual employees bore relatively high incidence of State lottery, especially in the urban area. The incidence seemed to be rather low on owner cultivators and on people engaged in professions.[76]

Shreekant and Mehta's study revealed that out of the total collection from State lotteries, about 25 per cent went into distribution costs by way of commission and bonus for distributors/dealers. About 10 per cent was spent on direct administrative expenses, 40 per cent was distributed as prizes (of which nearly 15 per cent went to the Union Government as income-tax). Thus, only 25 per cent of the gross collection was left with the State Government for any development expenditure.[77]

But a positive side of the lottery scheme appears to be the creation of employment opportunities to the unemployed masses and capital resources in the shape of prizes to the lucky and ambitious entrepreneurs. S.K. Biswas's study (1978) showed that more than 25,000 people of the Uttar Pradesh were directly or indirectly supporting their families through the lottery business. Hundreds of poor students had found new media of income by selling lottery tickets for pursuing their studies. The study also indicated that thousands of unknown persons had started business and industry of varied nature with the money acquired by winning lottery prizes. Even the small prizes had encouraged the poor labourers and economically handicapped persons to start a new life.[78]

Summing up, we may say that tax effort of a country may be measured by computing marginal tax rates, income elasticities, tax-income ratios, regression analysis and representative tax rates. But the technique of representative rates or average effective rates of a tax is considered superior to any other method. We have also applied the technique of representative rates. Almost all the studies have confirmed that there was a large range of variation in tax efforts among different countries and tax effort ratio for the developing or underdeveloped countries was invariably less than that of the developed countries. Similar variations in tax performances were observed in the case of different States in India. On the whole, tax performance of the Union and the State Governments was not quite satisfactory. Moreover, within the tax sources, the rate of growth of indirect taxes was higher than that of direct taxes. Tax-wise analysis showed that at the Union level, corporation tax, union excise duty and import duty were the most buoyant. But at the State level, sales tax, motor vehicles tax and entertainment tax were highly buoyant.

Almost all the studies relating to the State lottery scheme revealed that its incidence was regressive in character, notwithstanding the fact that the scheme provided some employment opportunities.

Technique of Analysis

The study has been based both on the primary and secondary data. To work out the scope of raising additional resources through existing and new tax and non-tax levies, the data have been culled from various issues of the *Reserve Bank of India Bulletin*, *Report of Currency and Finance*, *Statistical Abstract of Punjab* and State Budget of the Punjab Government. The data on State lotteries in Punjab regarding gross receipts, prizes, commission and bonus to agents, and other expenditure, have been gathered from the Directorate of Punjab State Lotteries. The State-wise figures on Net State Domestic Product were obtained from the Estimates of Net State Domestic Product as published by Central Statistical Organisation. Besides, the study has also made use of Census data.

To examine the economic implications of State lotteries, primary data from 250 selected households (140 participants[79] and 110 non-participants) were collected during April-June 1985. Wherever annual data were required these pertained to the year 1984-85. The methodology for the selection of households has been given in the relevant chapter *i.e.* Chapter VI.

The study covers a period of 16 years, 1967-68 through 1982-83[80] for secondary data. To study the shifts in the relative shares of various tax and non-tax sources in State's own revenue, we compared the three years' average of 1967-68 through 1969-70, 1973-74 through 1975-76 and 1979-80 through 1981-82. To analyse the relative growth of different sources of tax and non-tax revenues, compound growth rates were calculated by using the formula :

$$y = ab^t$$

where y is the revenue from a particular tax or non-tax source and t, the time period, a and b being constants. The growth rate is equal to (b-1).

With a view to examining the responsiveness of different tax and non-tax sources with respect to Net State Domestic Product, the buoyancy coefficients were worked out, using the equation :

$$y = ax^b \text{ or } \log y = \log a + b \log x$$

where y is the revenue from a tax or non-tax source, x the Net State Domestic Product and b the buoyancy coefficient, 'a' being a constant.

In order to study the scope of additional revenue mobilisation from different tax and non-tax sources, the existing effective rates in different States were compared with the representative rates based on certain assumptions (potential bases).[81]

Notes and References

1. Varma, C.R. Thiagaraja, "Taxation in Developing Countries", *Eastern Economist*, Vol. 58, No. 7, February 18, 1972, p. 267.
2. *Ibid.*, p. 267.

3. Srivastava, R.L., "Taxation in Underdeveloped Countries with Special Reference to India", *AICC Economic Review*, Vol. 16, No. 11, November 10, 1964, pp. 21-24.
4. Lotz, J.R. and Morss, E.R., "Measuring Tax Effort in Developing Countries", *IMF Staff Papers*, Vol. XIV, No. 3, November 1967, pp. 478-79.
5. *Ibid.*, p. 479.
6. Chelliah, Raja J., "Trends in Taxation in Developing Countries", *IMF Staff Papers*, Vol. XVIII, No. 2, 1971, pp. 257-58.
7. *Ibid.*, pp. 256-60.
8. *Ibid.*, p. 263.
9. *Ibid.*, p. 265.
10. *Ibid.*, p. 265.
11. Bahl Roy W., "A Regression Approach to Tax Effort and Tax Ratio Analysis", *IMF Staff Papers*, Vol. XVIII, No. 3, 1971, p. 571.
12. *Ibid.*, p. 572
13. *Ibid.*, p. 582.
14. *Ibid.*, pp. 593-97.
15. Bahl, Roy W., "A Representative Tax System Approach to Measuring Tax Effort in Developing Countries", *IMF Staff Papers*, Vol. XIX, No. 1, 1972, pp. 87-89.
16. *Ibid.*, pp. 88-89.
17. *Ibid.*, p. 90.
18. *Ibid.*, p. 92.
19. *Ibid.*, p. 105.
20. Rao, K.B.K., "Does the Indian Tax Policy Have a Rationale", *Margin*, Vol. 4, No. 3, April 1972, pp. 164-68.
21. *Ibid.*, pp. 164-68.
22. *Ibid.*, pp. 164-68.
23. *Ibid.*, pp, 164-68.
24. Varma, C.R. Thiagaraja, *op. cit.*, p. 268.
25. Srivastava, R.L., *op. cit.*, p. 22.
26. *Ibid.*, p. 22.
27. Ansari, M.M., "Resource Mobilisation through Taxation", *Yojana*, Vol. XXVIII, No. 16, September 16-30, 1984, pp. 8-12.
28. Rao, K.B.K., "Income Elasticity of Central and States Taxes", *Margin*, Vol. I, No. 3, April 1969, pp. 11-21,
29. *Ibid.*, pp. 11-21.
30. *Ibid.*, pp. 11-21.
31. Jain, M.M., "Income Elasticity of Indian Tax Structure 1955-56 to 1965-66", *Economic and Political Weekly*, Vol. IV, No. 18, May 3, 1969, pp. 769-71.
32. *Ibid.*, pp. 769-71.
33. *Ibid.*, pp. 769-71.
34. *Ibid.*, pp. 769-71.
35. Ansari, M.M., *op. cit.*, pp. 8-12.
36. Patil, J.F., "Central Taxation I—Level and Composition in States", *The Economic Times*, November 16, 1983, p. 5.

37. *Ibid.*, p. 5.
38. Patil, J.F., "Central Taxation II—Per Capita Revenue from Shared Taxes Received by States", *The Economic Times*, November 17, 1983, p. 5.
39. Srivastava, R.L., *op. cit.*, p. 22.
40. Nagaraja, N., "Tax Revenue in a Developing Economy", *AICC Economic Review*, Vol. XVI, No. 13-15, January 6, 1965, p. 139.
41. Srivastava, Suresh Chandra, "Is India the Highest Taxed Country in the World ?", *Capital*, Vol. 165, No. 4135, October 22, 1970, pp. 693-95.
42. Chandrasekhar, S., "Inter-State Disparities of Tax Incidence in India", *Economic and Political Weekly*, Vol. III, No. 22, June 1, 1968, pp. 845-49.
43. *Ibid.*, p. 846.
44. *Ibid.*, p. 847.
45. Chandrasekhar, S., "Tax Structure of State Government", *AICC Economic Review*, Vol. XX, No. 11, December 15, 1968, pp. 31-34.
46. Nambiar, K.V. and Rao, M. Govinda, "Tax Performance of States", *Economic and Political Weekly*, Vol. VII, No. 21, May 20, 1972, p. 1036.
47. *Ibid.*, p. 1037.
48. *Ibid.*, p. 1037.
49. Reddy, K.N., "Inter-State Tax Effort", *Economic and Political Weekly*, Vol. X, No. 50, December 13, 1975, pp. 1916-17.
50. *Ibid.*, p. 1918.
51. *Ibid.*, p. 1919.
52. *Ibid.*, p. 1921.
53. *Ibid.*, p. 1923.
54. *Ibid.*, p. 1923.
55. *Ibid.*, p. 1924.
56. Rao M. Govinda, "Economic and Political Determinants of States' Tax Revenue : A Case Study of Four States", *Economic and Political Weekly*, Vol. XIV, No. 47, November 24, 1979, p. 1925.
57. *Ibid.*, p. 1925.
58. *Ibid.*, p. 1927.
59. *Ibid.*, p. 1927.
60. *Ibid.*, p. 1932.
61. Chelliah Raja J. and Narain Sinha, *Measurement of Tax Effort of State Government 1973-76* (New Delhi, National Institute of Public Finance and Policy, 1983), p. 4.
62. *Ibid.*, pp. 8-9.
63. *Ibid.*, pp. 50-53
64. Dhesi, Autar S., and Ghuman, B.S., "Aspects of Financing State Plans (with Special Reference to Punjab)", *Margin*, Vol. 16, No. 3, April 1984, p. 33.
65. *Ibid.*, pp. 35-36.
66. Dandekar, V.M., "Government by Gambling", *Economic and Political Weekly*, Vol. V, Nos. 3, 4, 5 (Annual Number), January 1970, p. 83.
67. Singh, Rukhan, "A Case Study : What is the Response to the Lottery Scheme", *The Economic Times*, June 13, 1970, p. 5.

68. Shreekant G. Joag and Mehta, Subhash C., "Mismarketing of Dreams", *The Economic Times*, November 1, 1981, p. 4.
69. Dutta, A., "State Lotteries as Revenue Earners—An Analysis", *Yojana*, Vol. XVI, No. 2, February 6, 1972, pp. 119-21.
70. Bapat, L.G., "The Economics of State Lotteries", *Swarajya*, Vol. 16, No. 30, January 22, 1972, pp. 3-4.
71. Rangachari, A.V., "Economics of State Lotteries", *Southern Economic Review*, Vol. I, No. 4, June 1972, pp. 389-90.
72. *Ibid.*, p. 392.
73. *Ibid.*, p. 396.
74. *Ibid.*, p. 396.
75. Institute for Social and Economic Change, Bangalore, "Socio-Economic Impact of Removal of Prohibition, Socio-Economic Impact of State Lottery and Horse Racing in India", Mimeographed, February 1976, pp. 148-50.
76. *Ibid.*, p. 151.
77. Shreekant, G. Joag and Mehta, Subhash C., *op. cit.*, p. 4.
78. Biswas, S.K., "Lottery Scheme of Welfare Plans" *The Times of India*, July 12, 1978, p. 5.
79. A household whose any member ever purchased a State Lottery ticket was identified as participant.
80. However, in the case of certain States, *viz.* Himachal Pradesh, Manipur, Meghalaya, Nagaland and Tripura, data from 1967-68 through 1969-70 were not available.
81. Analyses of these potential bases and representative rates are given in the relevant chapters, Chapter II—Chapter IV.

2

INTER-STATE TAX EFFORT—AGGREGATE ANALYSIS

Different States in India are at different levels of development. Consequently, problems relating to resource mobilisation differ from State to State. It is generally felt that, to a large extent, the financial problems of the States arise from their lack of tax effort *i.e.* their failure to mobilise resources from sources within their own jurisdiction. One may not agree as to what constitutes a high or low tax effort in particular instances, but most would agree that inter-State comparisons are at least relevant, particularly in the context of fiscal transfers to the States under various Articles of the Constitution. The First Finance Commission was supposed to have taken note of tax effort of the States while recommending grants-in-aid under Article 275, but the Commission did not indicate the operational technique which it employed to measure the tax effort and the results it obtained from the use of that technique. The Second Finance Commission, too, conceded the importance of tax effort but avoided its measurement. The Third Finance Commission was relatively practical. It avoided measuring inter-State tax effort on the ground that its determination had to be related to the States' tax potential and, therefore, required special study. The Fourth Finance Commission also accepted the principle of considering how far the States had made efforts to raise resources in relation to their tax potential. Only the Fifth Finance Commission took the initiative and attempted for the first time, a measure of inter-State tax effort.[1]

In this chapter an attempt has been made to present an inter-State analysis of tax effort.

Table 2.1 explains the percentage share of States' own tax and non-tax revenue to total revenue. Considering the three years'

TABLE 2.1 : **Percentage Share of States' Own Tax and Non-tax Revenue to Total State Revenue**

State	*Three years' average of 1967-68 through 1969-70*	*Three years' average of 1973-74 through 1975-76*	*Three years' average of 1979-80 through 1981-82*
Andhra Pradesh	64.25	66.05	63.58
Assam	26.70	38.66	51.27
Bihar	54.67	49.63	39.46
Gujarat	69.05	70.47	71.73
Haryana	75.67	79.80	78.03
Himachal Pradesh	—	39.92	35.90
Jammu & Kashmir	30.55	41.20	44.16
Karnataka	66.73	75.99	71.77
Kerala	60.69	62.56	69.91
Madhya Pradesh	64.37	67.00	59.64
Maharashtra	74.47	77.04	77.65
Manipur	—	12.16	16.04
Meghalaya	—	14.93	20.21
Nagaland	—	9.70	22.34
Orissa	40.10	45.48	41.29
Punjab	79.59	77.03	79.22
Rajasthan	54.63	56.11	56.53
Tamil Nadu	69.68	74.03	67.27
Tripura	—	12.74	19.63
Uttar Pradesh	60.79	58.98	48.39
West Bengal	66.44	61.37	61.97
All States	54.12	64.02	60.96

average for 1967-68 through 1969-70, this percentage was found to be 54.12 for all the States taken together. This meant that the States had to depend on the Union Government to the tune of 45.88 per cent of their total revenue. During the period 1973-74 through 1975-76, this percentage share of States' own tax and non-tax revenue rose to 64.02. But it declined to 60.96 during 1979-80 through 1981-82.

The inter-State comparison showed that during the period 1967-68 through 1969-70, the percentage contribution of States' own tax and non-tax revenue was the highest in Punjab (79.59) and the lowest in Assam (26.70). Haryana was at number two and Maharashtra at number three in order of ranking, their percentage share being 75.67 and 74.47 respectively. However, during 1973-74 through 1975-76, while the percentage contribution of States' tax and non-tax revenue moved up in the case of Haryana (79.80) and Maharashtra (77.04), it declined in the case of Punjab (77.07). So, during the period 1973-74 through 1975-76, in respect of resource mobilisation from own sources, Haryana attained the first place and Maharashtra, the second but Punjab slipped down to the third place. Comparing the three years' average of 1973-74 through 1975-76 with that of 1967-68 through 1969-70, the percentage share of States' own tax and non-tax revenue to total revenue diminished only in two States (Punjab and Bihar) while in all other States it improved.

Looking at the three years' average of 1979-80 through 1981-82, it was found that the percentage share of States' own tax and non-tax revenue was again maximum in Punjab (79.22). During this period Haryana and Maharashtra moved to second and third places respectively in order of ranking. In all the periods, the States like Punjab, Haryana, Maharashtra, Gujarat, Karnataka and Tamil Nadu had the percentage share of States' own revenue more than the all States' average. In other words, these States consistently depended mainly on their own sources of revenue; on the other hand, the States like Assam, Bihar, Himachal Pradesh, Jammu and Kashmir, Meghalaya, Nagaland, and Orissa chiefly banked upon the Union assistance in terms of share from the Union taxes and grants-in-aid from the Union Government.

Table 2.2 depicts the percentage shares of States' own tax and non-tax revenue to States' own revenue. For all the States taken together these percentages were 71.81 and 28.19 respectively during the period 1967-68 through 1969-70. As between the States, the percentage share of States' own tax revenue varied

TABLE 2.2: **Percentage Shares of States' Own Tax and Non-tax Revenues**

State	*1967-68 through 1969-70*		*1973-74 through 1975-76*		*1979-80 through 1981-82*	
	Tax revenue	*Non-tax revenue*	*Tax revenue*	*Non-tax revenue*	*Tax revenue*	*Non-tax revenue*
Andhra Pradesh	82.96	17.04	72.16	27.84	72.30	27.70
Assam	76.12	23.88	72.85	27.15	38.45	61.55
Bihar	77.54	22.46	75.43	24.57	71.21	28.79
Gujarat	73.65	26.35	71.63	28.37	75.70	24.30
Haryana	68.78	31.22	64.13	35.87	66.17	33.83
Himachal Pradesh	—	—	43.30	56.70	40.32	59.68
Jammu & Kashmir	40.09	59.91	28.93	71.07	37.83	62.17
Karnataka	65.46	35.54	59.48	40.52	70.47	29.53
Kerala	71.92	28.08	70.62	29.38	68.79	31.21
Madhya Pradesh	61.21	38.79	60.13	39.87	57.67	42.33
Maharashtra	75.65	24.35	71.25	28.75	72.39	27.61
Manipur	—	—	39.20	60.80	20.22	79.78
Meghalaya	—	—	47.45	52.55	32.13	67.87
Nagaland	—	—	46.15	53.85	17.73	82.27
Orissa	63.48	36.52	52.11	47.89	57.86	42.14
Punjab	74.99	25.01	73.81	26.19	77.45	22.55
Rajasthan	71.67	28.33	59.66	40.34	59.32	40.68
Tamil Nadu	69.76	30.24	77.26	22.74	79.79	20.21
Tripura	—	—	32.08	67.92	21.52	78.48
Uttar Pradesh	66.19	33.81	64.97	35.03	71.81	28.19
West Bengal	78.43	21.57	80.74	19.26	78.65	21.35
All States	71.81	28.19	68.46	31.54	69.58	30.42

from 40.09 for Jammu and Kashmir to 82.96 for Andhra Pradesh. In the States of Assam, Bihar, Gujarat, Maharashtra, Punjab and West Bengal, the percentage contribution of States' own tax revenue was higher than all States' average.

However, during the period 1973-74 through 1975-76, the percentage contribution of tax revenue fell to 68.46 for all the States taken together. As between the States, this percentage had a range of 28.93 for Jammu and Kashmir to 80.74 for West Bengal. Tamil Nadu (77.26 per cent), Bihar (75.43 per cent) and Punjab (73.81 per cent) attained the second, third and fourth places respectively. However, there were two States, *viz.* Tamil Nadu and West Bengal, in whose case the percentage share of States' own tax revenue actually improved while for all other States, the share of non-tax revenue gained importance.

During the next period, 1979-80 through 1981-82, it was observed that the percentage contribution of States' own tax revenue again went up to 69.58 for all the States taken together and ranged between 17.73 for Nagaland and 79.79 for Tamil Nadu. West Bengal (78.65 per cent) and Punjab (77.45 per cent) stood at number two and number three respectively. The States of Andhra Pradesh, Bihar, Gujarat, Maharashtra, Punjab and West Bengal were consistently above all States' average. Thus, we can say that some of the relatively underdeveloped States, namely Himachal Pradesh, Jammu and Kashmir, Manipur, Meghalaya, Nagaland, Orissa, Rajasthan and Tripura, raised a lower proportion of revenue through States' own tax sources than some of the relatively developed States like Andhra Pradesh, Gujarat, Maharashtra, Punjab and West Bengal.

Table 2.3 relates to the composition of States' total tax revenue *i.e.* the share of States' own tax revenue *vis-a-vis* the share in Union taxes. For the period 1967-68 through 1969-70, while the average contribution of States' own tax revenue was 70.47 per cent, and that of Union tax revenue, 29.53 per cent. Across the States, the share of States' own tax revenue had variation from 42.72 per cent for Jammu and Kashmir to 84.74 per cent for Punjab. Haryana (79.17 per cent) and Maharashtra (76.67 per cent) occupied the second and third positions respectively. However, during the period 1973-74 through 1975-76, the average percentage share of States' own tax revenue dropped to 68.64 and that of Union tax transfers rose to 31.36. As between

TABLE 2.3 : **Percentage Share of States' Own Tax Revenue and the Share in Union Taxes**

State	1967-68 through 1969-70		1973-74 through 1975-76		1979-80 through 1981-82	
	State's own tax revenue	Share in Union taxes	State's own tax revenue	Share in Union taxes	State's own tax revenue	Share in Union taxes
1	2	3	4	5	6	7
Andhra Pradesh	71.40	28.60	71.20	28.80	66.55	33.45
Assam	64.13	35.87	57.85	42.15	43.24	56.76
Bihar	59.39	40.61	51.85	48.15	39.72	60.28
Gujarat	74.78	25.22	74.13	25.87	74.18	25.82
Haryana	79.17	20.83	81.39	18.61	79.75	20.25
Himachal Pradesh	—	—	61.47	38.53	61.23	38.77
Jammu & Kashmir	42.72	57.28	55.55	44.45	58.50	41.50
Karnataka	74.41	25.59	73.41	26.59	71.31	28.69
Kerala	73.85	26.15	70.80	29.20	68.58	31.42
Madhya Pradesh	66.48	33.52	63.89	36.11	56.34	43.66
Maharashtra	76.67	23.33	78.17	21.83	77.64	22.36
Manipur	—	—	36.48	63.52	28.38	71.62
Meghalaya	—	—	43.23	56.77	41.02	58.98
Nagaland	—	—	58.61	41.39	55.66	44.34
Orissa	55.73	44.27	50.94	49.06	45.43	54.57
Punjab	84.74	15.26	82.40	17.60	81.48	18.52

(*Contd.*)

1	2	3	4	5	6	7
Rajasthan	68.45	31.55	63.86	36.14	58.97	41.03
Tamil Nadu	74.38	25.62	74.59	25.41	69.00	31.00
Tripura	—	—	25.83	74.17	25.51	74.49
Uttar Pradesh	62.43	37.57	58.02	41.98	51.48	48.52
West Bengal	71.85	28.15	67.65	32.35	63.07	36.93
All States	70.47	29.53	68.64	31.36	64.17	35.83

the States, the percentage share of States' own tax revenue varied between 25.83 for Tripura and 82.40 for Punjab. The percentage contribution of States' own tax revenue stepped up only in the case of Haryana, Jammu and Kashmir, Maharashtra and Tamil Nadu. Haryana and Maharashtra remained at number two and number three respectively.

For the period 1979-80 through 1981-82, the percentage share of States' own tax revenue further stepped down to 64.17 and consequently the share of taxes shared with the Union stepped up to 35.83 for all the States taken together. The percentage share of States' own tax revenue ranged from 25.51 for Tripura to 81.48 for Punjab. The relative positions of Haryana and Maharashtra remained the same. The percentage share of States' own tax revenue improved only in the States of Gujarat and Jammu and Kashmir while for all other States it dwindled. In the States of Andhra Pradesh, Gujarat, Haryana, Karnataka, Kerala, Maharashtra, Punjab and Tamil Nadu, the contribution of States' own tax revenue was more than all States' average. Thus, these relatively developed States relied less on the share in Union taxes than the relatively underdeveloped States like Jammu and Kashmir, Uttar Pradesh, Bihar, Manipur, Meghalaya, Orissa and Tripura. On the whole, States' dependence on the Union Government, as far as shareable taxes were concerned, increased. This might partly be due to the ever-increasing pressure of the

States on the Union Government to widen the pool of shareable taxes.

Table 2.4 reveals the annual growth rate of States' revenue and Net State Domestic Product (NSDP) for the period 1967-68

TABLE 2.4: **Annual Compound Growth Rates of States' Revenues and Net State Domestic Products (1967-68 to 1982-83)**

(*Per cent*)

State	*NSDP*	*Total revenue*	*State's own total revenue*	*State's tax revenue*	*State's own tax revenue*	*Share in Union taxes*	*State's own non-tax revenue*
Andhra Pradesh	10.80	17.03	17.70	16.88	16.67	17.39	21.68
Assam	11.28	12.12	15.46	14.27	11.16	17.01	22.12
Bihar	9.91	15.88	13.79	15.47	12.67	18.34	16.83
Gujarat	12.08	16.61	17.34	17.26	17.54	16.34	16.35
Haryana	13.18	18 06	18.60	17.96	18.26	14.94	19.39
Himachal Pradesh	10.62	22.92	25.68	22.26	23.12	21.87	27.11
Jammu & Kashmir	13.16	15.61	18.58	15.69	18.75	12.22	18.40
Karnataka	9.64	15.75	16.59	17.15	17.07	17.37	16.03
Kerala	11.08	15.11	16.37	16.51	16.45	17.00	15.84
Madhya Pradesh	9.94	16.69	16.49	16.82	16.00	12.34	16.84
Maharashtra	12.84	16.52	17.33	16.21	16.63	14.80	20.00
Manipur	11.16	21.16	27.37	24.93	15.86	28.64	50.33
Meghalaya	—	17.75	32.93	19.88	33.03	25.28	32.55
Nagaland	—	14.55	32.90	15.97	27.77	18.27	36.55
Orissa	9.48	16.05	15.93	16.13	14.95	17.35	17.44
Punjab	12.73	15.34	15.63	15.89	15.80	16.45	15.15
Rajasthan	11.63	16.44	17.09	16.04	15.37	17.29	20.57
Tamil Nadu	9.58	14.39	14.17	15.84	15.42	16.89	9.95
Tripura	11.59	20.19	30.64	29.07	31.19	28.75	30.11
Uttar Pradesh	10.44	17.00	14.53	16.30	20.89	17.50	12.50
West Bengal	9.57	14.23	14.44	14.74	13.93	16.43	15.66
All States	10.92	16.15	16.21	16.30	15.93	19.88	16.92

through 1982-83. In each State, the total revenue (tax and non-tax) mounted at a much higher rate than the Net State Domestic Product. The annual rate of growth of Net State Domestic Product was the highest in Haryana (13.18 per cent) and the lowest in Orissa (9.48 per cent). Punjab, showing a growth rate of 12.73 per cent stood the fourth. For all the States taken together, the States' total revenue swelled at a rate of 16.15 per cent per annum and varied from 12.12 per cent for Assam to 22.92 per cent for Himachal Pradesh.

Considering the States' own total revenue, it was observed that it multiplied at a rate of 16.21 per cent per annum for all the States taken together and the rate varied from 13.79 per cent for Bihar to 32.93 per cent for Meghalaya. While examining All States' own tax and non-tax revenue, it was interesting to observe that States' own non-tax revenue increased at a higher rate (16.92 per cent) than own tax revenue (15.93 per cent). However, in the case of Punjab, the position was the reverse. The State's own tax revenue moved up at a higher rate (15.80 per cent) than the non-tax revenue (15.15 per cent). The growth rates of States' own tax revenues ranged between 11.16 per cent for Assam and 33.03 per cent for Meghalaya. The growth of revenue from share in Union taxes was higher (19.88 per cent) as compared to that of States' own tax revenue (15.93 per cent). The growth rate of States' tax revenue (*i.e.* including share from the Union) was higher (16.30 per cent) than that of total revenue (16.15 per cent) for all the States taken together. In Punjab, too, the tax revenue showed an upward trend at a higher rate (15.89 per cent) than the total revenue (15.34 per cent) for the period 1967-68 to 1982-83.

While the above results reveal that the tax revenue mobilisation efforts have been commendable as compared to the rise in Net State Domestic Product, the growth rates hide some significant characteristics of tax performance. The growth rates neither give any idea about the nature of tax base nor indicate the potential tax services that may be utilized for augmenting revenues without unduly burdening the taxpayers. Secondly, the growth rates point out nothing about the relative weights, or the extents of contribution of individual taxes, in the aggregate tax revenues. Since these aspects are imperative in tax analysis, we shall examine in the next chapter the intensity of use of different taxes and the relative contribution of each tax to the total revenue.

The growth in tax revenue may come about through 'automatic' response of the tax yield to changes in NSDP and/or through the imposition of new taxes, revision of the rate structure of existing taxes, expansion of the tax base, making tax compliance harder by law and other administrative measures backed by legal action.

Changes in tax yield resulting from modifying tax parameters (*i.e.* rate, base etc.) are called 'discretionary changes'. They are the result of legislative action. With tax parameters held constant (*i.e.* discretionary changes being eliminated) automatic changes in tax yield resulting from variations in NSDP measure the elasticity of a tax system. However, changes in the tax yield flowing from the combined effect of 'automatic' changes and 'discretionary' changes are a measure of the 'buoyancy' of a tax or a tax system.

An analysis of such buoyancy is important for many reasons. First, to the extent that the buoyancy is low, it would suggest a need for devising a tax structure which would overcome the deficiencies. Secondly, on the basis of such a study, a State Government can estimate the probable tax revenue, with unchanged base and rate of tax, consequent on mere increase in the NSDP. Thirdly, it would be helpful in indicating the extent of additional tax effort needed to increase the revenue of the government.

We have used the method of regression analysis to estimate buoyancies of tax revenue. The regression equation used was :

$$Y = aX^b$$

or

$$\log Y = \log a + b \log X,$$

where Y denotes tax revenue,

X dénotes Net State Domestic Product,

b is the regression coefficient or buoyancy.

The results derived from the regression analysis of various States' revenues for the period 1967-68 to 1981-82 are presented in Table 2.5. The buoyancy coefficient of total revenue for all the States taken together was 1.434, which meant that 1 per cent increase in NSDP was accompanied by roughly 1.434 per cent increase in total States' revenue. The buoyancy coefficient for total revenue was more than unity in every State indicating thereby that 1 per cent increase in NSDP resulted in more than 1 per cent increase in State's total revenue. This buoyancy coefficient was the highest for Himachal Pradesh (2.099) and the lowest for Assam (1.162).

The buoyancy coefficient of States' own total revenue for all the States taken together was slightly higher (1.444) than that of the total revenue (1.434). This meant that the States mobilised more resources from their own sources (tax and non-tax) than they obtained through Union Government transfers in terms of share from Union taxes and grants-in-aid. The buoyancy coefficient of States' own total revenues varied from 1.207 for Punjab to 2.745 for Manipur. In all the States, except Bihar, Madhya Pradesh, Tamil Nadu and Uttar Pradesh, the buoyancy coefficient of States' own revenue was more than that of States' total revenue.

TABLE 2.5: **Buoyancy Coefficients of the States' Revenue (1967-68 to 1981-82)**

State	*Total revenue*	*State's own total revenue*	*State's tax revenue*	*State's own tax revenue*	*Share in Union taxes*	*State's own non-tax revenue*
1	*2*	*3*	*4*	*5*	*6*	*7*
Andhra Pradesh	1.505	1.608	1.516	1.458	1.513	2.005
Assam	1.162	1.386	1.223	0.971	1.445	1.974
Bihar	1.513	1.325	1.469	1.246	1.704	1.580
Gujarat	1.315	1.360	1.362	1.379	1 307	1.303
Haryana	1.345	1.380	1.326	1.347	1.233	1.454
Himachal Pradesh	2.099	2.247	2.020	2.091	2.049	2.386

(*Contd.*)

1	2	3	4	5	6	7
Jammu & Kashmir	1.185	1.427	1.152	1.376	0.877	1.459
Karnataka	1.553	1.656	1.673	1.662	1.697	1.654
Kerala	1.349	1.455	1.444	1.439	1.461	1.474
Madhya Pradesh	1.553	1.513	1.536	1.494	1.641	1.578
Maha-rashtra	1.242	1.324	1.321	1.259	1.114	1.515
Manipur	1.741	2.745	2.179	1.288	2.395	5.061
Orissa	1.558	1.612	1.572	1 468	1.680	1.823
Punjab	1,189	1.207	1.219	1.214	1.256	1.190
Rajasthan	1.348	1.384	1.287	1.231	1.387	1.684
Tamil Nadu	1.410	1.383	1.540	1.489	1.664	1.038
Tripura	1.750	2.433	2.331	2.435	2.372	2.431
Uttar Pradesh	1.459	1.335	1.471	1.853	1.555	1.145
West Bengal	1.410	1.458	1 495	1.406	1.634	1.617
All States	1.434	1.444	1.448	1.407	1.497	1.536

Comparing All States' own tax and non-tax revenues, we found that the buoyancy coefficient was slightly more (1.536) for non-tax revenue than that for tax revenue (1.407). This indicated that the change in NSDP led to larger increase in States' non-tax revenue than in tax revenue. The buoyancy coefficient of States' own tax revenue varied from 0.971 for Assam to 2.435 for Tripura and that of State's own non-tax revenue, from 1.038 for Tamil Nadu to 5.061 for Manipur. The buoyancy coefficient of State's own non-tax revenue was more than State's own tax revenue in all the States except Gujarat, Karnataka, Punjab, Tamil Nadu, Tripura and Uttar Pradesh. All these States mobilised more resources from own tax sources than from non-tax sources. It was only in the case of Assam that the buoyancy coefficient of State's own tax revenue was less than unity, while for all other States it was more than unity. The buoyancy coefficient of share in Union taxes was 1.497 which was higher than that of the aggregate States' own tax revenue (1.407). This meant that with the increase in NSDP, the increase in revenue from share in Union taxes was more than in All States' own tax revenue. This was true of all the States' except Gujarat, Haryana, Himachal Pradesh, Jammu and Kashmir, Maharashtra, Tripura and Uttar Pradesh.

There is another way of looking at the tax effort of different States. It is generally believed that tax effort (or taxable capacity) should move with per capita income positively. Between two States with the same NSDP but with different per capita income, taxable capacity would be the greater in the State with the higher per capita income. It follows that if the two States have equal tax ratios, the poorer State would be making the greater tax effort.

In order to analyse the inter-State disparities in tax effort, we have presented in Table 2.6 per capita incomes and per capita tax revenues for different States. Almost during the entire period under study, the States of Gujarat, Haryana, Himachal Pradesh, Maharashtra, Punjab and West Bengal were found to be relatively well off. Punjab had the highest per capita income throughout. The per capita State tax for an average State was Rs. 23.80 during the period 1967-68 through 1969-70 and increased to Rs. 103.29 during the period 1979-80 through 1981-82. The per capita State tax ranged between Rs. 12.63 for Orissa and Rs. 50.03 for Punjab for the years 1967-68 through 1969-70. During 1979-80 through 1981-82, it varied from Rs. 20.59 for Tripura to Rs. 220.62 for Punjab. Thus, per capita State tax was the highest in Punjab throughout the period under study. Further, the per capita State tax increased in all the States over the period.

Taxable capacity is usually measured by the ratio of per capita tax revenue to per capita income. Under progressive tax structure, the State with higher per capita income is also expected to bear a higher tax burden. With this end in view, we calculated the proportions of per capita State's own tax revenue to per

TABLE 2.6 : **Per Capita Income and Per Capita State's Own Tax Revenue**

(*Rupees*)

State	*1967-68 through 1969-70*			*1973-74 through 1975-76*			*1979-80 through 1981-82*		
	Per capita income	*Per capita State tax*	*Per capita State tax as percentage of per capita income*	*Per capita income*	*Per capita State tax*	*Per capita State tax as percentage of per capita income*	*Per capita income*	*Per capita State tax*	*Per capita State tax as percentage of per capita income*
Andhra Pradesh	505.30	23.47	4.64	916.67	55.88	6.10	1338.67	112.72	8.42
Assam	502.60	18.77	3.73	751.17	28.36	3.77	1221.40	39.32	3.22
Bihar	390.00	15.62	4.01	641.00	24.63	3.84	909.33	41.22	4.53
Gujarat	650.00	25.77	3.96	1130.67	68.04	6.02	1887.00	163.91	8.69
Haryana	719.67	35.73	4.96	1316.67	89.86	6.81	2287.00	190.38	8.32
Himachal Pradesh	—	—	—	1020.67	36.53	3.58	1527.67	82.69	5.41
Jammu & Kashmir	464.20	13.61	2.93	824.67	28.54	3.46	1475.67	72.15	4.89
Karnataka	590.73	27.49	4.65	1018.50	61.86	6.04	1367.00	136.22	9.96

Kerala	502.00	28.63	5.70	891.67	55.94	6.27	1365.67	133.30	9.76
Madhya Pradesh	448.30	18.38	4.10	783.83	39.67	5.06	1075.67	77.01	7.16
Maharashtra	709.57	43.23	6.09	1278.33	90.50	7.08	2263.80	189.22	8.36
Manipur	—	—	—	738.73	11.64	1.58	1039.90	21.68	2.08
Orissa	463.33	12.63	2.73	714.50	23.08	3.23	1085.73	51.89	4.78
Punjab	901.67	50.03	5.55	1632.00	103.01	6.31	2848.67	220.62	7.74
Rajasthan	475.00	20.70	4.36	846.33	38.78	4.58	1236.33	75.73	6.13
Tamil Nadu	505.33	29.74	5.89	817.33	69.17	8.46	1260.00	137.32	10.89
Tripura	—	—	—	750.33	7.16	0.95	1095.00	20.59	1.88
U.P.	476.97	15.83	3.32	713.80	31.42	4.40	1186.07	62.28	5.25
West Bengal	673.57	27.56	4.09	1041.43	48.95	4.70	1520.23	99.47	6.54
All States	540.94	23.80	4.40	909.27	50.15	5.52	1421.83	103.29	7.26

capita income. During the period 1967-68 through 1969-70, this proportion was the highest for Maharashtra, and the lowest for Orissa. For Andhra Pradesh, Haryana, Karnataka, Kerala, Maharashtra, Punjab and Tamil Nadu, the tax-income ratio was found to be higher than the overall average. Although for Maharashtra and Tamil Nadu, the per capita income was less than that of Punjab, yet the tax-income ratio was higher. Interestingly, the States like Andhra Pradesh, Kerala and Tamil Nadu, which had the lower per capita income than the average State, carried a higher tax-income ratio.

Considering the three years' average for 1973-74 through 1975-76, it was observed that the proportion of per capita State tax revenue to per capita income was the highest for Tamil Nadu (8.46 per cent) and the lowest for Tripura (0.95 per cent). The States of Andhra Pradesh, Gujarat, Haryana, Karnataka, Kerala, Maharashtra, Punjab and Tamil Nadu had a comparatively high tax-income ratio.

For the period 1979-80 through 1981-82, the average tax-income ratio was found to be 7.26 per cent and it varied from 10.89 per cent for Tamil Nadu to 1.88 per cent for Tripura. Again, the States of Andhra Pradesh, Gujarat, Haryana, Karnataka, Kerala, Maharashtra, Punjab and Tamil Nadu recorded a comparatively high tax-income ratio. Further, although the per capita State tax revenue and per capita income in each of the States of Andhra Pradesh, Gujarat, Haryana, Karnataka, Kerala, Maharashtra and Tamil Nadu were lower than those for Punjab yet the tax-income ratio was higher. The tax-income ratios were in general, relatively low in the States with comparatively high per capita income *viz.*, Punjab, Haryana and Maharashtra. This indicated that these States were putting in inadequate efforts for raising revenue commensurate with their taxable capacities.

The use of the tax-income ratio as a measure of tax effort, however, involves the implicit assumption that total income, irrespective of other circumstances, is the appropriate indicator of relative taxable capacity. Such an assumption is simplistic for it may be readily seen that the capacity to pay as well as to collect taxes will be affected by the size of the population in relation to income, distribution of the income, capability of "tax handles", the degree of monetisation, etc. An allowance will have to be made for all such major factors. This can be done either by adjusting the actual tax ratios for variations in the tax capacity factors or by adjusting the amounts of taxes that could be collected through the use of the potential bases available to the States. In the former approach, regression analysis is used to estimate or measure the influence of capacity factors on tax effort; in the latter approach, a model or representative tax system is applied to potential bases to estimate the relative taxable capacity.

It may be hypothesized that the actual tax ratio depends on (i) the ability of the people to pay taxes, (ii) the ability of the administration to collect taxes, and (iii) the willingness on the part of the leaders of the government to tax *i.e.* their decision regarding the extent of the taxable capacity to be utilised. Factors affecting (i) and (ii) may be classified as tax capacity factors and those relating to (iii) may be grouped under tax effort factors. One can then attempt to explain variations in the tax ratios of the States through a regression analysis in which the tax ratio can be taken as the dependent variable, and the various tax capacity indicators of the tax and tax effort factors as the explanatory variables.

In the aggregate regression approach to the measurement of tax effort, per capita income is generally included among the explanatory factors. But per capita income, while representing in a broad sense the standard of living of the people, is only a summary measure of the stage of development and the other characteristics of the economy. If a more disaggregated picture of the economy could be brought into the computation of relative taxable capacities, the advantages or disadvantages, which the several States enjoy or suffer from in terms of availability and value of potential bases, could be more explicitly taken into account. In the regression approach, the tax capacity factors such as the degree of urbanisation, the share of agriculture in Net State Domestic Product and the degree of monetisation are used as proxies for the potential bases from which the taxes have to be collected. The representative tax system method makes a direct use of the potential bases themselves.

The representative tax system involves three major steps. First, for each tax an appropriate base has to be identified; this should not be the actual base as recorded in the official tax statistics, but rather the potential base which may be taken to represent the relative taxable capacity. Second, a representative set of tax rates, which may be said to constitute the representative tax system, has to be generated. The representative rate for a tax may be derived as the average of the effective rates (ER) of that tax, the effective rate in a State being computed as the ratio of the actual collections to the potential base. Third, the average effective rates (AER) of the taxes have to be applied to their respective bases in a State. The product of the AER and the potential base of a tax will indicate the revenue which the concerned State could raise from that source if its potential is used to the average extent. This is because the rate applied is the average for the States and the base used is the potential base (or its reasonable proxy). If the products of the AER and the potential bases for all the taxes levied by a government are added, the sum would represent the amount of revenue that the State could raise through the representative system. This may be called its relative taxable capacity.

The AER of a tax may be derived in two ways. One way is to regress the revenue series on the chosen bases, the regression coefficient of the base being taken to represent the AER. Alternatively, an arithmetic average of the effective rates of that tax in the several States may be worked out. We have adopted the second alternative.

The methodology may be described symbolically as follows :

If RA_{ij} and PB_{ij} are the actual revenue and the potential base respectively for the jth tax in the ith State, then the effective rate of the tax is

$$ER_{ij}=\frac{RA_{ij}}{PB_{ij}}.$$

The average effective rate for the jth tax is then obtained as follows :

$$AER_j=\frac{1}{S(j)}\sum_{i=1}^{S(j)} ER_{ij}$$

where $S(j)$ is the number of States in which the jth tax is being levied.

The set of AERs is applied to the corresponding tax base in a State to derive the yield of the representative tax structure in that State which is a measure of its relative taxable capacity ($\hat{T}$). In other words, $\hat{T}$ can be taken to represent the tax revenue that a State would have if it had made an average effort to exploit its potential bases. It follows that if $T_i > \hat{T}_i$, then the ith State can be said to be making more than the average tax effort. Thus, an index of relative tax effort can be derived by dividing the actual tax revenue of a State by the estimated relative taxable capacity, *i.e.*

$$E_i = \frac{T_i}{\hat{T}_i}$$

If $E_i > 1$, the State can be said to be making more than the average effort; and conversely, if $E_i < 1$. The States are then ranked according to the values of E_i. Thus, the efforts made by a State could be judged by its relative position in the order of ranking.[2]

Table 2.7 gives the effective rates, average effective rates and tax potentials for different States (for their own tax sources). For working out the tax potentials for different States, their Net State Domestic Product has been taken as the base. The effective rates of States' own tax revenues varied from 2.69 per cent for Orissa to 5.84 per cent for Tamil Nadu, average being 4.39 per cent for the period 1967-68 through 1969-70. Analysing the tax potentials of different States, it was found that while Kerala, Maharashtra, Punjab and Tamil Nadu had indices distinctly above the average; Bihar, Orissa and Uttar Pradesh had indices distinctly below. In order of ranking, Punjab occupied the fourth place.

For the period 1973-74 through 1975-76, the effective rate of States' own tax revenue ranged from 0.93 per cent for Tripura to 8.14 per cent for Tamil Nadu, the average being 5.06 per cent. Punjab move up to the third place while Tamil Nadu and Maharashtra continued to occupy the first and second positions respectively.

For the three years' average of 1979-80 through 1981-82, the average effective rate was 6.58 per cent and varied between 1.90 per cent for Tripura and 10.81 per cent for Tamil Nadu. The relative positions of different States with respect to tax effort

TABLE 2.7 : **Effective Rates and Tax Potentials for State's Own Tax Revenues**

State	*1967-68 through 1969-70*						*1973-74 through 1975-76*					
	Tax revenue (Rs. lakhs)	*Tax base (Rs. lakhs)*	*Effective rate (%)*	*Tax potential (Rs. lakhs)*	*Index of use of tax pontential (col. 2/col. 5)*	*Ranking in terms of col. 6*	*Tax revenue (Rs. lakhs)*	*Tax base (Rs. lakhs)*	*Effective rate (%)*	*Tax potential (Rs. lakhs)*	*Index of use of tax potential (col. 8/ col. 11)*	*Ranking in terms of col. 12*
1	*2*	*3*	*4*	*5*	*6*	*7*	*8*	*9*	*10*	*11*	*12*	*13*
Andhra Pradesh	9664.33	208788.67	4.63	9165.82	1.0544	7	25964.00	427166.67	6.08	21614.63	1.2012	6
Assam	2512.67	69025.00	3.64	3030.20	0.8292	12	4574.00	122180.00	3.74	6182.31	0.7399	14
Bihar	7189.33	208233.33	3.45	9141.44	0.7865	13	14858.00	386700.00	3.84	19567.00	0.7593	13
Gujarat	7993.00	162559.33	4.92	7136.35	1.1200	5	19610.67	324833.33	6.04	16436.57	1.1931	8
Haryana	3307.67	67629.33	4.89	2968.93	1.1141	6	9740.33	144974.67	6.72	7335.72	1.3278	4
Himachal Pradesh	—	—	—	—	—	—	1350.67	40026.67	3.37	2025.35	0.6669	16
Jammu & Kashmir	582.67	20099.67	2.90	882.38	0.6603	15	1429.33	41650.67	3.43	2107.62	0.6782	15
Karnataka	7565.00	163981.00	4.61	7198.77	1.0509	8	19523.67	320566.67	6.09	16220.67	1.2036	7

Kerala	5702.33	100812.00	5.66	4425.65	1.2885	3	12624.33	196866.67	6.41	9961.45	1.2673	5
Madhya Pradesh	7110.67	175576.67	4.05	7707.82	0.9225	11	17554.67	344533.33	5.15	17433.39	1.0184	9
Maharashtra	19073.00	337008.67	5.65	14794.67	1.2892	2	48871.33	703800.00	6.94	35612.28	1.3723	2
Manipur	—	—	—	—	—	—	136.67	9133.83	1.50	462.17	0.2957	18
Orissa	2591.33	96439.67	2.69	4233.70	0.6121	6	5368.00	167266.61	3.21	8463.69	0.6342	17
Punjab	6408.00	116510.00	5.50	5114.79	1.2528	4	14918.33	220700.00	6.76	11167.42	1.3359	3
Rajasthan	4960.33	112509.67	4.41	4939.17	1.0043	9	10920.00	237133.33	4.61	11998.95	0.9101	11
Tamil Nadu	11550.67	197696.67	5.84	8678.88	1.3309	1	29930.00	367833.33	8.14	18612.37	1.6081	1
Tripura	—	—	—	—	—	—	122.00	13151.00	0.93	665.44	0.1833	19
Uttar Pradesh	13260.67	402919.00	3.29	17688.67	0.7497	14	29833.67	679300.00	4.39	34272.58	0.8679	12
West Bengal	11385.67	280876.00	4.05	12330.46	0.9234	10	23149.33	501000.00	4.62	25350.60	0.9132	10
	Average effective rate = 4.39 per cent						Average effective rate = 5.06 per cent					

(Contd.)

State	1979-80 through 1981-82					
	Tax revenue (Rs. lakhs)	*Tax base (Rs. lakhs)*	*Effective rate (%)*	*Tax potential (Rs. lakhs)*	*Index of use of tax potential (col. 14/ col. 17)*	*Ranking in terms of col. 18*
	14	*15*	*16*	*17*	*18*	*19*
Andhra Pradesh	59256.00	712710.67	8.31	46896.36	1.2636	6
Assam	7603.67	240633.33	3.16	15833.67	0.4802	17
Bihar	28275.00	626700.00	4.51	41236.86	0.6857	16
Gujarat	54684.00	635526.33	8.60	41817.63	1.3077	4
Haryana	24061.00	292093.00	8.24	19219.72	1.2519	7
Himachal Pradesh	3469.67	64735.33	5.36	4259.58	0.8146	12
Jammu & Kashmir	4235.33	86717.33	4.88	5706.00	0.7423	14
Karnataka	49552.67	497809.00	9.95	32755.83	1.5128	2
Kerala	33384.00	345193.00	9.67	22713.70	1.4698	3
Madhya Pradesh	39399.67	557956.67	7.06	36713.55	1.8732	9
Maharashtra	116495.67	1399043.00	8.33	92057.02	1.2655	5
Manipur	300.67	14289.33	2.10	940.24	0.3198	18
Orissa	13463.33	284472.53	4.73	18718.29	0.7193	15

Punjab	36336.00	471195.67	7.71	31004.68	1.1720	8
Rajasthan	25300.00	418944.67	6.04	27566.56	0.9178	11
Tamil Nadu	65595.67	606656.00	10.81	39917.96	1.6433	1
Tripura	413.00	21713.00	1.90	1428.72	0.2891	19
Uttar Pradesh	67676.33	1303872.30	5.19	85794.80	0.7888	13
West Bengal	53264.33	821983.00	6.48	54086.48	0.9848	10

Average effective rate = 6.58 per cent.

indices showed a marked change. Punjab which had gone up to the third place was now relegated to the eighth place. Considerable improvement in ranking was found in the case of Kerala and Karnataka, which moved up from fifth and seventh places in the previous period to first two places respectively in the current period. It was interesting to find that during these two sub-periods the effective rates increased in all the States except Assam. This meant that the Net State Domestic Product in Assam improved faster than States' own tax revenue. Further, while the States of Andhra Pradesh, Gujarat, Haryana, Karnataka, Kerala, Maharashtra and Tamil Nadu had tax effort indices distinctly above the average; Assam, Manipur and Tripura had markedly lower indices. It may be added that throughout the period under study, there was no tendency for the indices of several States to cluster round the average, indicating that there were perceptible differences in the performance of the States in the tax field. It may also be mentioned that whereas Punjab was the richest State in terms of per capita income, it did not apply the highest effective rate for its tax revenue However, under progressivity, in a State with higher per capita income than an average State, as in Punjab, taxable capacity is also expected to be higher. This means that had Punjab applied some higher effective rate, as desired under progressivity, it could have mobilised more additional resources than it actually did.

Cost of Tax Collection

Closely related with aggregate tax efforts is the analysis of cost of tax collection whose minimisation must be an important objective of budgetary policy in the States. The cost of tax collection would reveal the relative performance of different States in net tax collection. All taxes do not have similar cost implications. Moreover, a given tax structure implies a certain level of fixed costs and any addition to the cost of collection would naturally be determined by the type of changes in the existing structure. This part of the study is aimed at analysing the cost of tax collection. Cost of tax collection is taken here to mean direct money costs. For example, a rising unit cost over time may not be due to any additional organisational and administrative requirements of a recurring or non-recurring nature associated with higher tax yield. It may simply be due to declining tax yield, without a corresponding decline in the cost of tax collection. Or, it may be the result of the strengthening and streamlining of the tax machinery with a view to coping with the potential increase in tax yield in the future.

Table 2.8 shows the cost of tax collection in different States. For the three years' average period, 1967-68 through 1969-70, 9.60 paise was spent on the collection of one rupee as State tax revenue for all the States taken together. The cost of tax collection was minimum for Haryana (4.25 paise) and maximum for Jammu and Kashmir (20.34 paise). The States of Jammu and Kashmir, Orissa, Maharashtra, Uttar Pradesh, Rajasthan, Gujarat and Assam, spent more than 10 per cent of the State tax receipts on their collection. On the other hand, the States of Haryana, Tamil Nadu, Andhra Pradesh and Punjab spent about 5 per cent only. For the next three years' average period 1973-74 through

TABLE 2.8 : **Cost of Tax Collection**

(*Per cent*)

State	*Three years' average of 1967-68 through 1969-70*	*Three years' average of 1973-74 through 1975-76*	*Three years' average of 1979-80 through 1981-82*	*Growth rate of State tax revenue*	*Growth rate of cost of State tax collection*
1	*2*	*3*	*4*	*5*	*6*
Andhra Pradesh	5.02	4.06	4.11	16.67	14.21
Assam	10.39	9.74	10.73	11.16	10.71
Bihar	9.07	8.80	9.27	12.67	12.10
Gujarat	10.61	2.52	2.49	17.54	3.24
Haryana	4.25	2.78	2.29	18.26	12.64
Himachal Pradesh	—	11.34	10.72	23.12	19.45

(*Contd*)

1	2	3	4	5	6
Jammu & Kashmir	20.34	17.38	13.67	18.75	14.26
Karnataka	6.16	5.84	4.72	17.07	13.83
Kerala	8.30	8.50	6.26	16.45	13.11
Madhya Pradesh	9.02	8.70	7.50	16.00	14.58
Maharashtra	14.94	5.82	4.13	16.63	4.37
Manipur	—	21.43	29.24	15.86	16.13
Meghalaya	—	12.93	17.82	32.93	63.68
Nagaland	—	12.71	16.51	27.77	26.46
Orissa	18.42	16.65	15.64	14.95	13.77
Punjab	5.66	2.88	2.36	15.80	10.43
Rajasthan	12.19	9.82	8.20	15.37	11.88
Tamil Nadu	4.31	3.83	3.07	15.42	12.36
Tripura	—	58.56	27.18	24.91	45.97
Uttar Pradesh	13.29	9.19	7.98	20.89	10.73
West Bengal	8.34	6.32	5.31	13.93	10.12
All States	9.60	5.97	5.35	15.93	11.16

1975-76, the average cost of tax collection per rupee declined to 5.97 paise and the cost varied from 2.52 paise for Gujarat to 58.56 paise for Tripura. The cost was more than 10 paise per rupee in the States of Tripura, Manipur, Jammu and Kashmir, Orissa, Meghalaya, Nagaland and Himachal Pradesh.

For the next three years' average period, 1979-80 through 1981-82, the cost of tax collection further dropped to 5.35 paise per rupee for All States. The cost was the highest for Manipur (29.24 paise) and the lowest for Haryana (2.29 paise). In Manipur, Tripura, Meghalaya, Nagaland, Orissa, Jammu and Kashmir, Himachal Pradesh, Assam and Bihar, the cost of tax collection was significantly higher than the overall average. It was lower than the average in the relatively developed States like Haryana, Gujarat, Punjab, Maharashtra and Tamil Nadu. It fell significantly in the States of Gujarat, Punjab, Uttar Pradesh and West Bengal over the period under study. It was a happy sign that for all the States taken together, the cost of tax collection grew at a lower rate (11.16 per cent) than the States' tax revenue (15.93 per cent). This phenomenon was true even for the individual States except Manipur, Meghalaya and Tripura. Punjab, too, was favourably placed in this regard.

From the above discussion, it may be concluded that almost all the States have made meagre tax efforts. The proportion of tax to per capita income was generally low in the States with relatively high per capita income, *viz.* Punjab, Haryana and Maharashtra. In other words, the burden of State taxes in these States was comparatively low. This indicates that the Punjab State has not been putting in adequate effort for raising revenue commensurate with the taxable capacity of the State. Punjab is the richest State in terms of per capita income but it does not apply the highest effective rate for the tax revenue. Under progressivity, the taxable capacity in a State like Punjab, with higher per capita income than an average State, is also expected to be high comparatively. This means that if Punjab applies some higher effective rate than that for the period under study, as suggested by progressivity, it can mobilise some additional resources from States' own tax revenue. It was, however, a happy augury that the cost of tax collection in relation to tax revenue was diminishing in all the States except Manipur, Meghalaya and Tripura. Punjab was particularly in a favourable position in this respect.

Notes and References

1. Reddy, K.N., *op. cit.*, p. 1916.
2. This methodology has been used in Chapters III and IV also.

3

INTER-STATE TAX EFFORT—INDIVIDUAL TAX ANALYSIS

So far, we have dealt with the aggregate tax analysis. It has not explicitly brought out the relationship between the individual taxes and the related economic variables. Information on these relationships will be quite useful in making inter-State comparisons of tax effort. It will also enable us to draw conclusions regarding the specific directions in which the tax efforts in a particular State should move. This chapter analyses individual taxes.

Agricultural Income Tax and Land Revenue

Table 3.1 examines the percentage share of agricultural income tax in States' own tax revenue along with their buoyancies and growth rates. Agricultural income tax was first levied in 1938; since then many States have incorporated it in their tax structure. Andhra Pradesh, Gujarat, Haryana, Himachal Pradesh, Jammu and Kashmir, Madhya Pradesh, Manipur, Meghalaya, Nagaland and Punjab do not have this tax. During the three years' average period 1967-68 through 1969-70, the overall percentage share of agricultural income-tax was only 0.98. It varied from 0.02 per cent for Rajasthan to 11.55 per cent for Assam. However, during the next three years, 1973-74 through 1975-76, the overall share declined to 0.62 per cent and this decline was true of all the States except Assam. Further, the proportion of agricultural income-tax to States' own tax revenue ranged between 0.07 per cent for Maharashtra and 15.52 per cent for Assam.

TABLE 3.1 : **Percentage Share of Agricultural Income Tax in States' Own Tax Revenue**

State	*Three years' average share for 1967-68 through 1969-70*	*Three years' average share for 1973-74 through 1975-76*	*Three years' average share for 1979-80 through 1981-82*	*Growth rate (per cent)*	*Buoyancy*
Andhra Pradesh	—	—	—	—	—
Assam	11.55	15.52	20.66	18.14	1.812
Bihar	0.25	0.11	—	—8.02	—0.781
Gujarat	—	—	—	—	—
Haryana	—	—	—	—	—
Himachal Pradesh	—	—	—	—	—
Jammu & Kashmir	—	—	—	—	—
Karnataka	2.23	1.03	2.42	17.37	1.734
Kerala	5.56	3.73	3.07	11.31	1.044
Madhya Pradesh	—	—	—	—	—
Maharashtra	0.20	0.07	0.02	8.00	0.623
Manipur	—	—	—	—	—
Meghalaya	—	—	—	—	—
Nagaland	—	—	—	—	—
Orissa	0.23	0.12	0.00	—8.122	—0.804
Punjab	—	—	—	—	—
Rajasthan	0.02	0.00	0.00	—	—
Tamil Nadu	1.58	0.74	0.86	8.98	1.134
Tripura	—	0.82	1.29	24.51	2.403
Uttar Pradesh	0.11	0.00	0.00	—	—
West Bengal	1.38	0.61	0.67	7.01	1.023
All States	0.98	0.62	0.69	13.28	1.375

During the period 1979-80 through 1981-82, a slight improvement (to 0.69 per cent) was observed in the overall percentage share of agricultural income-tax which had variation from 0.02 for Maharashtra to 20.66 for Assam. Again, it was only in the case of Assam that the percentage contribution of agricultural income-tax was significant.[1] Despite the fact that its contribution was not significant in most of the States, the growth rate recorded was quite high. For all the States taken together, it was 13.28 per cent per annum and it varied between 7.01 per cent for West Bengal and 24.51 per cent for Tripura. However, in the case of Bihar and Orissa, it was negative. The significantly high growth rate recorded in Tripura was because of low value in the base year. The growth rate of agricultural income-tax in the States of Assam (18.14 per cent) and Kerala (17.37 per cent) was also higher than All States' average. The buoyancy coefficients followed the pattern of growth rates.

The agricultural income-tax, which is under the jurisdiction of the States, was found to be less intensively used than warranted for. An analysis of the revenues from this source and the relevant proxy bases, *viz.* agricultural income and the level of agricultural production, indicated a considerable scope for raising revenue from this source. In other words, its rate of growth was estimated to be much lower than that of the relevant bases such as agricultural income and agricultural production. As the revenue requirements of the States are duly high, this source ought to be adequately tapped.

Land revenue is an old direct tax on land which has become inelastic owing to the non-revision of its assessment. Table 3.2 depicts the percentage share of land revenue in States' own tax revenue for different States. For the three years' period 1967-68 through 1969-70, this share was 8.53 per cent for all the States taken together and it varied from 2.83 per cent for Punjab to 17.87 per cent for Uttar Pradesh. During the next phase *i.e.* 1973-74 through 1975-76, the percentage share of land revenue dropped to 6.26 for all the States and it ranged between 0.80 for Punjab and 30.60 for Tripura. Further, the percentage share of land revenue increased only in Andhra Pradesh, Assam and Haryana, while for all other States it registered a fall.

From 1979-80 through 1981-82, the overall share of land revenue further dwindled to 2.45 per cent and it varied between

TABLE 3.2 : **Percentage Share of Land Revenue in States' Own Tax Revenue**

State	*Three years' average share for 1967-68 through 1969-70*	*Three years' average share for 1973-74 through 1975-76*	*Three years' average share for 1979-80 through 1981-82*	*Growth rate (per cent)*	*Buoyancy*
Andhra Pradesh	13.59	14.95	5.56	7.22	0.797
Assam	13.01	14.58	3.87	—2.71	—0.294
Bihar	12.02	10.17	4.69	8.07	0.783
Gujarat	8.70	3.90	2.21	3.90	0.356
Haryana	3.73	4.60	1.49	10.88	0.956
Himachal Pradesh	—	5.50	1.64	5.14	0.716
Jammu & Kashmir	10.76	4.66	1.72	2.13	0.167
Karnataka	8.65	3.30	1.49	1.54	0.165
Kerala	3.16	2.51	0.96	5.88	0.598
Madhya Pradesh	10.75	9.80	2.49	4.09	0.485
Maharashtra	4.43	3.57	1.64	7.61	0.579
Manipur	—	17.07	6.76	—0.15	—0.132
Meghalaya	—	3.52	1.92	12.64	—
Nagaland	4.88	1.73	0.98	10.69	—
Orissa	5.74	4.93	4.06	11.67	1.242
Punjab	2.83	0.80	0.66	2.98	0.130
Rajasthan	16.59	10.96	5.57	5.08	0.388
Tamil Nadu	3.40	2.35	1.35	5.33	0.542
Tripura	—	30.60	3.15	4.37	0.594
Uttar Pradesh	17.87	10.79	4.15	4.26	0.505
West Bengal	4.94	3.48	1.23	2.90	0.520
All States	8.53	6.26	2.45	4.95	0.503

0.66 per cent for Punjab and 6.70 per cent for Manipur. Interestingly, the pecentage share of land revenue during this period was low in all the States compared with the preceding period. Further, in the States of Haryana, Himachal Pradesh, Kerala, Maharashtra, Meghalaya, Nagaland, Orissa, Punjab, Tamil Nadu and West Bengal, the percentage share of land revenue was consistently less than all States' average. The diminishing role of land revenue in the process of resource mobilisation was conspicuous in view of the fact that its share was declining for all the States over the period.

No doubt, the share of land revenue in States' own tax revenue was on the decline, yet the amount collected in absolute term was on the increase. For all the States taken together, the growth rate of land revenue for the period 1967-68 through 1982-83 was 4.95 per cent per annum. The positive growth rates were in the range of 1.54 per cent for Karnataka to 12.64 per cent for Meghalaya. The significantly high growth rate recorded in Meghalaya was due to the lower base period value. In two States, *viz.* Assam and Manipur, land revenue recorded a negative growth rate. Further, for Gujarat, Jammu and Kashmir, Assam, Karnataka, Madhya Pradesh, Manipur, Punjab and West Bengal, the growth rates of land revenue actually were less than all States' average. The buoyancy coefficients for different States followed, more or less, the path of growth rates. It was only in case of Orissa that the buoyancy coefficient was more than unity (1.242), whereas for all other States it was less than unity. It meant that 1 per cent increase in NSDP was usually accompanied by less than 1 per cent increase in land revenue.

The land revenue being generally fixed for a long period, there is no reason to expect any functional relationship between income from agriculture (or NSDP) and the yield from land revenue. The variations in the collection of land revenue, if any, may be due to conversion of forest land and other waste land to cultivable land. But all these changes affect the yield from land revenue very little and are not related to the changes in income from agriculture. The reasons for the inadequate taxation of land are : political influence of land owners; failure to rectify the excessively low evaluation basis through higher rates; and the difficulty of making productivity assessment and keeping it up to date.

Theoretically, land revenue depends on the productivity of land *i.e.* on the net income from land. While carrying out the land revenue settlements, the net produce of land was taken into account. As resettlements were not carried out for a long period, land revenue payable might have become out of line with productivity or net incomes. Yet potentially, it is the net income from agriculture that sets a limit to the amount of land revenue that can be collected. In addition to land revenue, some States also levy agricultural income-tax. However, the greater part of agricultural income-tax is usually obtained from the taxation of plantations income.

A question arises—should we relate tax yield to NSDP or to some other related tax base ? In this connection the observation of J. Maxwell is relevant : "When measurement of overall built-in flexibility is in question, it seems proper to take national or gross national product as the base. But when particular taxes are being examined, it may seem appropriate to relate changes in tax yield to changes in the precise base upon which the tax is levied."[2] Hence, it seems reasonable to take the net income from agriculture *i.e.*, the NSDP originating in the agriculture sector, to be the potential base for land revenue and agricultural income tax. For our purposes, we have taken the sum total of yield from both these taxes.

Table 3.3 depicts the effective rates and average effective rates of land revenue and agricultural income-tax for three different periods. The effective rates of the two taxes combined varied from 1.65 per cent in Assam to 0.25 per cent in Punjab for the period 1967-68 through 1969-70. The average effective rate was less than 1 per cent *i.e.* 0.81 per cent. The indices of use of tax potential of land revenue and agricultural income-tax were significantly higher than unity in the case of Assam, Rajasthan and Andhra Pradesh. During the next period 1973-74 through 1975-76, the average effective rate came down to 0.71 per cent. The effective rates showed variation from 0.09 per cent in Punjab to 1.95 per cent in Assam. It was again in the case of Assam and Andhra Pradesh that indices of use of tax potential were significantly higher than unity.

For the period 1979-80 through 1981-82, the average effective rate further slid down to 0.56 per cent. The effective rates ranged between 0.11 per cent in Punjab and 1.56 per cent in Assam.

TABLE 3.3: **Effective Rates and Tax Potentials for Agricultural Income Tax and Land Revenue**

State	*1967-68 through 1969-70*						*1973-74 through 1975-76*					
	Revenue from land revenue and agricultural income-tax (Rs. lakhs)	*Tax base* (Rs. lakhs)*	*Effective rate (%)*	*Tax potentials (Rs. lakhs)*	*Index of use of tax potential (col. 2/col. 5)*	*Ranking in terms of col. 6*	*Revenue from land revenue and agricultural income-tax (Rs. lakhs)*	*Tax base* (Rs. lakhs)*	*Effective rate (%)*	*Tax potentials (Rs. lakhs)*	*Index of use of tax potential (col. 8/col. 11)*	*Ranking in terms of col. 12*
1	*2*	*3*	*4*	*5*	*6*	*7*	*8*	*9*	*10*	*11*	*12*	*13*
Andhra Predesh	1313.33	117833.67	1.11	954.45	1.3760	3	3882.00	231433.33	1.65	1443.18	2.3625	2
Assam	617.33	37400.00	1.65	302.94	2.0378	1	1377.00	70490.00	1.95	500.48	2.7514	1
Bihar	882.00	106700.00	0.83	864.27	1.0205	8	1526.67	219766.67	0.69	1560.34	0.9784	9
Gujarat	695.33	69485.33	1.00	562.83	1.2354	4	765.30	121433.33	0.63	862.18	0.8877	10
Haryana	123.33	43925.33	0.28	355.80	0.3466	14	449.00	89017.67	0.50	632.03	0.7104	11
Himachal Pradesh	—	—	—	—	—	—	74.33	18833.33	0.39	133.72	0.5559	15
Jammu and Kashmir	62.67	11401.33	0.55	92.35	0.6786	13	66.97	21216.00	0.31	150.85	0.4420	16

Karnataka	823.00	92112.00	0.89	746.11	1.1031	7	846.67	177633.33	0.48	1261.20	0.6713	12
Kerala	497.33	52437.67	0.95	424.75	1.1709	6	787.33	93833.33	0.84	666.22	1.1818	4
Madhya Pradesh	764.67	99563.33	0.77	806.46	0.9482	10	1740.33	194600.00	0.89	1381.66	1.2596	3
Maharashtra	864.67	106532.00	0.81	864.67	1.0000	9	1778.00	221400.00	0.80	1571.94	1.1311	6
Manipur	—	—	—	—	—	—	23.33	5466.67	0.43	38.81	0.6011	14
Orissa	154.67	57145.33	0.27	462.88	0.3341	15	271.33	108463.33	0.25	770.09	0.3523	17
Punjab	181.33	73198.00	0.25	592.90	0.3058	16	121.67	131566.67	0.09	934.12	0.1303	18
Rajasthan	824.00	64442.67	1.28	521.99	1.5786	2	1197.00	144966.67	0.83	1029.26	1.1630	5
Tamil Nadu	575.00	76761.67	0.75	621.77	0.9248	11	926.00	131066.67	0.71	926.00	1.0000	8
Uttar Predesh	2384.33	238628.67	1.00	1932.89	1.2336	5	3220.67	387966.67	0.83	2754.56	1.0437	7
West Bengal	719.67	116393.67	0.62	942.79	0.7633	12	947.67	204400.00	0.46	1451.24	0.6530	13
Average effective rate=0.81 per cent							Average effective rate=0.71 per cent					

*Tax base=Agricultural income

(*Contd.*)

State	1979-80 through 1981-82					
	Revenue from land revenue and agricultural income tax (Rs. lakhs)	*Tax base* (Rs. lakhs)*	*Effective rate (%)*	*Tax potential (Rs. lakhs)*	*Index of use of tax potential (Col. 14/ col. 17)*	*Ranking in terms of col. 18*
	14	*15*	*16*	*17*	*18*	*19*
Andhra Pradesh	3292.33	342024.00	0.96	1915.33	1.7189	3
Assam	1865.33	119200.00	1.56	667.52	2.7944	1
Bihar	1327.00	278800.00	0.48	1561.28	0.8489	9
Gujarat	1208.00	199695.00	0.60	1118.29	1.0802	7
Haryana	357.33	148005.33	0.24	828.83	0.4314	15
Himachal Pradesh	57.00	27463.67	0.21	153.80	0.3706	17
Jammu and Kashmir	73.00	33310.67	0.22	186.54	0.3913	16
Karnataka	1938.33	223125.00	0.87	1249.50	1.5513	4
Karala	1346.00	129032.33	1.04	722.58	1.8628	2
Madhya Pradesh	980.33	253926.67	0.39	1421.99	0.6890	11
Maharashtra	1941.67	373744.67	0.52	2092.97	0.9278	8
Manipur	20.33	8206.33	0.25	45.96	0.4423	14
Orissa	547.67	157368.33	0.35	881.26	0.6215	13

Punjab	238.00	211899.67	0.11	1186.64	0.2006	18
Rajasthan	1410.33	208986.00	0.67	1170.32	1.2051	6
Tamil Nadu	1297.67	168836.00	0.77	945.48	1.3725	5
Uttar Pradesh	2809.33	592149.67	0.47	3316.04	0.8472	10
West Bengal	1013.33	285249.00	0.37	1541.39	0.6574	12

Average effective rate=0.56 per cent

*Tax base=Agricultural income

For Assam, Kerala, Andhra Pradesh and Karnataka, the use indices were found to be significantly above unity. It was found that the States which did not impose agricultural income-tax had invariably low effective rates. Land revenue did not move with the growth of its base *i.e.* agricultural income. Further, the effective rates of the two taxes in question declined over the period under study in all the States. The States of Punjab, Haryana, Himachal Pradesh and Jammu and Kashmir could easily mobilise more resources from these taxes by applying the average effective rate.

Punjab has a predominantly agricultural economy. For the year 1981-82, the contribution of agriculture to the NSDP was 44 per cent as against 35 per cent for the country as a whole. It is, therefore, necessary that adequate resources should be raised from the agricultural sector. There is abundant evidence to show that in recent years the tax-paying capacity of the agricultural sector, especially the large landholders, has increased considerably owing to increase in agricultural income. There has also been a substantial increase in the yield per hectare of all major crops during the last two decades. Moreover, the State Government has spent more than 50 per cent of its total plan expenditure on agricultural programmes, irrigation and power projects. Besides, the State Government has been giving various kinds of subsidies from time to time to this sector.

In Punjab, the only taxes that are levied on the agricultural sector are land revenue and surcharge on cash crops. The contribution of these taxes to the State tax structure has been diminishing progressively. From 3.69 per cent in 1967-68, their contribution shrank to 0.69 per cent in 1982-83. Land revenue is levied at a flat rate and has been fixed in money term for a number of years. Pending a fresh land settlement, a surcharge on land revenue can be levied in the State on a sliding scale.

Profession Tax

The formal name of this tax is 'tax on professions, trade callings and employment'. It is required to be paid by all those who are engaged in some profession or trade or are in some gainful employment. This tax is mostly confined to urban areas. Table 3.4 exhibits the percentage share of profession tax to States' own tax revenue. While in some States, *viz.* Andhra Pradesh, Bihar,

TABLE 3.4 : **Percentage Share of Profession Tax in States' Own Tax Revenue**

State	*Three years' average share for*			*Growth rate (per cent)*	*Buoyancy*
	1967-68 through 1969-70	*1973-74 through 1975-76*	*1979-80 through 1981-82*		
Andhra Pradesh	—	—	—	—	—
Assam	0.84	0.92	1.18	13.66	1.134
Bihar	—	—	—	—	—
Gujarat	—	—	1.47	19.30	1.468
Haryana	0.60	0.48	0.01	—10.37	—0.954
Himachal Pradesh	—	—	—	—	—
Jammu & Kashmir	—	—	—	—	—
Karnataka	—	—	1.55	23.59	1.928
Kerala	0.02	0.03	0.11	27.20	2.214
Madhya Pradesh	0.76	0.69	0.73	12.67	1.382
Maharashtra	—	2.35	2.73	18.13	1.364
Manipur	—	—	3.60	—	—
Meghalaya	—	1.76	2.38	23.57	—
Nagaland	—	2.30	5.04	35.53	—
Orissa	—	—	—	—	—
Punjab	0.13	—	—	—	—
Rajasthan	—	—	—	—	—
Tamil Nadu	—	—	—	—	—
Tripura	—	2.72	6.86	14.26	1.119
Uttar Pradesh	1.10	0.14	0.03	—23.08	—2.460
West Bengal	—	—	1.93	—	—
All States	0.20	0.25	0.32	24.90	1.854

Himachal Pradesh, Jammu and Kashmir, Orissa and Rajasthan, this tax is not levied at all, in other States, *viz.* Karnataka, Kerala and Tamil Nanu, it is levied by the local bodies. In Punjab, this tax was abolished in 1968. Kerala and Haryana also discontinued this tax after 1981. The States of Gujarat, Karnataka and West Bengal levied this tax after 1975. During the three years' average for 1967-68 through 1969-70, the overall share of profession tax to States' own tax revenue was 0.20 per cent, which varied from 0.02 per cent for Kerala to 1.10 per cent for Uttar Pradesh.

For the three years' average of 1973-74 through 1975-76, the overall share of profession tax went up to 0.25 per cent, and it ranged from 0.03 per cent for Kerala to 2.72 per cent for Tripura. The share of profession tax was significant in the States of Tripura, Maharashtra, Nagaland and Meghalaya. During the three years' average of 1979-80 through 1981-82, the share of profession tax further mounted to 0.32 per cent, and varied between 0.03 per cent for Uttar Pradesh and 6.86 per cent for Tripura.

Thus, on the whole, the share of profession tax was consistently on the increase. Further, it was only the States of Assam, Kerala, Maharashtra, Meghalaya, Negaland and Tripura, which followed the all States pattern. The other States either discontinued this tax or relied relatively little on this tax as a source of revenue. The overall growth rate of profession tax was found to be 24.90 per cent per annum. The positive growth rates ranged between 12.67 per cent for Madhya Pradesh and 35.33 per cent for Nagaland. Haryana and Uttar Pradesh experienced a negative growth rate. Although buoyancy coefficients followed, more or less, the trends in growth rates, yet they revealed that this tax was highly buoyant as a source of revenue.

The effective rates of this tax (Table 3.5) have been computed by taking the incomes from public administration, trade, hotels and resturants, banking and insurance and other sources as the tax base. During the three years' average period 1967-68 through 1969-70, the average effective rate worked out to only 0.15 per cent. The States with indices of use of tax potential markedly above unity were Assam, Haryana, Uttar Pradesh and Madhya Pradesh. For the next three years' period *i.e.* 1973-74 through 1975-76, the average effective rate rose to 0.31 per cent and the States of Assam, Haryana, Maharashtra and Tripura were found to be having indices of use of tax potential significantly higher than unity.

For the next three years' period, 1979-80 to 1981-82, the average effective rate increased marginally to 0.32 per cent. For the States levying this tax, the effective rates showed variations from 0.03 per cent for Haryana to 0.77 per cent for Maharashtra. The States of Maharashtra, Karnataka, Tripura, West Bengal and Gujarat, had indices of use of tax potential notably higher than unity. Thus, it is evident that the States, except Maharashtra, Karnataka, Tripura, West Bengal and Gujarat were not earnestly exploiting this source of revenue. For all the States taken together, the total yield during this period was only Rs. 62.64 crores. Had all the States imposed this tax and an average effective rate of 1 per cent was reached, the total yield would have been as much as Rs. 236.59 crores. Punjab, too, could have mobilised Rs. 4.27 crores additionally, if it had imposed profession tax at the average effective rate. At an effective rate of 1 per cent, however, the total yield could have reached the level of Rs. 13.55 crores.

Stamp Duty and Registration Fee

These taxes cover the duties levied on various deeds and documents, executed as a proof or record of certain legal transactions. In India, stamp duty is of two types—judicial and non-judicial. The former is regulated under the Court Fee Act, 1870, and the latter, under Indian Stamp Act, 1899. Registration fee is collected in the course of the registration of various types of instruments or deeds relating to financial transactions under the Indian Registration Act, 1908.

Percentage share of stamp duty and registration fee in the States' own tax revenue is given in Table 3.6. For the three years' average period, 1967-68 through 1969-70, the overall share of stamp duty and registration fee was 8.60 per cent, and ranged from 5.23 per cent for Rajasthan to 13.61 per cent for Haryana. The percentage share for the States of Haryana, Tamil Nadu, Bihar, Punjab and Kerala, was significantly higher than all States' average. During the next three years' average period, *i.e.* 1973-74 through 1975-76, the overall contribution of this tax moved down to 6.80 per cent and this downward movement was true of all

TABLE 3.5: **Effective Rates and Tax Potentials for Profession Tax**

State	*1967-68 through 1969-70*						*1973-74 through 1975-76*					
	Tax revenue (Rs. lakhs)	*Tax base* (Rs. lakhs)*	*Effective rate (%)*	*Tax potential (Rs. lakhs)*	*Index of use of tax potential (col. 2/col. 5)*	*Ranking in terms of col. 6*	*Tax revenue (Rs. lakhs)*	*Tax base* (Rs. lakhs)*	*Effective rate (%)*	*Tax potential (Rs. lakhs)*	*Index of use of tax potential (col. 8/col. 11)*	*Ranking in terms of col. 12*
1	*2*	*3*	*4*	*5*	*6*	*7*	*8*	*9*	*10*	*11*	*12*	*13*
Andhra Pradesh	—	43810.00	—	65.72	—	—	—	97893.00	—	303.47	—	—
Assam	21.00	7325.00	0.29	10.99	1.9108	1	42.00	21473.33	0.20	66.57	1.5850	4
Bihar	—	41533.33	—	62.30	—	—	—	50900.00	—	157.79	—	—
Gujarat	—	38435.33	—	57.65	—	—	—	84600.00	—	262.26	—	—
Haryana	20.00	9913.33	0.20	14.87	1.3633	2	46.33	25912.00	0.18	80.33	1.7339	3
Himachal Pradesh	—	3726.67	—	5.59	—	—	—	7700.00	—	23.87	—	—
Jammu and Kashmir	—	4020.33	—	6.03	—	—	—	8936.67	—	27.70	—	—

Karnataka	—	29256.67	—	43.89	—	—	—	60333.33	—	187.03	—	—
Kerala	1.00	24265.67	0.004	36.40	0.0274	6	4.00	46066.67	0.009	142.81	0.0280	7
Madhya Pradesh	54.33	27150.00	0.20	40.73	1.3339	3	123.00	57733.33	0.21	178.97	0.6873	5
Maha-rashtra	—	82320.00	—	123.48	—	—	1376.00	183933.33	0.75	570.19	2.4132	1
Manipur	—	1016.67	—	1.53	—	—	—	2166.67	—	6.72	—	—
Orissa	—	17060.67	—	25.59	—	—	—	23966.67	—	74.30	—	—
Punjab (67-69)	8.50	23144.00	0.04	34.72	0.2448	5	—	45233.35	—	140.22	—	—
Rajasthan	—	23292.00	—	34.94	—	—	—	42600.00	—	132.06	—	—
Tamil Nadu	—	55483.67	—	83.23	—	—	—	95433.33	—	295.84	—	—
Tripura	—	1644.67	—	2.47	—	—	17.00	2134.00	0.80	8.61	1.9744	2
Uttar Pradesh	145.67	76737.33	0.19	115.11	1.2655	4	43.00	135633.33	0.03	420.46	0.1023	6
West Bengal	—	66947.33	—	100.42	—	—	—	119766.67	—	371.28	—	—
	Average effective rate=0.15 per cent						Average effective rate=0.31 per cent					

(Contd.)

State	1979-80 through 1981-82					
	Tax reveuue (Rs. lakhs)	*Tax base* (Rs. lakhs)*	*Effective rate (%)*	*Tax potential (Rs. lakhs)*	*Index of use of tax potential (col. 14/ col. 17)*	*Ranking in terms of col. 18*
	14	*15*	*16*	*17*	*18*	*19*
Andhra Pradesh	—	164668.35	—	526.94	—	—
Assam	89.67	44946.67	0.20	143.83	0.6234	8
Bihar	—	131366.67	—	420.37	—	—
Gujarat	806.67	186178.00	0.43	595.77	1.3540	5
Haryana	2.00	67266.67	0.003	215.25	0.0093	11
Himachal Pradesh	—	14048.33	—	44.95	—	—
Jammu and Kashmir	—	18510.00	—	59.23	—	—
Karnataka	766.67	111850.67	0.69	357.92	2.1420	2
Kerala	36.00	97535.00	0.04	312.11	0.1153	9
Madhya Pradesh	289.33	104183.33	0.28	333.39	0.8678	7
Maharashtra	3182.33	415831.67	0.77	1330.67	2.3915	1
Manipur	14.00	4200.33	0.33	13.44	1.0417	6
Orissa	—	53306.33	—	170.58	—	—
Punjab (67-69)	—	133473.67	—	427.12	—	—

Rajasthan	—	100770.67	—	322.47	—	—
Tamil Nadu	—	164693.67	—	527.02	—	—
Tripura	28.33	5407.00	0.52	17.30	1.6376	3
Uttar Pradesh	18.33	330493.00	0.005	1057.58	0.0173	10
West Bengal	1030.33	217130.67	0.48	694.82	1.4829	4

Average effective rate=0.32 per cent

*Tax base=Income from public administration, trade, hotels and resturants, banking and insurance and other services.

TABLE 3.6: **Percentage Share of Stamp Duty and Registration Fee in States' Own Tax Revenue**

State	*Three years' average share for 1967-68 through 1969-70*	*Three years' average share for 1973-74 through 1975-76*	*Three years' average share for 1979-80 through 1981-82*	*Growth rate (per cent)*	*Buoyancy*
Andhra Pradesh	9.15	6.08	5.87	12.49	1.105
Assam	5.48	4.45	3.85	6.91	0.620
Bihar	11.61	10.33	5.85	6.37	0.663
Gujarat	6.67	5.34	5.67	15.61	1.136
Haryana	13.61	8.17	8.16	12.93	0.936
Himachal Pradesh	—	6.86	5.54	21.31	1.802
Jammu and Kashmir	8.58	5.11	4.87	12.35	0.857
Karnataka	7.62	5.32	5.42	13.35	1.297
Kerala	9.67	9.32	7.82	14.32	1.276
Madhya Pradesh	6.80	5.79	5.80	14.08	1.321
Maharashtra	6.36	3.89	3.62	11.28	0.852
Manipur	—	7.56	6.10	8.23	0.709
Meghalaya	—	4.58	3.44	16.53	—
Nagaland	—	1.34	1.20	19.04	—
Orissa	8.43	8.13	6.02	11.70	1.150
Punjab	10.94	10.89	10.34	14.95	1.140
Rajasthan	5.23	4.39	5.34	14.79	1.173
Tamil Nadu	12.23	8.38	7.03	10.30	0.997
Tripura	—	24.59	13.72	16.12	1.356
Uttar Pradesh	8.69	8.28	10.85	17.60	1.568
West Bengal	8.49	7.56	5.52	10.59	1.087
All States	8.60	6.80	6.37	13.02	1.151

States. However, it varied between 1.34 per cent for Nagaland and 24.59 per cent for Tripura.

For the three years' average period, 1979-80 through 1981-82, the percentage share of stamp duty and registration fee further dipped to 6.37 for all the States taken together. And this share had a range of 1.20 per cent for Nagaland to 13.72 per cent for Tripura. However, over the period under study, the percentage share slipped down in every State except Rajasthan and Uttar Pradesh. Further, the growth rate of revenue from this tax was the highest for Himachal Pradesh (21.31 per cent) and the lowest for Bihar (6.37 per cent). Buoyancy coefficients, though these followed the pattern of growth rates, were more than unity for the States of Himachal Pradesh, Uttar Pradesh, Tripura, Madhya Pradesh, Karnataka, Kerala, Rajasthan, Orissa, Punjab, Gujarat, Andhra Pradesh and West Bengal. This meant that in all these States 1 per cent increase in NSDP was accompanied by more than 1 per cent increase in revenue for stamp duty and registration fee.

To estimate the effective rates, NSDP has been used as the potential base. The results are given in Table 3.7. For the three years' average period 1967-68 through 1969-70, the effective rates varied from 0.19 per cent for Assam to 0.71 per cent for Tamil Nadu, the overall being 0.39 per cent. The States of Tamil Nadu, Haryana, Punjab and Kerala, had indices of use of tax potential significantly higher than unity. For the next period *i.e.* 1973-74 through 1975-76, the average effective rate worked out to 0.36 per cent. The effective rates ranged from 0.11 per cent for Manipur to 0.74 per cent for Punjab. During this period, the abovementioned four States *i.e.* Punjab, Tamil Nadu, Kerala and Haryana, continued to exploit the tax potential markedly. For the period 1979-80 through 1981-82, the average effective rate stepped up to 0.43 per cent and this rate varied between 0.12 per cent for Assam and 0.80 per cent for Punjab. The same four States maintained indices of use of tax potential notably higher than unity. On the other hand, the States of Assam, Manipur, Jammu and Kashmir and Bihar, had indices significantly lower than unity. Although in relation to NSDP, Punjab, Tamil Nadu, Kerala and Haryana, exploited this source rather intensively, yet the relative importance of this tax was on the decline.

TABLE 3.7: **Effective Rates and Tax Potentials for Stamp Duty and Registration Fee**

State	1967-68 through 1969-70						1973-74 through 1975-76					
	Tax revenue (Rs. lakhs)	Tax base* (Rs. lakhs)	Effective rate (%)	Tax potential (Rs. lakhs)	Index of use of tax potential (col. 2/col. 5)	Ranking in terms of col. 6	Tax revenue (Rs. lakhs)	Tax base* (Rs. lakhs)	Effective rate (%)	Tax potential (Rs. lakhs)	Index of use of tax potential (col. 8/col. 11)	Ranking in terms of col. 12
1	2	3	4	5	6	7	8	9	10	11	12	13
Andhra Pradesh	884.33	208788.67	0.42	814.28	1.0860	5	1577.33	427166.67	0.37	1537.80	1.0257	6
Assam	137.67	69025.00	0.19	269.20	0.9114	8	203.67	122180.00	0.17	439.85	0.4630	17
Bihar	835.00	208233.33	0.40	812.11	1.0282	6	1534.67	386700.00	0.40	1392.12	1.1024	5
Gujarat	533.33	162559.33	0.33	633.98	0.8412	11	1047.33	324833.33	0.32	1169.40	0.8956	9
Haryana	450.33	67629.33	0.67	263.75	1.7074	2	796.00	144974.67	0.55	521.91	1.5252	4
Himachal Pradesh	—	—	—	—	—	—	92.67	40026.67	0.23	144.10	0.6431	14
Jammu and Kashmir	50.00	20099.67	0.25	78.39	0.6378	14	73.00	41650.67	0.18	149.94	0.4869	16
Karnataka	576.33	163981.00	0.35	639.53	0.9012	9	1038.67	320566.67	0.32	1154.04	0.9000	8
Kerala	551.67	100812.00	0.55	393.17	1.4031	4	1177.00	196866.67	0.60	708.72	1.6607	3

Madhya Pradesh	483.67	175576.67	0.28	684.75	0.7063	13	1028.00	344533.33	0.30	1240.32	0.8288	10
Maharashtra	1212.33	337008.83	0.36	1314.33	0.9224	7	1901.33	703800.00	0.28	2533.68	0.7504	12
Manipur	—	—	—	—	—	—	10.33	9133.33	0.11	32.95	0.3135	18
Orissa	218.33	96439.67	0.23	376.11	0.5805	16	436.67	167266.67	0.26	602.16	0.7252	13
Punjab	701.00	116510.00	0.61	454.39	1.5427	3	1625.00	220700.00	0.74	794.52	2.0453	1
Rajasthan	259.67	112509.67	0.23	438.79	0.5918	15	479.67	237133.33	0.20	853.68	0.5619	15
Tamil Nadu	1413.00	197696.67	0.71	771.02	1.8326	1	2509.33	367833.33	0.68	1324.20	1.8950	2
Uttar Pradesh	1152.33	402919.00	0.29	1571.38	0.7333	12	2471.00	679300.00	0.36	2471.00	1.0000	7
West Bengal	966.33	280876.00	0.34	1095.42	0.8822	10	1750.33	501000.00	0.35	1803.60	0.7827	11
		Average effective rate=0.39 per cect						Average effective rate=0.36 per cent				

*Tax base=Net State Domestic Product.

(*Contd.*)

State	1979-80 through 1981-82					
	Tax revenue (Rs. lakhs)	*Tax base* (Rs. lakhs)*	*Effective rate (%)*	*Tax potential (Rs. lakhs)*	*Index of use of tax potential (col. 14/ col. 17)*	*Ranking in terms of col. 18*
	14	*15*	*16*	*17*	*18*	*19*
Andhra Pradesh	3477.67	712710.67	0.49	3064.66	1.1348	7
Assam	292.67	240633.33	0.12	1034.72	0.2828	18
Bihar	1653.67	626700.00	0.26	2694.81	0.6136	15
Gujarat	3099.00	635526.33	0.49	2732.76	1.1340	8
Haryana	1964.33	292093.00	0.67	1255.99	1.5640	4
Himachal Pradesh	192.33	64735.33	0.30	278.36	0.6910	13
Jammu and Kashmir	206.33	86717.33	0.24	372.88	0.5533	16
Karnataka	2684.67	497809.00	0.54	2140.58	1.2542	6
Kerala	2611.67	345193.33	0.76	1484.33	1.7595	3
Madhya Pradesh	2286.67	557956.67	0.41	2399.21	0.9531	9
Maharashtra	4215.00	1399043.00	0.30	6015.88	0,7006	12
Manipur	18.33	14289.33	0.13	61.44	0.2983	17

Orissa	810.33	284472.33	0.28	1223.23	0.6625	14
Punjab	3758.67	471195.67	0.80	2026.14	1.8551	1
Rajasthan	1350.33	418944.67	0.32	1801.46	0.7496	11
Tamil Nadu	4611.00	606656.00	0.76	2608.62	1.7676	2
Uttar Pradesh	7341.00	1303872.30	0.56	5606.65	1.3093	5
West Bengal	2939.67	821983.00	0.36	3534.53	0.8317	10
Average effective rate=0.43 per cent						

*Tax base=Net State Domestic Product.

Sales Tax

The origin of modern general sales tax is traceable to the Government of India, Act, 1935. Entry 48 on List II (Provincial Legislative List) of the Seventh Schedule to the Government of India Act, 1935, granted exclusive powers to a State Government to impose tax on the sale and purchase of goods other than newspapers within the States. Acting under these powers, the province of Bombay was the first to levy a tax on the sale of tobacco in a limited way in 1938. In the same year, the Central Provinces also levied a retail tax on motor spirit and this was followed by the levy of a general sales tax in Madras in 1939. General Sales Tax was introduced in the erstwhile State of Punjab in 1941.

Sales tax, which has become almost number one as a source of State tax revenue, includes receipts under general sales tax, central sales tax, sales tax on motor spirits and purchase tax on sugar cane. The share of sales tax to States' own tax revenue is given in Table 3.8. For the three years' period 1967-68 through

TABLE 3.8: **Percentage Share of Sales Tax in States' Own Tax Revenue**

State	*Three years' average share for 1967-68 throngh 1969-70*	*Three years' average share for 1973-74 through 1975-76*	*Three years' average share for 1979-80 through 1981-82*	*Growth rate (per cent)*	*Buoyancy*
1	*2*	*3*	*4*	*5*	*6*
Andhra Pradesh	41.12	42.23	47.70	18.49	1.602
Assam	45.40	46.73	52.53	11.72	1.029
Bihar	48.52	49.02	69.47	16.07	1.554
Gujarat	58.25	65.33	67.40	18.85	1.482
Haryana	36.85	40.91	46.33	20.50	1.510

(*Contd.*)

1	*2*	*3*	*4*	*5*	*6*
Himachal Pradesh	—	27.89	40.48	28.70	2.535
Jammu and Kashmir	30.78	33.30	41.53	21.02	1.530
Karnataka	45.37	47.76	50.85	18.24	1.771
Kerala	51.08	59.95	61.11	17.96	1.562
Madhya Pradesh	45.53	48.84	52.62	17.45	1.579
Maha-rashtra	59.10	62.06	65.81	17.48	1.331
Manipur	—	48.05	50.44	18.13	1.591
Meghalaya	—	53.55	46.26	29.02	—
Nagaland	—	37.62	47.63	31.32	—
Orissa	51.61	54.53	58.65	16.17	1.582
Punjab	38.30	42.23	43.81	17.11	1.313
Rajasthan	45.96	51.90	61.84	18.02	1.445
Tamil Nadu	54.76	59.50	67.69	20.39	1.716
Tripura	—	—	52.95	10.40	1.023
Uttar Pradesh	39.47	49.70	54.51	18.42	1.678
West Bengal	50.50	55.56	60.06	19.85	1.988
All States	48.73	53.10	58.44	17.66	1.558

1969-70, the overall share of sales tax to States' own tax revenue was 48.73 per cent ; in the States, the share varied from 30.78 per cent for Jammu and Kashmir to 59.10 per cent for Maharashtra. The share of sales tax was more than 50 per cent in the States of Maharashtra, Gujarat, Tamil Nadu, Orissa and West Bengal. During the next phase, *i.e.* 1973-74 through 1975-76, the overall share of sales tax coursed upward to 53.10 per cent and the share ranged from 27.89 per cent for Himachal Pradesh to 65.73 per cent for Gujarat. During this period, three more States, *viz.*,

Kerala, Meghalaya and Rajasthan joined the category for which the share of sales tax was more than 50 per cent. In fact, the share of sales tax increased for all the States.

The overall share of sales tax further expanded to 58.44 per cent during the period 1979-80 through 1981-82. This share varied between 40.48 per cent for Himachal Pradesh and 69.47 per cent for Bihar. During this period, the share of sales tax was more than 50 per cent in as many as 14 States. In Punjab, the share of sales tax was 43.81 per cent which was one of the lowest in the country. However, barring Meghalaya, the percentage share of sales tax to total tax revenue has consistently improved in all the States. We may conclude that the States having more than 50 per cent share of sales tax were generally those where the share of non-agricultural sector to NSDP was relatively high.

The overall growth rate of sales tax revenue was found to be 17.66 per cent and the rate had a range of 10.40 per cent for Tripura to 31.32 per cent for Nagaland. In Punjab, the growth rate of sales tax (17.11 per cent) was less than all States' average. The important role which sales tax has come to occupy in a State's fiscal structure is because of its productivity. The buoyancy coefficient of sales tax for all the States taken together was found out to be 1.558. That is, 1 per cent change in NSDP led to 1.558 per cent additional revenue from sales tax. The buoyancy coefficients varied from 1.023 for Tripura to 2.535 for Himachal Pradesh. The States like Himachal Pradesh, West Bengal, Karnataka, Tamil Nadu, Uttar Pradesh and Andhra Pradesh, had higher buoyancy coefficients than all States' average. Further, although in the case of States like Tripura (1.023), Assam (1.029), Punjab (1.313) and Maharashtra (1.331), the buoyancy coefficients were considerably low yet they were above unity.

In the studies conducted so far, NSDP has been taken as the potential base for sales tax.[3] In the present study, however, we have examined the relative propriety of NSDP and non-agricultural State domestic product as the potential base for sales tax. We fitted in two linear regression equations given below. While in the first equation, we took NSDP as the explanatory variable, in the second, non-agricultural State domestic product was treated as the explanatory variable. The following results were obtained :

$$T = -9.7845 + 0.05203X_1 \qquad (R^2 = 0.9823),$$

$$T = -5.9458 + 0.08115X_2 \qquad (R^2 = 0.9938),$$

where T = revenve from sales tax,

X_1 = NSDP,

X_2 = non-agricultural State domestic product.

We naturally considered the non-agricultural State domestic product relatively appropriate potential base for sales tax.

Table 3.9 depicts the effective rates for sales tax. For the period 1967-68 through 1969-70, the average effective rate worked out to 4.33 per cent. The effective rate was the maximum for Kerala (6.02 per cent) and the minimum for Jammu and Kashmir (2.06 per cent). For Kerala, Punjab, Tamil Nadu, and Haryana, the indices of use of tax potential were significantly higher than unity. During the next three years' period, 1973-74 through 1975-76, the average effective rate rose to 5.25 per cent. The effective rate was the maximum for Tamil Nadu (7.52 per cent) and the minimum for Himachal Pradesh (1.78 per cent). The indices of use of tax potential were markedly above unity in the same four States as in the earlier period.

During the period 1979-80 through 1981-82, the average effective rate of sales tax further mounted to 6.46 per cent. The effective rate was the maximum for Tamil Nadu (10.14 per cent) and the minimum for Manipur (2.49 per cent). The indices of use of tax potential were notably higher than unity in the States of Tamil Nadu, Kerala, Karnataka, Gujarat and Haryana. After reaching the unitary limit in the earlier two periods, the index of use of tax potential fell below unity in Punjab. Perhaps, this State could not maintain the high effective rate on account of the growth of agricultural sector at a relatively fast rate.[4] Had Punjab applied the average effective rate, it could have mobilised about Rs. 8.32 crores additional revenue per annum.

State Excise Duty

The state excise duty is levied on all kinds of alcoholic liquor, opium, hemp, and other narcotics. Next to sales tax, it dominates States' tax structure. The contribution of state excise duty in each State is shown in Table 3.10. For the three years'

TABLE 3.9: **Effective Rates and Tax Potentials for Sales Tax**

State	1967-68 through 1969-70						1973-74 through 1975-76					
	Revenue from sales tax (Rs. lakhs)	*Tax base* (Rs. lakhs)*	*Effective rate (%)*	*Tax potential (Rs. lakhs)*	*Index of use of tax potential (col. 2/col. 5)*	*Ranking in term of col. 6*	*Revenue from sales tax (Rs. lakhs)*	*Tax base* (Rs. lakhs)*	*Effective rate (%)*	*Tax potential (Rs. lakhs)*	*Index of use of tax potential (col. 8/col. 11)*	*Ranking in terms of col. 12*
1	*2*	*3*	*4*	*5*	*6*	*7*	*8*	*9*	*10*	*11*	*12*	*13*
Andhra Pradesh	3973.67	90955.00	4.37	3938.35	1.0089	9	10964.33	195733.33	5.60	10275.99	1.0660	10
Assam	1140.67	31625.00	3.61	1369.36	0.8330	11	2137.33	51690.00	4.13	2713.73	0.7876	15
Bihar	3488.33	101533.33	3.44	4396.39	0.7935	13	7283.33	166933.33	4.36	8763.99	0.8311	13
Gujarat	4656.00	93074.00	5.00	4030.10	1.1553	5	12811.33	203400.00	6.30	10678.50	1.1997	6
Haryana	1219.00	23704.00	5.14	1026.38	1.1377	4	3984.67	55957.00	7.12	2937.74	1.3564	3
Himachal Pradesh	—	—	—	—	—	—	376.67	21193.33	1.78	1112.64	0.3385	18
Jammu & Kashmir	179.33	8698.33	2.06	376.64	0.4761	16	476.00	20404.67	2.33	1071.25	0.4443	16
Karnataka	3432.00	71869.00	4.78	3111.93	1.1029	7	9324.33	142933.34	6.52	7504.00	1.2426	5
Kerala	2913.00	48374.33	6.02	2094.61	1.3907	1	7568.00	103033.34	7.35	5409.25	1.3991	2

Madhya Pradesh	3237.33	76013.33	4.26	3291.38	0.9837	10	8671.67	149933.33	5.78	7871.50	1.1017	9
Maharashtra	11272.67	230476.33	4.89	9979.63	1.1296	6	30330.33	482400.00	6.29	25326.00	1.1976	7
Manipur	—	—					65.67	3666.67	1.79	192.50	0.3411	17
Orissa	1337.33	39294.34	3.40	1701.44	0.7860	14	2927.33	58803.33	4.98	3087.17	0.9482	12
Punjab	2454.00	43312.00	5.67	1875.41	1.3085	2	6300.67	89133.33	7.07	4679.50	1.3464	4
Rajasthan	2280.00	48067.00	4.74	2081.30	1.0955	8	5667.33	92166.67	6.15	4838.50	1.7712	8
Tamil Nadu	6325.00	120935.00	5.23	5236.49	1.2079	3	17809.00	236766.67	7.52	12430.25	1.4327	1
Uttar Pradesh	5234.00	164290.00	3.19	7113.77	0.7358	15	14828.67	291333.33	5.09	15295.00	0.9695	11
West Bengal	5750.00	164482.33	3.50	7112.08	0.8085	12	12862.67	296600.00	4.34	15571.50	0.8261	14
	Average effective rate=Rs. 4.33 per cent						Average effective rate=Rs. 5.25 per cent					

*Tax base=Non-agricultural State Domestic Product

(*Contd.*)

State	1979-80 through 1981-82					
	Revenue from sales tax (Rs. lakhs)	Tax base* (Rs. lakhs)	Effective rate (%)	Tax potential (Rs. lakhs)	Index of use of tax potential (col. 14/ col. 17	Ranking in terms of col. 18
	14	15	16	17	18	19
Andhra Pradesh	28270.00	370686.67	7.63	23946.36	1.1806	6
Assam	3994.33	121433.33	3.29	7844.59	0.5092	17
Bihar	19643.33	347900.00	5.65	22474.34	0.8740	13
Gujarat	36854.33	435831.33	8.46	28154.70	1.3090	4
Haryana	11147.33	144087.67	7.74	9308.06	1.1976	5
Himachal Pradesh	1404.67	37271.67	3.77	2407.75	0.5834	15
Jammu & Kashmir	1759.00	53406.67	3.29	3450.07	0.5099	16
Karnataka	25200.00	274684.00	9.17	17744.59	1.4202	3
Kerala	20402.33	216161.00	9.44	13964.00	1.4611	2
Madhya Pradesh	20733.00	304330.00	6.81	19659.72	1.0546	9
Maharashtra	76671.00	1025298.33	7.48	66234.27	1.1576	7
Manipur	151.67	6083.00	2.49	392.96	0.3860	18
Orissa	7895.67	127104.00	6.21	8210.92	0.9616	10
Punjab	15918.00	259296.00	6.14	16750.52	0.9503	11

Rajasthan	15646.00	209958.67	7.45	13563.33	1.1536	8
Tamil Nadu	44400.67	437820.00	10.14	28283.17	1.5699	1
Uttar Pradesh	36890.67	711722.63	5.18	45977.28	0.8024	14
West Bengal	31988.67	546734.00	5.85	35319.02	0.9057	12

Average effective rate=6.46 per cent

*Tax base=Non-agricultural State Domestic Product

average period 1967-68 through 1969-70, the state excise duty contributed 12.77 per cent to States' own tax revenue for all the States taken together. Its share varied from 0.80 per cent for Tamil Nadu to 33.58 per cent for Jammu and Kashmir. Tamil Nadu and Gujarat were two States where the share of state excise duty was negligible. This was primarily due to the policy of prohibition pursued in these two States. In the States of Jammu and Kashmir, Punjab, Haryana and Andhra Pradesh, it contributed more than 20 per cent. During the next three years', 1973-74 through 1975-76, the share of state excise duty slightly increased to 13.47 per cent for all the States taken together. It was maximum (48.37 per cent) for Nagaland and minimum (0.53

TABLE 3.10: **Percentage Share of State Excise Duty in States' Own Tax Revenue**

State	*Three years' average share for 1967-68 through 1969-70*	*Three years' average share for 1973-74 through 1975-76*	*Three years' average share for 1979-80 through 1981-82*	*Growth rate (per cent)*	*Buoyancy*
1	*2*	*3*	*4*	*5*	*6*
Andhra Pradesh	20.48	22.78	25.96	19.37	1.654
Assam	11.25	6.25	5.40	4.13	0.398
Bihar	15.40	14.93	7.35	3.98	0.397
Gujarat	0.91	0.53	0.62	15.44	1.235
Haryana	22.27	18.85	17.94	16.03	1.165
Himachal Pradesh	—	39.63	30.97	19.69	1.828
Jammu & Kashmir	33.58	38.97	27.46	16.21	1.228

(*Contd.*)

1	*2*	*3*	*4*	*5*	*6*
Karnataka	16.83	23.42	19.19	18.16	1.803
Kerala	16.19	12.98	17.99	17.92	1.563
Madhya Pradesh	18.44	16.46	14.91	13.82	1.302
Maharashtra	2.25	6.10	7.78	27.17	2.013
Manipur	—	8.54	11.09	29.56	2.423
Meghalaya	—	13.91	25.35	38.06	—
Nagaland	—	48.37	33.84	32.80	—
Orissa	14.47	10.39	6.93	8.45	0.816
Punjab	31.01	26.81	27.28	14.71	1.117
Rajasthan	16.98	15.10	8.90	11.08	0.836
Tamil Nadu	0.80	9.44	6.51	24.11	2.029
Tripura	—	15.30	7.59	22.90	1.886
Uttar Pradesh	17.06	13.89	13.77	13.11	1.189
West Bengal	12.57	9.99	9.62	11.03	1.113
All States	12.77	13.47	12.86	15.86	1.380

per cent) for Gujarat. Further, the States where the share of state excise duty was more than 20 per cent were Nagaland, Himachal Pradesh, Jammu and Kashmir, Punjab, Karnataka and Andhra Pradesh.

For the three years' period, 1979-80 through 1981-82, the overall contribution of state excise duty declined to 12.86 per cent. Its share ranged from 0.62 per cent for Gujarat to 33.84 per cent for Nagaland. Further, while in the States of Andhra Pradesh, Karnataka, Kerala, Maharashtra, Manipur, Meghalaya and Tamil Nadu, the percentage contribution of state excise duty consistently improved, for all other States it registered some decline. In Punjab, the share of state excise duty fell from 31.01 per cent to 27.28 per cent. This means that state excise duty, though the second largest source of State tax revenue in Punjab, lost its importance over the period.

TABLE 3.11: **Effective Rates and Tax Potentials for State Excise Duty (First Variant)**

State	1967-68 through 1969-70						1973-74 through 1975-76					
	Revenne from state excise duty (Rs. lakhs)	*Tax base* (lakhs of L.P.L.)*	*Effective rate (Rs. per L.P.L.)*	*Tax potential (Rs. lakhs)*	*Index of use of tax potential (col. 2/ col. 5)*	*Ranking in terms of col. 6*	*Revenue from state excise duty (Rs. lakhs)*	*Tax base* (lakhs of L.P.L.)*	*Effective rate (Rs. per L.P.L.)*	*Tax potential (Rs. lakhs)*	*Index of use of tax potential (Col. 8/ col. 11)*	*Ranking in terms of Col. 12*
1	*2*	*3*	*4*	*5*	*6*	*7*	*8*	*9*	*10*	*11*	*12*	*13*
Andhra Pradesh	1979.33	305.98	6.47	2903.75	0·6816	9	5915.67	305.98	19.33	5050.48	1.0658	6
Assam	282.67	13.84	20.42	131.34	2.1522	2	285.67	13.84	20.64	251.06	1.1379	4
Bihar	1107.33	663.47	1.67	6296.33	0.1759	11	2218.67	663.47	3.34	12035.35	0.1843	12
Haryana	736.67	78.88	9.34	748.57	0.9841	6	1836.33	78.88	23.28	1430.88	1.2834	2
Karnataka	1273.00	495.54	2.57	4702.67	0.2707	10	4573.00	495.54	9.23	8989.10	0.5087	10
Kerala	923.00	38.18	24.17	362.33	2.5476	1	1638.33	38.18	42.91	692.59	2.3655	1
Madhya Pradesh	1311.33	142.65	9.19	1353.75	0.9687	7	2923.00	142.65	20.49	2587.67	1.1296	5
Maharashtra	563.33	479.33	1.18	4548.84	0.1238	12	2981.33	479.33	6.22	8695.05	0.3429	11

Punjab	1987.00	174.30	11.40	1654.11	1.2013	3	4000.33	174·30	22.95	3161.80	1.2652	3
Rajasthan	842.33	111.05	7.59	1053.81	0.7993	8	1649.00	111.05	14.85	2014.45	0.8186	9
Uttar Pradesh	2262.00	214.92	10.52	2039.59	1.1090	4	4143.67	214.92	19.28	3898.65	1.0628	7
West Bengal	1431.67	152.17	9.41	1444.09	0.9414	5	2312.00	152.17	15.19	2760.36	0.8376	8
	Average effective rate=Rs. 9.49 per L.P.L.						Average effective rate=Rs. 18.14 per L.P.L.					

(*Contd.*)

State	1979-80 through 1981-82					
	Revenue from state excise duty (Rs. lakhs)	*Tax base* (lakhs of L.P.L.)*	*Effective rate (Rs. per L.P.L.)*	*Tax potential (Rs. lakhs)*	*Index of use of tax potential (col. 14/col. 17)*	*Ranking in terms of col. 18*
	14	*15*	*16*	*17*	*18*	*19*
Andhra Pradesh	15384.00	305.98	50.78	13478.42	1.1414	4
Assam	410.33	13.84	29.65	609.65	0.6734	8
Bihar	2078.33	663.47	3.13	29225.85	0.0711	12
Haryana	4316.53	78.88	54.72	3474.66	1.2422	3
Karnataka	9509.67	495.54	19.19	21828.54	0.4357	10
Karala	6007.88	38.18	157.33	1681.83	3.5717	1
Madhya Pradesh	5876.00	142.65	41.19	6283.73	0.9311	6
Maharashtra	9066.00	479.33	18.91	21114.49	0.4294	11
Punjab	9922.67	174.30	56.87	7677.92	1.2911	2
Rajasthan	2251.67	111.05	20.28	4891.75	0.4603	9
Uttar Pradesh	9318.67	214.92	43.36	9467.23	0.9843	5
West Bengal	5124.00	152.17	33.67	6703.09	0.7644	7

Average effective rate=Rs. 44.05 per L.P.L.

*Tax base=Total consumption of country spirit, Indian made foreign liquor and beer in the state during 1973-74 to 1975-76.

L.P.L.=London Proof Litre.

The growth rate of state excise duty for all the States taken together worked out to 15.86 per cent per annum. It was the highest for Meghalaya (38.06 per cent) and the lowest for Bihar (3.98 per cent). The significantly high growth rates recorded in the States of Meghalaya, Nagaland, Manipur, and Tamil Nadu were because of low values in the base year. In the States of Assam, Bihar and Orissa, the growth rates were much less than the overall average. In Punjab, also the growth rate was below all States' average. The overall buoyancy coefficient was 1.380. This meant that 1 per cent increase in State income was accompanied by 1.380 per cent additional revenue from state excise duty. The buoyancy coefficients varied between 0.397 for Bihar and 2.423 for Manipur. The States of Manipur, Tamil Nadu, Maharashtra, Tripura, Karnataka, and Andhra Pradesh possessed higher buoyancy coefficient than all States' average. For Bihar, Assam, Orissa and Rajasthan, the buoyancy coefficients were less than unity, whereas in all other States these were above unity. For Punjab, though the buoyancy coefficient was less than all States' average, it was higher than unity.

For estimating the effective rates of state excise duty, either the total quantity of consumption of liquor and narcotics or the total value of consumption of liquor and other goods subject to state excise duty could be taken as the potential base. The value of the consumption of liquor and narcotics in a State would change if the prices or the quantities of goods consumed change. Since the state excise duty is generally levied on specific basis, its yield does not respond to price changes, it is preferable to take the quantities consumed as the base. Further, the tax rates vary with different brands of liquor, *viz.* country liquor, foreign liquor, beer, etc. Therefore, it would be preferable to calculate the effective rates for these brands separately. But non-availability of relevant data compelled us to rely on aggregate figures. In the present analysis, we have used the consumption figures as given in a recent study conducted by Indian Institute of Public Finance and Policy.[5] Further, we have worked out two variants of the effective rates. In the first instance, we have assumed the potential base to be constant for the period under study (Table 3.11). Second time, we have assumed that the per capita consumption of liquor and narcotics is constant throughout the period of analysis and accordingly we have worked out the total

TABLE 3.12 : **Effective Rates and Tax Potentials for State Excise Duty (Second Variant)**

State	*1967-68 through 1969-70*						*1979-80 through 1981-82*					
	Revenue from state excise duty (Rs. (lakhs)	*Tax base (lakhs of L.P.L.)*	*Effective rate (Rs. per L.P.L.)*	*Tax potential (Rs. lakhs)*	*Index of use of tax potential (col. 2/ col. 5)*	*Ranking in terms of col. 6*	*Revenue from state excise duty (Rs. lakhs)*	*Tax base (lakhs of L.P.L.)*	*Effective rate (Rs. per L.P.L.)*	*Tax potential (Rs. lakhs)*	*Index of use of tax potential (col. 8/ col. 11)*	*Ranking in terms of col. 12*
1	*2*	*3*	*4*	*5*	*6*	*7*	*8*	*9*	*10*	*11*	*12*	*13*
Andhra Pradesh	1979.33	149.56	13.23	2708.53	0.7308	8	15384.00	510.52	30.13	12446.48	1.2360	2
Assam	282.67	7.82	36.15	141.62	1.9960	1	410.33	27.26	15.05	664.60	0.6173	9
Bihar	1107.33	357.27	3.10	6470.16	0.1711	11	2078.33	1075.24	1.93	26214.35	0.0793	12
Haryana	736.67	36.80	20.02	666.45	1.1054	3	4316.33	158.93	27.16	3874.71	1.1140	3
Karnataka	1273.00	253.49	5.02	4590.70	0.2773	10	9509.67	769.53	12.36	18761.14	0.5069	10
Kerala	923.00	19.55	47.21	354.05	0.3836	9	6007.00	66.95	89.72	1632.24	3.6802	1
Madhya Pradesh	1311.33	72.69	18.04	1316.42	0.9961	4	5876.00	231.02	25.44	5632.27	1.0433	5

Maharashtra	563.33	229.52	2.45	4156.61	0.1355	12	9066.00	952.62	9.52	23224.88	0.3904	11
Punjab	1987.00	92.01	21.60	1666.30	1.1925	2	9912.67	371.73	26.67	9062.78	1.0938	4
Rajasthan	842.33	52.69	15.99	954.22	0.8827	7	2251.67	196.19	11.48	2345.11	0.9599	6
Uttar Pradesh	2262.00	127.48	17.74	2308.66	0.9798	5	9318.67	412.52	22.59	10057.24	0.9266	7
West Bengal	1431.67	85.31	16.78	1545.15	0.9266	6	5124.00	249.66	20.52	6086.71	0.8418	8
	Average effective rate=Rs. 18.11 per L.P.L.						Average effective rate=Rs. 24.38 per L.P.L.					

consumption figures (Table 3.12). One more limitation of this exercise is that the consumption data was available only for 12 States and, as such, we could calculate the effective rates only for these States.

Table 3.11 shows the results based on the first variant. For the three years' period 1967-68 through 1969-70, the average effective rate worked out to Rs. 9.49 per London Proof Litre (L.P.L.). The effective rate was the maximum for Kerala (Rs. 24.17 per L.P.L.) and the minimum for Maharashtra (Rs. 1.18 per L.P.L.). It was only in the case of Kerala, Assam, Punjab and Uttar Pradesh that the indices of use of tax potential were higher than unity. During the next three years', 1973-74 through 1975-76, the average effective rate per L.P.L increased to Rs. 18.14. The effective rate had a range of Rs. 3.34 per L.P.L. for Bihar to Rs. 42.91 per L.P.L. for Kerala. During this period, the indices of use of tax potential were higher than unity for the States of Kerala, Haryana, Punjab, Assam, Madhya Pradesh, Uttar Pradesh and Bihar. For the next three years' period, 1979-80 through 1981-82, the average effective rate further mounted to Rs.44.65 per L.P.L. The effective rates varied between 3.13 per L.P.L. for Bihar and Rs. 157.33 per L.P.L. for Kerala. During this period, the indices of use of tax potential were above unity only in the case of Kerala, Punjab, Haryana and Andhra Pradesh.

Assuming the per capita consumption of liquor to be constant (second variant), the effective rates were re-worked out and are given in Table 3.12. For the three years' period 1967-68 through 1969-70, the average effective rate was worked out to be Rs. 18.11 per L.P.L. The effective rate varied from Rs. 2.45 per L.P.L. for Maharashtra to Rs. 36.15 per L.P.L. for Assam. Further, for Assam, Punjab and Haryana, the indices of use of tax potential were higher than unity. For the three-year period, 1979-80 through 1981-82, the average effective rate swelled to Rs. 24.38 per L.P.L. The effective rate ranged from Rs. 1.93 per L.P.L. for Bihar to Rs. 89.72 per L.P.L. for Kerala. Further, for Kerala, Andhra Pradesh, Haryana, Punjab and Madhya Pradesh, the indices of use of tax potential were higher than unity. The effective rates over the period under study actually dwindled in the case of Bihar and Rajasthan. It may be added that the results of this exercise did not vary much from those of the previous exercise.

Motor Vehicles Tax

This tax was first levied on all-India basis in the form of a fee under the Indian Motor Vehicles Act, 1914. However, in the course of time the different States fixed different rates of the motor vehicles tax. The percentage contribution of motor vehicles tax to the total tax revenue in different States is given in Table 3.13. During the period 1967-68 through 1969-70, the overall percentage contribution of this tax was 7.10, which varied from 1.89 for Punjab to 14.46 for Tamil Nadu. In Tamil Nadu, Andhra Pradesh, Karnataka, Kerala, Orissa, and Jammu and Kashmir, the percentage share was higher than all States' average. However, for Punjab, Haryana and Bihar, the percentage share

TABLE 3.13 : **Percentage Share of Motor Vehicles Tax in States' Own Tax Revenue**

State	*Three years' average share for 1967-68 through 1969-70*	*Three years' average share for 1973-74 through 1975-76*	*Three years' average share for 1979-80 through 1981-82*	*Growth rate (per cent)*	*Buoyancy*
1	*2*	*3*	*4*	*5*	*6*
Andhra Pradesh	12.46	9.45	8.96	13.34	1.185
Assam	6.30	4.77	5.02	7.57	0.671
Bihar	2.80	4.48	4.91	18.23	1.636
Gujarat	6.90	5.32	4.19	7.98	1.013
Haryana	2.50	5.42	4.10	22.41	1.720
Himachal Pradesh	—	4.42	4.28	25.99	2.406

(*Contd.*)

1	*2*	*3*	*4*	*5*	*6*
Jammu & Kashmir	7.26	6.44	6.01	15.67	1.175
Karnataka	9.95	6.88	9.89	16.91	1.615
Kerala	9.42	5.99	6.07	12.74	1.116
Madhya Pradesh	4.72	3.65	7.32	18.73	1.718
Maharashtra	6.17	4.32	4.22	12.63	0.942
Manipur	—	7.08	10.53	20.13	1.411
Meghalaya	—	9.51	8.01	23.69	—
Nagaland	—	5.76	7.31	16.21	—
Orissa	9.21	8.68	7.45	13.06	1.278
Punjab	1.89	3.26	3.43	21.49	1.640
Rajasthan	5.60	5.56	5.50	15.79	1.130
Tamil Nadu	14.49	12.31	11.34	13.47	1.405
Tripura	—	13.11	8.23	16.61	1.420
Uttar Pradesh	4.52	4.73	4.09	15.97	1.334
West Bengal	5.47	4.11	3.59	10.91	1.025
All States	7.10	6.04	6.05	14.18	1.261

of this tax was much less than all States' average. During the next three years' period, 1973-74 through 1975-76, the overall share of motor vehicles tax dropped to 6.04 per cent. Further, this share had variations from 3.26 per cent for Punjab to 13.11 per cent for Tripura. It was interesting to find that whereas its contribution stepped up in States with comparatively low share of motor vehicles tax, it stepped down where its share was already on the higher side.

For the period 1979-80 through 1981-82, the overall contribution of this tax marginally rose to 6.05 per cent. It was the maximum for Tamil Nadu (11.34 per cent) and the minimum for Punjab (3.43 per cent). For the States of Tamil Nadu, Manipur, Karnaṭaka, Andhra Pradesh, Tripura and Meghalaya, its contribution was significantly higher than all States' average. Further, its contribution showed an upward trend in the case of Bihar, Haryana, Madhya Pradesh, Manipur, Nagaland and Punjab, whereas for other States it diminished. It should be mentioned here that two States, *viz.* Andhra Pradesh and Tamil Nadu, do not impose a separate tax on passengers and goods. Instead, they collect motor vechicles tax at an enhanced rate. The percentage contribution of motor vehicles tax was naturally high in these States.

The overall growth rate worked out to 14.18 per cent per annum. It varied from 7.57 per cent for Assam to 25.99 per cent for Himachal Pradesh. Meghalaya, Haryana, Punjab, Manipur and Bihar experienced significantly higher growth rates than all States' average. The buoyancy coefficient of motor vehicles tax was found to be 1.261 for all the States taken together and it ranged from 0.671 for Assam to 2.406 for Himachal Pradesh. It was less than unity only in two States, *viz.* Assam and Maharashtra.

As motor vehicles of different types, ranging from two-wheelers to trucks, are taxed at varying rates, it is not possible to take the total number of vehicles as the potential base to estimate the effective tax rate. From the tax point of view, the vehicles may be classified into the following broad categories :

(i) two-wheelers with registered laden weight as the basis of the tax,
(ii) three-wheelers and four-wheelers including cabs taxed on the basis of seating capacity,
(iii) buses,
(iv) trucks, and
(v) Government vehicles which are taxed on the basis of unladen weight.

We had access to data on the total motor vehicles tax collections for all the States. In addition, we were able to collect information on the number of vehicles for different categories. However, the break up of the tax revenue by these categories of vehicles was not available, nor we could get data according to range of laden weights, seating capacity etc. for different vehicles. As such, we could not compute the effective rates for different

TABLE 3.14 : **Index of use of Tax Potentials of Motor Vehicles Tax**

State	1967-68 through 1969-70				1973-74 through 1975-76				1979-80 through 1981-82			
	Revenue from motor vehicles tax (Rs. lakhs)	Tax potential (Rs. lakhs)	Index of use of tax potential (col. 2/ col. 3)	Ranking in terms of col. 4	Revenue from motor vehicles tax (Rs. lakhs)	Tax potential (Rs. lakhs)	Index of use of tax potential (col. 6/ col. 7)	Ranking in terms of col. 8	Revenue from motor vehicles tax (Rs. lakhs)	Tax potential (Rs. lakhs)	Index of use of tax potential (col. 10/ col. 11)	Ranking in terms of col. 12
1	2	3	4	5	6	7	8	9	10	11	12	13
Assam	158.33	128.77	1.2296	3	218.00	479.24	0.4549	13	381.33	314.12	1.2140	4
Bihar	201.00	517.46	0.3884	13	665.00	961.17	0.6914	10	1388.33	2035.41	0.6821	11
Gujarat	551.33	822.63	0.6702	11	1042.67	1430.39	0.7289	8	2291.00	3619.73	0.6329	13
Haryana	83.00	156.56	0.5301	12	528.00	384.60	1.3729	1	986.00	756.49	1.3034	3
Himachal Pradesh	—	—	—	—	59.67	184.27	0.3238	14	148.33	181.93	0.8153	8
Jammu & Kashmir	42.33	31.76	1.3328	2	92.00	297.56	0.3092	15	254.67	193.25	1.3178	2
Karnataka	753.00	930.44	0.8093	9	1343.67	1469.17	0.9146	4	4898.67	4173.90	1.1736	5
Kerala	537.33	631.87	0.8504	8	756.00	639.01	1.1831	3	2028.00	2199.63	0.9220	7
Madhya Pradesh	336.00	383.34	0.8765	7	647.33	1071.16	0.6043	11	2885.33	3750.68	0.7693	9

Maharashtra	1176.67	1204.53	0.9769	6	2109.67	2635.63	0.8004	6	4920.00	4926.62	0.9987	6
Manipur	—	—	—	—	9.67	157.92	0.0612	17	31.67	148.17	0.2137	17
Orissa	238.67	215.44	1.1078	5	4 6.00	389.87	1.1953	2	1003.00	674.66	1.4867	1
Punjab	121.33	411.69	0.2947	14	485.33	681.62	0.7120	9	1245.67	2116.13	0.5887	14
Rajasthan	277.67	227.89	1.2184	4	606.67	1008.53	0.6015	12	1391.00	1936.62	0.7183	10
Tripura	—	—	—	—	16.00	183.01	0.0874	16	34.00	110.33	0.3082	16
Uttar Pradesh	599.00	419.59	1.4276	1	1411.67	1725.09	0.8183	5	2771.00	4102.66	0.6754	12
West Bengal	622.33	837.74	0.7429	10	952.00	1295.71	0.7347	7	1910.00	3485.56	0.5480	15

categories and a weighted effective rate for all the vehicles in each State. Hence, regression analysis, taking motor vehicles tax collections as the dependent variable and the number of vehicles under each category as the independent variables, could be used. However, there was one problem. As already stated, Andhra Pradesh and Tamil Nadu collected motor vehicles tax at enhanced rate because they did not impose a separate tax on passengers and goods. Therefore, the figures of motor vehicles tax collections for these two States were not comparable with the corresponding figures of other States. For estimating the effective rates of motor vehicles tax, we left out these two States.

The following regression equation has been used :[6]

$$MVT = \beta_o + \beta_1 N_1 + \beta_2 N_2 + \beta_3 N_3,$$

where MVT = motor vehicles tax in Rs. lakhs,

N_1 = the number of two-wheelers,

N_2 = the number of three-wheelers, cars and cabs,

N_3 = the number of buses and trucks.

β_1, β_2 and β_3 are regression coefficients and β_o is the intercept.

Table 3.14 gives the tax revenue, the tax potential and the index of use of tax potential of the motor vehicles tax. For the three years' average period, 1967-68 through 1969-70, the States of Uttar Pradesh, Jammu and Kashmir, Assam, Rajasthan and Orissa had the index of use of tax potential higher than unity. Punjab was at the bottom with an index of merely 0.2947. During the next three years', 1973-74 through 1975-76, Haryana (1.3729) had the highest index, followed by Orissa (1.1953) and Kerala (1.1831). For every other State, the index of use of tax potential was less than unity. Punjab, with an index of 0.7120, occupied the ninth place. For the next three years' average period, 1979-80 through 1981-82, the index was above unity in the States of Orissa, Jammu and Kashmir, Haryana, Assam and Karnataka. Punjab, with the index at 0.5887, was relegated to the 14th place.

Thus, we could say that although the growth rate and buoyancy coefficient for Punjab were significantly higher than all States' average, yet the motor vehicles tax had not been optimally exploited. Punjab has untapped potentials for this tax. If the State could attain the index of use of tax potential equal to unity, it would mobilise additional revenue to the tune of Rs. 860 lakhs per annum.

Passengers and Goods Tax

Under Indian Motor Vehicles Act, 1914, this tax is levied in all the States except Andhra Pradesh, Manipur, Nagaland, Tripura and Tamil Nadu. The State-wise share of passengers and goods tax in total tax revenue is given in Table 3.15. For the three years' average period, 1967-68 through 1969-70, the percentage share of passengers and goods tax was found to be 4.72 for all the States taken together. It varied from 1.43 per cent for Orissa to 12.53 per cent for Haryana. The other States where its share was comparatively good were Gujarat (6.67 per cent) and Rajasthan (6.38 per cent). In Orissa (1.43 per cent), Bihar (1.48 per cent), and Kerala (1.52 per cent), its share was comparatively low. During the period 1973-74 through 1975-76, its share went up to 5.99 per cent for all the States taken together. Haryana (13.47 per cent) continued to be at the top. Next was Himachal Pradesh (12.47 per cent), followed by Punjab (8.69 per cent). For Gujarat, Rajasthan and West Bengal also the share was significantly higher than all States' average. The percentage share of passengers and goods tax was the minimum for Assam (1.52).

However, for the next three years' period, 1979-80 through 1981-82, its overall share came down to 5.27 per cent. Haryana with 14.02 per cent share of passengers and goods tax retained the top position. Orissa with 1.58 per cent share was at the bottom. As already stated, Andhra Pradesh and Tamil Nadu did not impose this tax separately. And Kerala, too, merged this tax with motor vehicles tax with effect from 1977. Over the period under study, its share moved up in all the States except Assam, Gujarat, Himachal Pradesh, Karnataka and Maharashtra.

For all the States taken together, the growth rate of the passengers and goods tax was found to be 16.65 per cent per annum. Haryana (36.33 per cent) recorded the highest growth, followed by Himachal Pradesh (33.83 per cent) and Meghalaya (25.44 per cent). Bihar (17.16 per cent), Madhya Pradesh (18.79 per cent), Orissa (22.70 per cent), Uttar Pradesh (17.11 per cent)

TABLE 3.15 : **Percentage Share of Passengers and Goods Tax in States' Own Tax Revenue**

State	*Three years' average share for 1967-68 through 1969-70*	*Three years' average share for 1973-74 through 1975-76*	*Three years' average share for 1979-80 through 1981-82*	*Growth rate (per cent)*	*Buoyancy*
Assam	2.15	1.52	1.88	10.66	0.926
Bihar	1.48	2.81	3.75	17.16	2.014
Gujarat	7.51	8.43	5.05	14.33	1.081
Haryana	12.53	13.47	14.02	36.33	1.949
Himachal Pradesh	—	12.98	10.21	33.83	2.079
Jammu & Kashmir	2.97	4.92	12.02	11.50	1.261
Karnataka	2.84	3.18	1.64	—4.41	—1.279
Kerala	1.52	2.53	—	—24.45	—2.254
Madhya Pradesh	6.67	6.27	8.09	18.79	1.737
Maharashtra	5.45	5.57	2.35	10.84	0.690
Meghalaya	—	4.40	6.62	25.44	—
Orissa	1.43	2.87	1.58	22.70	2.272
Punjab	7.31	8.69	7.53	15.43	1.197
Rajasthan	6.38	7.48	7.49	15.42	1.344
Uttar Pradesh	5.34	4.20	6.36	17.11	1.504
West Bengal	2.26	7.10	9.17	24.25	2.450
All States	4.72	5.99	5.27	16.65	1.454

and West Bengal (24.25 per cent) also had relatively high growth ates. Karnataka and Kerala registered negative growth rates.

The minimum positive growth rate of passengers and goods tax was observed in Assam (10.66 per cent). Punjab (15.43 per cent), too, had lower growth rate than all States' average.

The overall buoyancy coefficient of passengers and goods tax was estimated to be 1.454 and it varied between 0.690 for Maharashtra and 2.450 for West Bengal. Leaving aside Kerala, buoyancy coefficient was negative only in Karnataka. In Punjab, though the buoyancy coefficient (1.197) was more than unity, yet it was less than all States' average. For Maharashtra (0.690) and Assam (0.926), the buoyancy coefficient was less than unity.

For estimating the effective rates of passengers and goods tax, the total number of buses and trucks in the State was taken as the potential base. Information on the tax yield separately for trucks and buses for most of the States was not available. The effective rates were, therefore, calculated for the two types of vehicles taken together. To the extent that a truck represents a greater taxable potential than a bus, taking them together would understate the taxable capacity of the States in which the proportion of trucks was relatively large.

Table 3.16 shows the effective rates of passengers and goods tax for different States. For the three years' average period, 1967-68 through 1969-70, the overall effective rate was Rs. 1640.55 per vehicle which ranged from Rs. 5374.04 per vehicle for Haryana to Rs. 90.23 per vehicle for Jammu and Kashmir. In Haryana, Punjab, Uttar Pradesh, Madhya Pradesh and Gujarat, the effective rates were significantly higher than unity, while in Jammu and Kashmir, Assam, Orissa, Kerala and Bihar, these were much lower than unity. During the next three-year period, 1973-74 through 1975-76, the overall effective rate per vehicle coursed upward to Rs. 4970.50 and the rate ranged between Rs. 19672.16 for Haryana and Rs. 665.30 for Assam. In Haryana, Punjab, Himachal Pradesh and Gujarat, the effective rates were considerably higher than unity, while in Assam, Jammu and Kashmir, Kerala, Bihar, Orissa and Karnataka, they were markedly lower than unity.

For the period 1979-80 through 1981-82, the average effective rate further multiplied to Rs. 7138.05 per vehicle. Here again Haryana touched the top with an effective rate of Rs. 23685.42 per vehicle. Assam had again the lowest effective rate of Rs. 771.06 per vehicle. Haryana, Punjab, Uttar Pradesh, West

TABLE 3.16 : **Effective Rates and Tax Potential for Passengers and Goods Tax**

State	*1967-68 through 1969-70*						*1973-74 through 1975-76*					
	Revenue from passengers and goods tax (Rs. lakhs)	*Tax base* (number)*	*Effective rate (Rs. per vehicle)*	*Tax potential (Rs. lakhs)*	*Index of use of tax potential (col. 2/col. 5)*	*Ranking in terms of col. 6*	*Revenue from passengers and goods tax (Rs. lakhs)*	*Tax base* (number)*	*Effective rate (Rs. per vehicle)*	*Tax potential (Rs. lakhs)*	*Index of use of tax potential (col. 8/col. 11)*	*Ranking in terms of col. 12*
1	*2*	*3*	*4*	*5*	*6*	*7*	*8*	*9*	*10*	*11*	*12*	*13*
Assam	54.00	15475	348.95	253.88	0.2127	13	69.33	13385	517.97	655.30	0.1043	15
Bihar	106.67	18243	584.72	299.29	0.3564	10	417.00	25665	1624.78	1275.68	0.3269	12
Gujarat	600.33	31166	1926.23	511.29	1.1741	5	1653.33	25266	6543.70	1255.85	1.3165	4
Haryana	414.50	7713	5374.04	126.54	3.2756	1	1312.33	6671	19672.16	331.58	3.9578	1
Himachal Pradesh	—	—	—	—	—	—	175.33	2310	7590.04	114.82	1.5270	3
Jammu and Kashmir	17.33	5500	315.09	90.23	0.1921	14	70.33	5338	1317.53	265.33	0.2651	14
Karnataka	214.67	23884	898.80	391.83	0.5479	8	621.67	28538	2178.39	1418.39	0.4383	10
Kerala	86.67	17814	486.37	292.25	0.2966	11	320.00	19985	1601.20	993.35	0.3221	13
Madhya Pradesh	474.00	21961	2158.37	360.28	1.3156	4	1113.67	21432	5196.30	1065.28	1.0454	5

Maharashtra	1038.67	60789	1708.65	997.27	1.0415	6	2720.67	74170	3668.15	3686.62	0.7380	7
Orissa	37.00	9964	371.34	163.46	0.2264	12	154.00	7646	2014.13	380.04	0.4052	11
Punjab	468.33	10337	4530.62	169.58	2.7617	2	1295.67	11011	11767.05	547.30	2.3674	2
Rajasthan	316.33	23665	1336.70	388.24	0.8148	7	817.33	22984	3556.08	1142.42	0.7154	9
Uttar Pradesh	708.33	31987	2214.43	524.76	1.3498	3	1254.00	34773	3606.25	1728.39	0.7255	8
West Bengal	257.33	42236	609.27	692.90	0.3714	9	1644.67	44405	3703.79	2207.15	0.7452	6
	Average effective rate = Rs. 1640.55 per vehicle						Average effective rate = Rs. 4970.50 per vehicle					

(*Contd.*)

State	*1979-80 through 1981-82*					
	Revenue from passegers and goods tax (Rs. lakhs)	*Tax base* (number)*	*Effective rate (Rs. per vehicle)*	*Tax potential (Rs. lakhs)*	*Index of use of tax potential (col. 14/ col. 17)*	*Ranking in terms of col. 18*
	14	*15*	*16*	*17*	*18*	*19*
Assam	142.67	18503	771.06	1320.75	0.1080	14
Bihar	1060.67	31740	3341.75	2265.62	0-4682	10
Gujarat	2762.00	35169	7853.51	2510.38	1.1002	5
Haryana	3372.33	14238	23685.42	1016.32	3.3182	1
Himachal Pradesh	354.33	7848	4514.91	560.19	0.6325	9
Jammu and Kashmir	509.00	6844	7437.17	488.53	1.0409	7
Karnataka	814.50	44022	1850.21	3142.51	0.2592	12
Kerala	—	—	—	—	—	—
Madhya Pradesh	3188,33	44242	7206.57	3158.02	1.0096	8
Maharashtra	2736.00	104796	2610.79	7480.39	0.3658	11
Orissa	213.00	12414	1715.80	886.12	0.2404	13
Punjab	2735.33	21254	12869.72	1517.12	1.8030	2
Rajasthan	1895.00	24718	7666.48	1764.38	1.0740	6
Uttar Pradesh	4305.00	45858	9266.43	3273.37	1.3152	3
West Bengal	4883.33	53411	9142.93	3812.50	1.2809	4

Average effective rate = Rs. 7138.05 per vehicle.

*Tax base = Total number of buses and trucks in the State

Bengal, and Gujarat were the States where the effective rates were significantly higher than unity. Throughout the period under study, Punjab occupied the second position as far as the index of use of tax potential was concerned. The State had no scope to raise additional revenue from passengers and goods tax.[7]

Electricity Duty

This tax is imposed on the consumption of electricity in a State. It was levied first in Bombay in 1932. At present, electricity duty is levied in all the States except Tripura and Nagaland. Andhra Pradesh does not have separate electricity duty and Tamil Nadu has a nominal duty at the rate of 0.18 paise per unit on large industrial consumers only. But the level of electricity tariff in either of these two States is perceptibly higher than that in any of the remaining States.

Table 3.17 indicates the yield from electricity duty. For the three years' average period, 1967-68 through 1969-70, the share of electricity duty was 4.44 per cent for all the States taken together and it had a range from 0.02 per cent for Andhra Pradesh to 8.71 per cent for Orissa. Further, the percentage share of electricity duty for Maharashtra, West Bengal, Tamil Nadu, Gujarat and Bihar, was more than that of an average State. During the three-year period 1973-74 through 1975-76, the overall share of electricity duty to States' own tax revenue dipped to 3.25 per cent. Again, the share was maximum for Orissa (8.36 per cent) and the minimum for Andhra Pradesh (0.03 per cent). For Bihar, Gujarat, Haryana, Madhya Pradesh, Maharashtra, Orissa, Punjab and West Bengal, the percentage share of electricity duty was more than that of an average State. For the period 1979-80 through 1981-82, its overall share moved up slightly to 3.35 per cent. Orissa and Andhra Pradesh with 12.96 per cent and 0.05 per cent shares continued to occupy the uppermost and lowermost positions respectively. In Orissa, Gujarat, Haryana, Maharashtra, Madhya Pradesh, Punjab, Manipur and Bihar, the percentage share of electricity duty was more than all States' average.

As far as the growth rate of electricity duty is concerned, it was 13.36 per cent per annum for all the States taken together. It was the highest for Himachal Pradesh (34.34 per cent) and the lowest (though positive) for West Bengal (5.86 per cent). Tamil

TABLE 3.17: **Percentage Share of Electricity Duty in States' Own Tax Revenue**

State	*Three years' average share for 1967-68 through 1969-70*	*Three years' average share for 1973-74 through 1975-76*	*Three years' average share for 1979-80 through 1981-82*	*Growth rate (per cent)*	*Buoyancy*
Andhra Pradesh	0.02	0.03	0.05	21.66	1.977
Assam	1.47	0.81	0.89	11.79	1.050
Bihar	5.56	5.37	3.54	6.90	0.741
Gujarat	6.31	5.49	7.43	19.74	1.530
Haryana	4.16	3.64	5.21	21.67	1.558
Himachal Pradesh	—	0.67	1.11	34.34	2.279
Jammu & Kashmir	1.66	1.45	2.94	16.62	1.675
Karnataka	3.33	3.05	2.37	14.08	1.240
Kerala	2.58	2.35	2.79	17.91	1.477
Madhya Pradesh	3.68	3.80	4.89	18.23	1.623
Maharashtra	7.40	5.31	5.00	12.37	0.956
Manipur	—	—	4.21	—	—
Meghalaya	—	1.06	0.99	11.59	—
Orissa	8.71	8.36	12.96	19.10	1.836
Punjab	3.98	3.44	4.28	16.30	1.292
Rajasthan	1.29	1.50	2.09	20.56	1.522
Tamil Nadu	6.70	0.47	0.51	−5.32	−0.771
Uttar Pradesh	0.94	1.92	1.48	18.48	1.131
West Bengal	7.24	5.01	3.07	5.86	0.677
All States	4.44	3.25	3.35	13.36	1.158

Nadu recorded even a negative growth rate. In Punjab, however, the growth rate of electricity duty was higher than all States' average.

The buoyancy coefficient of electricity duty was computed to be 1.158 for all the States taken together. The positive buoyancy coefficients had variations from 0.677 for West Bengal to 2.279 for Himachal Pradesh. Tamil Nadu naturally recorded a negative buoyancy coefficient. The buoyancy coefficient was more than unity in all the States except West Bengal, Bihar and Maharashtra. For Punjab, the buoyancy coefficient, too, was more than that of all States.

Electricity duty is levied on purpose-wise consumption of electricity. However, the State-wise data on the consumption of electricity for different purposes and the revenue therefrom were not available. Hence, the total consumption of electricity was taken as the potential base.[8] The effective rates (Table 3.18) were obtained by dividing the total revenue from this tax by the total electricity consumption. For the three-year period, 1967-68 through 1969-70, the average effective rate worked out to 1.41 paise per unit. The effective rate varied from 0.01 paise per unit for Andhra Pradesh to 2.20 paise per unit for Maharashtra. For Maharashtra, Haryana, Assam, Gujarat, West Bengal, Tamil Nadu, Bihar and Orissa, the indices of use of tax potential were higher than unity. For Punjab, the effective rate worked out to 1.11 paise per unit, which was a little less than the average effective rate. For the next three years' period, 1973-74 through 1975-76, the average effective rate pushed forward to 1.58 paise per unit. The maximum and the minimum effective rates were again observed for Maharashtra (2.82 paise per unit) and Andhra Pradesh (0.03 paise per unit) respectively. For the States of Bihar, Gujarat, Haryana, Madhya Pradesh, Maharashtra, Orissa, Punjab and West Bengal, the effective rates were found to be more than the average effective rate.

For the period 1979-80 through 1981-82, the average effective rate of electricity duty jumped up to 2.81 paise per unit. While Andhra Pradesh continued to occupy the bottom position, the topmost position went to Orissa. The effective rates of electricity duty per unit were significantly high for Orissa (6.92 paise), Gujarat (5.31 paise), Haryana (4.56 paise), Maharashtra (4.16 paise) and Madhya Pradesh (4.16 paise). Andhra Pradesh and

TABLE 3.18: **Effective Rates and Tax Potentials for Electricity Duty**

State	1967-68 through 1969-70						1973-74 through 1975-76					
	Revenue from electricity duty (Rs. lakhs)	*Tax base* (KWH in lakhs)*	*Effective rate (paise/KWH)*	*Tax potential (Rs. lakhs)*	*Index of use of tax potential (col. 2/col. 5)*	*Ranking in terms of col. 6*	*Revenue from electricity duty (Rs. lakhs)*	*Tax base* (KWH in lakhs)*	*Effective rate (Paise/KWH)*	*Tax potential (Rs. lakhs)*	*Index of use of tax potential (col. 8/col. 11)*	*Ranking in terms of col. 12*
1	*2*	*3*	*4*	*5*	*6*	*7*	*8*	*9*	*10*	*11*	*12*	*13*
Andhra Pradesh	2.33	16311.00	0.01	299.99	0.0078	16	8.67	26127.13	0.03	412.81	0.0210	17
Assam	37.00	1879.73	1.97	26.50	1.3962	3	37.00	4136.33	0.89	65.35	0.5662	13
Bihar	400.00	23564.67	1.70	332.26	1.2039	8	798.33	31110.02	2.57	491.54	1.6241	2
Gujarat	504.00	26583.03	1.90	374.82	1.3446	4	1076.33	46166.97	2.33	729.44	1.4756	5
Haryana	137.50	6585.17	2.09	92.85	1.4809	2	354.67	14140.20	2.51	223.42	1.5875	4
Himachal Pradesh	—	—	—	—	—	—	9.00	2100.87	0.43	33.19	0.2712	15
Jammu and Kashmir	9.67	1416.10	0.68	19.96	0.4845	14	20.67	2534.70	0.82	40.05	0.5161	14
Karnataka	252.00	19743.87	1.28	278.39	0.9052	10	595.33	39294.93	1.52	620.86	0.9589	10

Kerala	147.33	13080.87	1.13	184.44	0.7988	11	296.33	18728.60	1.58	296.00	1.0011	9
Madhya Pradesh	261.67	15685.27	1.67	221.16	1.1832	9	675.00	29022.13	2.33	458.55	1.4720	6
Maharashtra	1411.33	64111.73	2.20	903.98	3.5612	1	2597.53	92246.57	2.82	1457.50	1.7820	1
Orissa	225.67	11982.87	1.88	168.96	1.3356	5	449.00	17611.33	2.55	278.26	1.6136	3
Punjab	255.33	22960.93	1.11	323.75	0.7887	12	513.00	27905.80	1.84	440.91	1.1635	8
Rajasthan	64.00	6242.07	1.03	88.01	0.7272	13	164.33	15699.67	1.05	248.05	0.6625	12
Tamil Nadu	774.53	43681.37	1.77	615.90	1.2572	7	139.33	57590 07	0.24	909.92	0.1531	16
Uttar Pradesh	124.33	40080.27	0.31	515.13	0.2414	15	574.67	49196.13	1.17	777.30	0.7393	11
West Bengal	824.67	45452.33	1.87	640.87	1.2868	6	1159.67	52206.67	2.22	824.87	1.4049	7
	Average effective rate=1.41 paise per kwh						Average effective rate=1.58 paise per kwh					

(*Contd.*)

State	1979-80 through 1981-82					
	Revenue from electricity duty (Rs. lakhs)	Tax base* (KWH in lakhs)	Effective rate (Paise/KWH)	Tax potential (Rs. lakhs)	Index of use of tax potential (col. 14/col. 17)	Ranking in terms of col. 18
	14	15	16	17	18	19
Andhra Pradesh	27.33	52196.90	0.05	1466.73	0.0186	17
Assam	67.33	6536.67	1.03	183.68	0.3666	15
Bihar	1001.00	40648.13	2.46	1142.21	0.8764	10
Gujarat	4065.00	76558.43	5.31	2151.29	1.8896	2
Haryana	1254.33	27511.97	4.56	773.09	1.6225	3
Himachal Pradesh	38.67	2660.77	1.45	74.77	0.5172	13
Jammu and Kashmir	124.50	4489.50	2.77	126.15	0.9869	9
Karnataka	1173.33	54449.60	2.15	1530.04	0.7669	11
Kerala	930.00	27044.80	3.44	759.96	1.2242	6
Madhya Pradesh	1928.33	46399.33	4.16	1303.82	1.4790	5
Maharashtra	5820.33	139859.00	4.16	3930.04	1.4810	4
Orissa	1744.33	25195.53	6.92	707.99	2.4638	1
Punjab	1554.00	49875.07	3.12	1401.49	1.1088	7

Rajasthan	529.33	29970.43	1.77	842.17	0.6285	12
Tamil Nadu	333.67	86147.27	0.38	2420.74	0.1378	16
Uttar Pradesh	1003.67	79772.33	1.26	2241.60	0.4477	14
West Bengal	1633.33	58598.93	2.79	1646.63	0.9919	8
		Average effective rate=2.81 paise per kwh				

*Tax base=Total electricity consumed in the State.

Tamil Nadu do not levy electricity duty on total consumption but impose enhanced electricity tariff. The effective rates were comparatively low in the States of Assam, Uttar Pradesh, Himachal Pradesh and Rajasthan. For Punjab, the effective rate was worked out to be 3.12 paise per unit which was slightly more than the average effective rate.

However, as already mentioned, we have calculated the effective rate on the basis of total consumption of electricity. But the electricity duty differs for different categories of consumers. On account of the lack of relevant data, we could not calculate effective rates for different categories of consumers. Consequently, the applicability of our results is limited to that extent. For example, although in Punjab the index of use of tax potential for electricity duty was more than unity, the agricultural sector here paid less duty than the non-agricultural sector.[9] Had Punjab levied electricity duty equivalent to Haryana, it would have realised additional revenue to the tune of Rs. 720 lakhs.

Entertainment Tax

The entertainment tax forms part of a composite tax head comprising taxes on luxury, betting, show and amusement. Of these, only the entertainment tax levied on tickets for admission to cinemas, theatrical performance, etc. and the show tax are important. Entertainment tax was first levied in Bengal in 1929. Later on, other States, too, imposed this tax and at present it is found in all the States.

The percentage share of entertainment tax to States' own tax revenue is given in Table 3.19. For the three years' average period, 1967-68 through 1969-70, the overall share of entertainment tax was 2.94 per cent. It ranged from 0.74 per cent for Kerala to 4.84 per cent for Maharashtra. It contributed more than all States' average in Maharashtra (4.84 per cent), Uttar Pradesh (4.05 per cent), Gujarat (3.48 per cent), Assam (3.42 per cent), West Bengal (3.37 per cent) and Jammu and Kashmir (3.26 per cent). During the three years' period 1973-74 through 1975-76, its overall contribution rose to 4.29 per cent and it varied between 1.37 per cent for Kerala and 11.70 per cent for Manipur.

TABLE 3.19: **Percentage Share of Entertainment Tax in States' Own Tax Revenue**

State	*Three years' average share for 1967-68 through 1969-70*	*Three years' average share for 1973-74 through 1975-76*	*Three years' average share for 1979-80 through 1981-82*	*Growth rate (per cent)*	*Buoyancy*
Andhra Pradesh	1.59	4.37	4.31	29.00	2.508
Assam	3.42	3.13	4.23	9.92	0.888
Bihar	2.74	2.75	2.28	9.30	0.908
Gujarat	3.48	4.35	4.15	19.31	1.529
Haryana	2.52	3.42	2.59	17.84	1.361
Himachal Pradesh	—	2.49	1.68	11.34	1.030
Jammu & Kashmir	3.26	4.76	3.44	20.06	1.456
Karnataka	2.09	4.87	4.52	25.64	2.541
Kerala	0.74	1.37	0.63	−8.72	−0.891
Madhya Pradesh	2.81	3.36	3.02	16.37	1.504
Maharashtra	4.84	5.51	4.79	16.31	1.234
Manipur	—	11.70	9.31	13.15	1.189
Meghalaya	—	7.92	4.30	21.36	—
Nagaland	—	2.88	2.71	13.92	—
Orissa	1.14	1.97	2.30	21.52	2.088
Punjab	2.30	3.33	2.45	15.01	1.291
Rajasthan	1.94	2.67	2.87	18.74	1.516
Tamil Nadu	2.40	5.79	5.02	31.07	2.358
Tripura	—	9.84	5.45	28.38	2.775
Uttar Pradesh	4.05	4.79	5.18	16.74	1.508
West Bengal	3.37	4.83	4.02	15.68	1.648
All States	2.94	4.29	3.85	17.80	1.631

For the period 1979-80 through 1981-82, the overall share of entertainment tax to States' own tax revenue declined to 3.85 per cent. Its minimum and maximum shares were again observed in the case of Kerala (0.63 per cent) and Manipur (9.31 per cent). It contributed more than the all States' average in Manipur (9.31 per cent), Tripura (5.45 per cent), Uttar Pradesh (5.18 per cent), Tamil Nadu (5.02 per cent), Maharashtra (4.79 per cent), Karnataka (4.52 per cent), Andhra Pradesh (4.31 per cent), Meghalaya (4.30 per cent), Assam (4.23 per cent), Gujarat (4.15 per cent) and West Bengal (4.02 per cent). It may be noted that the contribution of this tax fell in the States of Bihar, Himachal Pradesh, Kerala, Maharashtra, Manipur, Meghalaya, Nagaland and Tripura over the period under study. In Punjab, the share of this tax was always less than all States' average.

The growth rate of entertainment tax was calculated to be 17.80 per cent per annum for all the States taken together. Kerala was the only State which experienced a negative growth rate. For the other States, growth rates had a range of 9.30 per cent for Bihar to 31.07 per cent for Tamil Nadu. A comparatively low growth rate was observed in Assam, Bihar, Himachal Pradesh, Kerala, Madhya Pradesh, Maharashtra, Manipur, Nagaland, Punjab, Uttar Pradesh and West Bengal.

The buoyancy coefficient worked out to 1.631 for all the States taken together and it varied between 0.888 for Assam and 2.775 for Tripura, leaving aside Kerala, which had a negative buoyancy coefficient (—0.891). It was a happy sign that for all the States except Assam and Bihar, the buoyancy coefficient was more than unity. Punjab experienced a buoyancy coefficient of 1.291 which, however, was less than all States' average. Looking at the percentage share, growth rate and buoyancy coefficient of this tax in Punjab, we may say that there existed a scope for additional revenue from entertainment tax.

Total seating capacity measured in terms of number of seats in cinemas was considered to be an appropriate potential base to compute the effective rates for entertainment tax. But we could not get time series data for total seating capacity in cinemas for different States. Here again we have made use of a recently conducted research study by Chelliah and Sinha.[10] However, this study pertains to the period 1973-74 through 1975-76. In order to work out the estimates (effective rates) backward as well as forward we applied two alternatives. First, we assumed that seating capacity for all other average periods was the same as that for 1973-74 through 1975-76. Secondly, assuming that the cinemas were mostly located in urban areas, we adjusted the seating capacity with the changes in urban population of a State.

The effective rates of entertainment tax based on the first alternative are given in Table 3.20. For the period 1967-68 through 1969-70, the average effective rate was calculated to be Rs. 83.32 per seat per annum. Uttar Pradesh (Rs. 246.46) had the highest rate and Kerala (Rs. 10.87) the lowest. For Uttar Pradesh, Maharashtra, Punjab and Bihar, the index of use of tax potential was markedly higher than unity. During the period 1973-74 through 1975-76, the average effective rate zoomed up to Rs. 261.73 per seat per annum. The effective rates had variations from Rs. 488.45 per seat for Maharashtra to Rs. 44.52 per seat for Kerala. During this period, the index of use of tax potential was more than unity in the States of Maharashtra, Uttar Pradesh, Punjab, Haryana, Rajasthan and West Bengal. For the next three years' average period 1979-80 through 1981-82, the average effective rate further shot up to Rs. 559.12 per cent per annum. Uttar Pradesh (Rs. 1183.13) had the highest rate and Kerala (Rs. 43.75) the lowest. The index of use of tax potential was consistently and significantly higher than unity in the case of Haryana, Maharashtra, Punjab, Rajasthan and Uttar Pradesh. On the other hand, the States of Andhra Pradesh, Assam and Kerala had notably lower yield than all States' average.

In the above case, we have assumed the total seating capacity to be constant at the level of 1973-74 through 1975-76. Assuming that seating capacity changed directly in proportion to urban population, the effective rates were re-worked out and incorporated in Table 3.21. For the three years' average period, 1967-68 through 1969-70, the average effective rate worked out to Rs. 103.28 per seat and the effective rate varied from Rs. 13.12 per seat in Kerala to Rs. 226.90 per seat in Uttar Pradesh. During the period 1979-80 through 1981-82, the average effective rate mounted to Rs. 439.17 per seat. Again, Uttar Pradesh (Rs. 890.30) had the highest rate and Kerala (Rs. 45.18) the lowest. Considering Tables 3.20 and 3.21 together, we may say that the relative positions of different States did not alter.

TABLE 3.20: **Effective Rates and Tax Potentials for Entertainment Tax (First variant)**

State	*1967-68 through 1969-70*						*1973-74 through 1975-76*					
	Revenue from entertainment tax (Rs. lakhs)	*Tax base* (number)*	*Effective rate (per seat)*	*Tax potential (Rs. lakhs)*	*Index of use of tax potential (col. 2/ col. 5)*	*Ranking in terms of col. 6*	*Revenue from entertainment tax (Rs. lakhs)*	*Tax base* (number)*	*Effective rate (per seat)*	*Tax potential (Rs. lakhs)*	*Index of use of tax potential (col. 8/ col. 11)*	*Ranking in terms of col. 12*
1	*2*	*3*	*4*	*5*	*6*	*7*	*8*	*9*	*10*	*11*	*12*	*13*
Andhra Pradesh	153.33	726301	21.11	605.15	0.2534	14	1134.67	726301	156.23	1900.95	0.5969	13
Assam	86.00	104965	81.93	87.46	0.9833	8	143.00	104965	136.24	274.72	0.5205	14
Bihar	127.33	181797	108.54	151.47	1.3028	4	408.00	181797	224.43	475.82	0.8575	9
Gujarat	278.33	375014	74.22	312.46	0.8908	10	853.00	375014	227.46	981.52	0.8691	8
Haryana	83.50	89233	93.58	74.35	1.1231	6	333.00	89233	373.18	233.55	1.4258	4
Karnataka	158.00	536100	29.47	446.68	0.3537	13	951.00	536100	177.39	1403.13	0.6778	11
Kerala	42.33	389245	10.87	324.32	0.1305	15	173.33	389245	44.52	1018.77	0.1701	15
Madhya Pradesh	200.00	254591	78.55	212.12	0.9429	9	597.33	254591	234.62	666.34	0.8964	7

Maharashtra	922.67	551545	167.32	459.55	2.0078	2	2694.00	551545	488.45	1443.56	1.8662	1
Orissa	29.67	61650	48.13	51.37	0.5776	11	106.00	61650	171.94	161.36	0.6569	12
Punjab	147.33	110817	132.95	92.33	1.5957	3	497.00	110817	448.49	290.04	1.7136	3
Rajasthan	96.33	96666	99.65	80.54	1.1961	5	291.67	96666	301.73	253.00	1.1528	5
Tamil Nadu	277.67	893566	31.07	744.52	0.3730	12	1732.C0	893566	193.13	2338.73	0.7406	10
Uttar Pradesh	537.67	296164	181.54	246.76	2.1789	1	1429.33	296164	482.61	775.15	1.8439	2
West Bengal	384.67	422065	90.90	351.66	1.0910	7	1117.33	422065	264.73	1104.67	1.0115	6
	Average effective rate=Rs. 83.32 per seat						Average effective rate=Rs. 261.73 per seat					

(*Contd.*)

State	1979-80 through 1981-82					
	Revenue from entertainment tax (Rs. lahks)	*Tax base* (number)*	*Effective rate (per seat)*	*Tax potential (Rs. lakhs)*	*Index of use of tax potential (col. 14/ col. 18)*	*Ranking in terms of col. 18*
	14	*15*	*16*	*17*	*18*	*19*
Andhra Pradesh	2555.67	726301	351.87	4060.89	0.6293	13
Assam	322.40	104965	306.77	586.88	0.5487	14
Bihar	645.67	181797	355.16	1016.46	0.6352	12
Gujarat	2271.67	375014	605.76	2096.78	1.0834	6
Haryana	624.00	89233	699.29	498.92	1.2507	5
Karnataka	2240.67	536100	417.96	2997.44	0.7475	10
Kerala	213.00	389245	54.72	2176.35	0.0979	15
Madhya Pradesh	1188.00	254591	466.63	1423.47	0.8346	9
Maharashtra	5579.00	551545	1011.52	3083.80	1.8091	2
Orissa	309.67	61650	502.30	344.70	0.8983	8
Punjab	891.67	110817	804.63	619.60	1.4391	3

Rajasthan	726.67	96666	751.73	540.48	1.3445	4
Tamil Nadu	3290.67	893566	368.26	4996.11	0.6586	11
Uttar Pradesh	3504.00	296164	1183.13	1655.91	2.1161	3
West Bengal	2140.33	422065	507.11	2359.85	0.9070	7

Average effective rate=Rs. 559.12 per seat

*Tax base=Total seating capacity in cinemas in the State.

TABLE 3.21 : **Effective Rates and Tax Potentials for Entertainment Tax (Second Variant)**

State	*1967-68 through 1969-70*						*1979-80 through 1981-82*					
	Revenue from entertainment tax (Rs. lakhs)	*Tax base* (number)*	*Effective rate (per seat)*	*Tax potential (Rs. lakhs)*	*Index of use of tax potential (col. 2/ col. 5)*	*Ranking in terms of col. 6*	*Revenue from entertainment tax (Rs. lakhs)*	*Tax base* (number)*	*Effective rate (per seat)*	*Tax potential (Rs. lakhs)*	*Index of use of tax potential (col. 9/ col. 11)*	*Ranking in terms of col. 12*
1	*2*	*3*	*4*	*5*	*6*	*7*	*8*	*9*	*10*	*11*	*12*	*13*
Andhra Pradesh	153.33	593091	25.85	750.12	0.2044	14	2525.67	913848	279.66	4013.35	0.6368	12
Assam	86,00	80790	106.45	83.44	1.0307	7	322.00	136374	236.12	598.91	0.5376	14
Bihar	197.33	142958	138.03	147.65	1.3365	4	645.67	236244	273.31	1037.51	0.6223	13
Gujarat	278.33	322594	86.28	333.18	0.8354	10	2271.67	461671	492.05	2027.52	1.1204	6
Haryana	83.50	71706	116.45	74.06	1.1275	6	624.00	118071	528.50	518.53	1.2034	5
Karnataka	158.00	432952	36.49	447.15	0.3533	13	2240.67	685496	326.87	3010.49	0.7443	10
Kerala	42.30	322633	13.12	333.22	0.1270	15	213.00	471416	45.18	2070.32	0.1029	15
Madhya Pradesh	200.00	198563	100.72	205.08	0.9752	9	1188.00	332497	357.30	1460.23	0.8136	9

Maharashtra	922.67	450010	205.03	464.77	1.9852	2	5579.00	674884	826.66	2963.89	1.8823	2
Orissa	29.67	45367	65.40	46.86	0.6332	11	309.67	83876	369.20	368.66	0.8407	8
Punjab	147.33	92700	158.93	95.74	1.5359	3	891.67	138202	645.19	606.94	1.4691	3
Rajasthan	96.33	76298	126.25	78.80	1.2225	5	726.67	127545	569.74	560.14	1.2963	4
Tamil Nadu	277.67	752496	36.90	777.18	0.3573	12	3290.67	1036047	317.62	4549.99	0.7232	11
Uttar Pradesh	537.67	236954	226.90	244.73	2.1970	1	3504.00	393575	890.30	1728.46	2.0272	1
West Bengal	383.67	360455	106.44	372.28	1.0306	8	2140.33	497968	429.81	2186.93	0.9787	7
	Average effective rate=Rs. 103.28 per seat						Average effective rate=Rs. 439.17 per seat					

*Tax base=Total seating capacity in 1973-74 through 1975-76 has been taken as the base and the figures for 1979-80 through 1981-82 and 1967-68 through 1969-70 have been calculated taking into account the change in urban population during the period.

Haryana, Maharashtra, Punjab, Rajasthan and Uttar Pradesh continued to have indices of use of tax potential significantly higher than unity. Obviously, there did not exist much scope for mobilising additional revenue from this tax in these States.

From the above discussion, it may be concluded that Punjab State can easily mobilise additional resources from such taxes as profession tax, sales tax, motor vehicles tax and electricity duty. In addition, the State can also mobilise some resources by levying a surcharge on land revenue because Punjab's is predominantly an agricultural economy. Agriculture income-tax may also be imposed on large farmers.

Notes and References

1. The bulk of this tax is collected in the States where plantations like tea, rubber and coffee are grown.
2. Maxwell, J., *Fiscal Policy*, (New York, Henry Holt and Company, 1955), p. 108.
3. Chelliah, Raja J. and Sinha, Narain, *op. cit.*, p. 37.
4. Agriculture products in India receive a preferential treatment so far as the sales tax is concerned.
5. Chelliah, Raja J., and Sinha, Narain, *op. cit.*, p. 67.
6. *Ibid.*, p. 42.
7. However, it may be added that this conclusion pertains to the data as we have used in the study. Since presently in some States the road transport is a State undertaking, this conclusion does not hold good in respect of that part of revenue which is realised as fare.
8. See, for example, Chelliah, Raja J., and Sinha, Narain, *op. cit.*, p. 25.
9. Gupta, J.R., *Burden of Tax in Punjab* (New Delhi, Concept Publishing Company, 1983), p. 72.
10. Chelliah, Raja J. and Sinha, Narian, *op. cit.*, p. 41.

4

REVENUE FROM NON-TAX SOURCES—AN INTER-STATE COMPARISON

Apart from taxes, the States can mobilise resources from non-tax sources. Two types of non-tax sources are availabe to the States. One is the transfer from the Union Government in the form of grants-in-aid and other contributions. The trends of these transfers would reveal the degree of dependence of the States on the Union Government for the execution of their planned and non-planned projects. The other source, which is the more relevant of the two from the viewpoint of resource mobilisation, is the administrative and commercial revenues from States' own sources.

Non-tax receipts mainly accrue from fees and charges collected by various departments on account of different kinds of services rendered to the people. Thus, though non-tax receipts also add to the total revenue of the State, they are different from tax receipts in the sense that the burden of non-tax receipts falls only on the beneficiaries of the various services. So, while there is no direct relationship between the taxes paid by the people and the benefits they get from the government, some relationship certainly exists between the payment of various non-tax fees and charges and the services rendered by the government in return. Further, there is no doubt that the growing needs of a developing economy must necessarily be met through taxation measure, yet in a developing economy, taxation, whether direct or indirect, has a limit beyond which it cannot be resorted to without adversely affecting the pace of economic development. To the extent that the non-tax receipts can be augmented, the need for placing an additional burden of tax on the people can be obviated.[1] We have already examined in the last chapter that Punjab has a potential for additional resource mobilisation only in ths case of such taxes as profession tax, sales tax, motor vehicles tax, electricity duty and land revenue, which together accounted for 52.44 per cent of the States' own tax revenue in 1981-82. Obviously, the States have to look towards non-tax sources for financing its developmental efforts.

The non-tax receipts are generally made up of numerous small items. The important constituents of the non-tax revenue are administrative receipts, social and developmental services, civil works, multipurpose river schemes, road and water transport schemes, dividends from commercial undertakings, debt services, forests, irrigation and grants-in-aid from the Union Government.[2]

In the present chapter, an attempt has been made to analyse the growth and contribution of various sources of non-tax revenue in different States. The scope of resource mobilisation through various non-tax sources has also been examined in this chapter.

Table 4.1A depicts the percentage share of a State's non-tax revenue in its total revenue. For the three years' average period, 1967-68 through 1969-70, this share was 36.06 per cent for all the States taken together. The percentage share of non-tax revenue varied from 26.52 in Maharashtra to 71.33 in Jammu and Kashmir. The contribution of non-tax sources was more than 50 per cent in the States of Jammu and Kashmir (71.33 per cent), Assam (56.76 per cent) and Orissa (54.32 per cent). On the other hand, it was less than 30 per cent in Maharashtra, West Bengal, Bihar and Punjab. However, a look at Table 4.1B would reveal that in the States of Assam, Jammu and Kashmir and Orissa a major proportion of State non-tax revenue came from the Union Government. It was only in the case of Haryana, Maharashtra, Punjab, Madhya Pradesh, Tamil Nadu, Uttar Pradhsh, Gujarat, Karnataka and West Bengal that a significant part (*i.e.* more than 50 per cent) of non-tax revenue was raised from their own sources.

For the next three years' period, 1973-74 through 1975-76, the percentage share of non-tax revenue declined to 30.20 for all the States taken together and it ranged from 23.33 in Tamil Nadu to 92.37 in Nagaland (Table 4.1A). The non-tax sources contri-

TABLE 4.1A: **Percentage Share of State's Non-Tax Revenue in Total Revenue**

State	*Three years' average for 1967-68 through 1969-70*	*Three years' average for 1973-74 through 1975-76*	*Three years' average for 1979-80 through 1981-82*
Andhra Pradesh	30.50	33.05	30.92
Assam	56.76	51.32	54.40
Bihar	28.63	27.79	29.26
Gujarat	32.00	31.91	26.79
Haryana	34.27	36.97	35.26
Himachal Pradesh	—	71.88	76.36
Jammu and Kashmir	71.33	78.44	71.44
Karnataka	41.30	38.43	29.08
Kerala	40.90	37.60	29.87
Madhya Pradesh	40.74	36.94	38.95
Maharashtra	26.52	29.78	27.60
Manipur	—	86.94	88.57
Meghalaya	—	83.61	84.17
Nagaland	—	92.37	92.88
Orissa	54.32	53.47	47.41
Punjab	29.56	31.00	24.40
Rajasthan	42.80	47.58	43.13
Tamil Nadu	34.64	23.33	22.21
Tripura	—	84.18	83.44
Uttar Pradesh	35.54	33.94	32.51
West Bengal	27.48	26.75	22.72
All States	36.06	30.20	33.90

TABLE 4.1B: **Percentage Share of State's Own Non-Tax Revenue in Total Non-Tax Revenue**

State	*Three years' average for 1967-68 through 1969-70*	*Three years' average for 1973-74 through 1975-76*	*Three years' average for 1979-80 through 1981-82*
Andhra Pradesh	33.48	55.62	56.96
Assam	15.33	20.45	58.01
Bihar	42.90	43.87	38.83
Gujarat	56.85	62.65	62.96
Haryana	68.95	77.61	74.87
Himachal Pradesh	—	31.49	28.06
Jammu and Kashmir	25.66	37.27	38.43
Karnataka	55.81	77.10	72.89
Kerala	41.66	48.89	73.04
Madhya Pradesh	61.30	72.31	64.81
Maharashtra	68.37	74.38	77.67
Manipur	—	8.50	14.45
Meghalaya	—	9.38	16.30
Nagaland	—	5.65	19.78
Orissa	26.96	40.73	36.70
Punjab	67.32	64.99	72.24
Rajasthan	36.16	47.58	53.32
Tamil Nadu	60.83	72.19	61.20
Tripura	—	10.28	18.46
Uttar Pradesh	57.83	60.87	41.96
West Bengal	52.15	44.19	58.20
All States	42.05	55.87	54.69

buted more than 50 per cent in the States of Nagaland (92.37 per cent), Manipur (86.94 per cent), Tripura (84.18 per cent), Meghalaya (83.16 per cent), Jammu and Kashmir (78.44 per cent), Himachal Pradesh (71.44 per cent), Orissa (53.47 per cent) and Assam (51.32 per cent). However, the share of State's own non-tax revenue in its total non-tax revenue (Table 4.1B) was 55.87 per cent for all the States taken together. The contribution of the Union Government to State's non-tax revenue, *i.e.* grants-in-aid and other contributions, was significant (about 90 per cent) in the States of Nagaland, Manipur, Meghalaya and Tripura.

For the three-year period, 1979-80 through 1981-82, the percentage share of non-tax revenue mounted to 33.90 (Table 4.1A). This share was the maximum in Nagaland (92.88 per cent) and the minimum in Tamil Nadu (22.21 per cent). It contributed more than 50 per cent in the States of Nagaland (92.88 per cent), Manipur (88.57 per cent), Meghalaya (84.17 per cent), Tripura (83.44 per cent), Himachal Pradesh (76.36 per cent), Jammu and Kashmir (71.44 per cent) and Assam (54.40 per cent). The share of non-tax sources was less than 30 per cent in the States of Tamil Nadu (22.21 per cent), West Bengal (22.72 per cent), Punjab (24.40 per cent), Gujarat (26.79 per cent), Maharashtra (27.60 per cent), Karnataka (29.08 per cent), Bihar (29.26 per cent) and Kerala (29.87 per cent).

However, the overall percentage share of States' own non-tax revenue in total non-tax revenue slightly fell to 54.69 (Table 4.1B). It was the maximum in Maharashtra (77.67 per cent) and the minimum in Manipur (14.45 per cent). The States' own non-tax sources contributed more than 70 per cent in the States of Maharashtra (77.67 per cent), Haryana (74.87 per cent), Kerala (73.04 per cent), Karnataka (72.89 per cent) and Punjab (72.24 per cent). On the other hand, the grants-in-aid and other contributions from the Union Government had more than 70 per cent share in the States of Manipur, Meghalaya, Tripura, Nagaland and Himachal Pradesh.

From the above we may infer that the percentage share of grants-in-aid and other contributions made by the Union Government to State's non-tax revenue was much more in the relatively underdeveloped States than in the developed States. Further, the States of Andhra Pradesh, Assam, Gujarat, Haryana, Karnataka, Kerala, Maharashtra, Punjab and Rajasthan, consistently

TABLE 4.2: **Growth Rates and Buoyancy Coefficients of States' Non-Tax Revenue**

State	*Total non-tax revenue*		*States' own non-tax revenue*		*Grants-in-aid and otherc ontributions*		*States' own tax revenue*	
	Growth rate (%)	*Buoyancy coefficient*	*Growth rate (%)*	*Buoyancy coefficient*	*Growth rate (%)*	*Buoyancy coefficient*	*Growth rate (%)*	*Buoyancy coefficient*
Andhra Pradesh	17.39	1.605	21.68	2.005	3.95	1.270	16.67	1.458
Assam	12.21	1.107	22.12	1.974	8.08	0.706	11.16	0.971
Bihar	17.06	1.621	16.83	1.580	17.18	1.648	12.67	1.246
Gujarat	15.33	1.224	16.35	1.303	13.11	1.037	17.54	1.379
Haryana	18.27	0.513	19.39	1.454	15.47	1.201	18.26	1.347
Himachal Pradesh	25.00	2.129	27.11	2.386	24.97	2.123	23.12	2.091
Jammu and Kashmir	15.55	1.193	18.40	1.459	14.39	1.081	18.75	1.376

Karnataka	13.23	1.344	16.03	1.654	9.18	0.875	17.07	1.662
Kerala	12.15	1.166	15.84	1.474	7.46	0.746	16.45	1.439
Madhya Pradesh	16.52	1.509	16.84	1.578	15.30	1.382	16.00	1.494
Maharashtra	17.38	1.334	19.99	1.515	12.55	0.900	16.63	1.259
Manipur	20.87	1.703	50.33	5.061	20.08	1.582	15.86	1.288
Meghalaya	18.18	—	32.55	—	16.46	—	32.93	—
Nagaland	14.00	—	36.55	—	12.58	—	27.77	—
Orissa	15.88	1.533	17.44	1.823	15.23	1.400	14.95	1.468
Punjab	13.90	1.106	15.15	1.190	11.52	0.951	15.80	1.214
Rajasthan	16.95	1.424	20.57	1.684	14.07	1.223	15.37	1.231
Tamil Nadu	10.52	1.068	9.95	1.038	11.34	1.111	15.42	1.489
Tripura	19.23	1.601	30.11	2.431	18.88	1.508	24.91	2.435
Uttar Pradesh	15.69	1.440	12.50	1.145	19.02	1.733	20.89	1.853
West Bengal	13.08	1.313	15.66	1.617	12.03	1.172	13.93	1.406
All States	16.27	1.426	16.92	1.536	14.85	1.316	15.93	1.407

depended more and more on their own sources as far as non-tax revenue was concerned.

Table 4.2 depicts the growth rates and buoyancy coefficients of non-tax revenues. For all the States taken together, the growth rate of non-tax revenue worked out to 16.27 per cent per annum. It varied between 10.52 per cent in Tamil Nadu and 25.00 per cent in Himachal Pradesh. Overall growth rate of grants-in-aid and other contributions (14.85 per cent) was less than that of all States' own non-tax revenue (16.92 per cent). Barring Bihar, Tamil Nadu, and Uttar Pradesh, this phenomenon was true of even individual States. The buoyancy coefficients followed the pattern of growth rates. This meant that the majority of States increasingly mobilised resources from their own non-tax sources rather than depend on the Union Government for grants-in-aid and other contributions. Comparing States' own tax and non-tax revenues, we found that the former had a higher growth rate (16.92 per cent) than the latter (15.93 per cent) for all the States taken together. The same was the case with individual States except Gujarat, Jammu and Kashmir, Karnataka, Kerala, Meghalaya, Punjab, Tamil Nadu and Uttar Pradesh.

Like tax revenue, the average effective rates for different kinds of non-tax revenue were calculated and applied to the corresponding potential bases so as to work out the prospects for additional resources mobilisation. Two bases, *viz*. NSDP and population, were tried. Table 4.3 presents the results based on the first variant *i.e.* NSDP.

For the period 1967-68 through 1969-70, the average effective rate for State's own non-tax revenue was computed to be 1.93 per cent. The effective rate ranged between 0.95 per cent in Andhra Pradesh and 4.33 per cent in Jammu and Kashmir. The index of use of non-tax potential, which has been defined to mean the ratio of actual revenue to potential revenue, revealed that the States of Jammu and Kashmir, Madhya Pradesh, Tamil Nadu, Karnataka, Haryana and Kerala performed comparatively well. Punjab occupied the seventh place in order of ranking.

For the next three years' period, 1973-74 through 1975-76, the average effective rate for non-tax revenue swelled to 2.98 per cent. The effective rate had variations from 1.10 per cent in West Bengal to 8.43 per cent in Jammu and Kashmir. The indices of use of non-tax potential were higher than unity in the

States of Jammu and Kashmir, Himachal Pradesh, Karnataka, Haryana, Madhya Pradesh and Rajasthan. On the other hand, the States of West Bengal, Bihar and Assam, had indices significantly lower than unity. During this period Punjab moved down to the tenth position.

For the next three years' period, 1979-80 through 1981-82, the average effective rate went up to 4.17 per cent. The effective rate was the maximum in Manipur (8.30 per cent) and the minimum in West Bengal (1.76 per cent). The indices of use of non-tax potential were above unity in the States of Manipur, Jammu and Kashmir, Himachal Pradesh, Assam, Madhya Pradesh, Kerala and Haryana. For the States of West Bengal, Bihar, Uttar Pradesh and Punjab, these indices were below unity. During this period, Punjab was pushed almost to the lowest position. Thus, in Punjab, there existed a great scope for additional resource mobilisation from non-tax sources.

Realising that non-tax revenue accrued mainly from fees and charges collected by various departments on account of different kinds of services rendered to the people, the second variant, *i.e.* population, was also tried for estimating the potential revenue from non-tax sources. Table 4.4 presents the results on this account.

For the period 1967-68 through 1969-70, the per capita average effective rate was calculated to be Rs. 10.88. The per capita effective rate had a range from Rs. 3.92 in Bihar to Rs. 20.38 in Jammu and Kashmir. For Jammu and Kashmir, Punjab, Haryana, Karnataka and Maharashtra, the indices of use of non-tax potential were significantly higher than unity. On the other hand, these indices were significantly lower than unity in the States of Bihar, Andhra Pradesh, Assam and Orissa. During the next three years' period, 1973-74 through 1975-76, the per capita average effective rate multiplied to Rs. 28.67 and it was the maximum in Jammu and Kashmir (Rs.70.33) and the minimum in Bihar (Rs. 8.05). The indices of use of non-tax potential were above unity in Jammu and Kashmir, Haryana, Himachal Pradesh, Karnataka, Maharashtra and Punjab. The indices were markedly below unity in Bihar, Assam and West Bengal. Punjab, which occupied the second position in the previous period with respect to index of use of non-tax potential, slid down to the sixth position.

TABLE 4.3 : **Effective Rates and Revenue Potentials for States' Non-tax Revenue (based on Net State Domestic Product)**

State	*1967-68 through 1969-70*						*1973-74 through 1975-76*					
	Non-tax revenue (Rs. lakhs)	*Revenue base (Rs. lakhs)*	*Effective rate (%)*	*Revenue potential (Rs. lakhs)*	*Index of use of revenue potential (col. 2/ col. 5)*	*Ranking (based on col. 6)*	*Non-tax revenue (Rs. lakhs)*	*Revenue base (Rs. lakhs)*	*Effective rate (%)*	*Revenue potential (Rs. lakhs)*	*Index of use of revenue potential (col. 8/ col. 11)*	*Ranking (based on col. 12)*
1	*2*	*3*	*4*	*5*	*6*	*7*	*8*	*9*	*10*	*11*	*12*	*13*
Andhra Pradesh	1985.67	208788.67	0.95	4029.62	0.4928	16	10010.67	427166.67	2.34	12729.57	0.7864	14
Assam	788.33	69025.00	1.14	1332.18	0.5918	13	1704.33	122180.00	1.39	3640.96	0.4681	16
Bihar	2083.00	208233.33	1.00	4018.90	0.5183	15	4838.67	386700.00	1.25	11523.67	0.4199	17
Gujarat	2859.33	162559.33	1.76	3137.40	0.9114	9	7765.33	324833.33	2.39	9680.03	0.8022	12
Haryana	1501.67	67629.33	2.22	1305.25	1.1505	5	5448.67	144974.67	3.76	4320.25	1.2612	4
Himachal Pradesh	—	—	—	—	—	—	1768.33	40026.67	4.42	1192.79	1.4825	2
Jammu & Kashmir	870.67	20099.67	4.33	387.92	2.2450	1	3511.00	41650.67	8.43	1241.19	2.8287	1
Karnataka	3991.67	163981.00	2.43	3164.83	1.2613	4	13301.33	320566.67	4.15	9552.89	1.3924	3

Kerala	2226.33	100812.00	2.21	1945.67	1.1442	6	5252.00	196866.67	2.67	5866.63	0.8952	9
Madhya Pradesh	4506.67	175576.67	2.57	3388.63	1.3299	2	11771.00	344533.33	3.42	10267.09	1.1465	5
Maharashtra	6139.33	337008.33	1.82	6504.26	0.9439	8	19724.00	703800.00	2.80	20973.24	0.9404	8
Manipur	—	—	—	—	—	—	212.00	9133.33	2.32	272.17	0.7789	15
Orissa	1490.67	96439.67	1.55	1861.29	0.8009	12	4932.67	167266.67	2.95	4984.55	0.9896	7
Punjab	2136.67	116510.00	1.83	2248.64	0.9502	7	5293.33	220700.00	2.40	6576.86	0.8048	10
Rajasthan	1961.00	112509.67	1.74	2171.44	0.9031	10	7384.67	237133.33	3.11	7066.57	1.0450	6
Tamil Nadu	5006.67	197696.67	2.53	3815.55	1.3122	3	8811.33	367833.33	2.40	10961.43	0.8038	11
Uttar Pradesh	6774.33	402919.00	1.68	7776.34	0.8711	11	16085.00	679300.00	2.37	20243.14	0.7946	13
West Bengal	3131.00	280876.00	1.11	5420.91	0.5776	14	5522.33	501000.00	1.10	14929.80	0.3699	18
		Average effective rate=1.93 per cent						Average effective rate=2.98 per cent				

(*Contd.*)

State	*1979-80 through 1981-82*					
	Non-tax revenue (Rs. lakhs)	*Revenue base (Rs. lakhs)*	*Effective rate (%)*	*Revenue potential (Rs. lakhs)*	*Index of use of revenue potential (col. 14/col. 17)*	*Ranking (based on col. 18)*
	14	*15*	*16*	*17*	*18*	*19*
Andhra Pradesh	22704.00	712710.67	3.19	29720.04	0.7639	11
Assam	13290.00	240633.33	5.52	10034.41	1.3244	4
Bihar	11433.67	626700.00	1.82	26133.39	0.4375	17
Gujarat	17553.33	635526.33	2.76	26501.45	0.6624	13
Haryana	12302.33	292093.00	4.21	12180.28	1.0100	7
Himachal Pradesh	5136.33	64735.33	7.93	2699.46	1.9027	3
Jammu & Kashmir	6959.67	86717.33	8.03	3616.11	1.9246	2
Karnataka	20769.33	497809.00	4.17	20769.33	1.0000	8
Kerala	15146.33	345193.33	4.39	14394.56	1.0522	6
Madhya Pradesh	28919.00	557956.67	5.18	23266.79	1.2429	5
Maharashtra	44434.67	1399043.03	3.18	58340.09	0.7616	12
Manipur	1186.00	14289.33	8.30	595.87	1.9904	1

Orissa	9804.67	284472.33	3.45	11862.50	0.8265	10
Punjab	10396.67	471195.67	2.21	19648.56	0.5291	15
Rajasthan	17351.00	418944.67	4.14	17469.99	0.9932	9
Tamil Nadu	16612.00	606656.00	2.74	25297.56	0.6567	14
Uttar Pradesh	26563.33	1303872.30	2.04	54371.48	0.4886	16
West Bengal	14455.33	821983.00	1.76	34276.69	0.4217	18

Average effective rate=4.17 per cent

TABLE 4.4 : **Effective Rates and Revenue Potentials for States' Own Non-Tax Revenue (based on population)**

State	1967-68 through 1969-70						1973-74 through 1975-76					
	Non-tax revenue (Rs. lakhs)	*Revenue base (population in lakhs)*	*Effective rate (per capita)*	*Revenue potential (Rs. lakhs)*	*Index of use of revenue potential (col. 2/col. 5)*	*Ranking (based on col. 6)*	*Non-tax revenue (Rs. lakhs)*	*Revenue base (population in lakhs)*	*Effective rate (per capita)*	*Revenue potential (Rs. lakhs)*	*Index of use of revenue potential (col. 8/col. 11)*	*Ranking (based on col. 12)*
1	*2*	*3*	*4*	*5*	*6*	*7*	*8*	*9*	*10*	*11*	*12*	*13*
Andhra Pradesh	1985.67	411.00	4.83	4471.68	0.4441	15	10010.67	463.08	21.62	13276.50	0.7540	11
Assam	788.33	133.71	5.90	1454.76	0.5419	14	1704.33	160.45	10.62	4600.10	0.3705	17
Bihar	2083.00	531.85	3.92	5786.53	0.3600	16	4838.67	601.26	8.05	17238.12	0.2807	18
Gujarat	2859.33	247.17	11.57	2689.21	1.0633	8	7765.33	287.33	27.03	8237.75	0.9427	7
Haryana	1501.67	92.32	16.27	1004.44	1.4950	3	5448.67	108.29	50.32	3104.67	1.7550	2
Himachal Pradesh	—	—	—	—	—	—	1768.33	36.89	47.94	1057.64	1.6720	3
Jammu & Kashmir	870.67	42.72	20.38	464.79	1.8733	1	3511.00	49.92	70.33	1431.21	2.4532	1
Karnataka	3991.67	274.58	14.54	2987.43	1.3362	4	13301.33	314.64	42.27	9020.73	1.4745	4

Kerala	2226.33	199.07	11.18	2165.88	1.0279	9	5252.00	225.07	23.33	6452.76	0.8139	10
Madhya Pradesh	4506.67	386.28	11.67	4202.73	1.0723	7	11771.00	445.74	26.41	12779.37	0.9211	8
Maha-rashtra	6139.33	468.83	13.10	5100.87	1.2036	5	19724.00	538.52	36.63	15439.37	1.2775	5
Manipur	—	—	—	—	—	—	212.00	11.67	18.17	334.58	0.6336	14
Orissa	1490.67	205.25	7.26	2233.12	0.6675	13	4932.67	231.91	21.27	6648.86	0.7419	12
Punjab	2136.67	127.77	16.72	1390.14	1.5370	2	5293.33	144.53	36.62	4143.68	1.2774	6
Rajasthan	1961.00	239.41	8.19	2604.78	0.7528	10	7384.67	280.73	26.31	8048.53	0.9175	9
Tamil Nadu	5006.67	387.90	12.91	4220.35	1.1863	6	8811.33	432.45	20.38	12398.34	0.7107	13
Uttar Pradesh	6774.33	836.95	8.09	9106.02	0.7439	11	16085.00	945.85	17.01	27117.52	0.5932	15
West Bengal	3131.00	412.66	7.59	4489.74	0.6974	12	5522.33	471.78	11.71	13525.93	0.4083	16
	Average effective rate=Rs. 10.88 per capita						Average effective rate=Rs. 28.67 per capita					

(*Contd.*)

State	1979-80 through 1981-82					
	Non-tax revenue (Rs. lakhs)	*Revenue base (population in lakhs)*	*Effective rate (per capita)*	*Revenue potential (Rs. lakhs)*	*Index of use of revenue potential (col. 14/col. 17)*	*Ranking (based on col. 18)*
	14	*15*	*16*	*17*	*18*	*19*
Andhra Pradesh	22704.00	524.56	43.28	31924.72	0.7112	13
Assam	13290.00	187.15	71.01	11389.95	1.1668	6
Bihar	11433.00	684.34	16.71	41648.93	0.2745	18
Gujarat	17553.33	332.70	52.76	20248.12	0.8669	11
Haryana	12302.33	126.03	97.61	7670.19	1.6039	3
Himachal Pradesh	5136.33	41.91	122.56	2532.38	2.0283	1
Jammu & Kashmir	6959.67	58.35	119.27	3551.18	1.9598	2
Karnataka	20769.33	362.73	57.26	22075.75	0.9408	9
Kerala	15146.33	250.13	60.55	15222.91	0.9950	8
Madhya Pradesh	28919.00	510.25	56.68	31053.82	0.9313	10
Maharashtra	44434.67	614.31	72 33	37386.91	1.1885	5
Manipur	1186.00	13.82	85.82	841.09	1.4101	4
Orissa	9804.67	258.93	37.87	15758.48	0.6222	14

Punjab	10396.67	164.36	63.26	10002.95	1.0394	7
Rajasthan	17351.00	333.08	52.09	20271.25	0.8559	12
Tamil Nadu	16612.00	476.33	34.87	28989.44	0.5730	15
Uttar Pradesh	26563.33	1083.87	24.51	65964.33	0.4027	17
West Bengal	14455.33	534.63	27.04	32537.58	0.4443	16

Average effective rate=Rs. 60.86 per capita

For the period 1979-80 through 1981-82, the per capita average effective rate shot up to Rs. 60.86. The per capita effective rate varied from Rs. 16.71 in Bihar to Rs. 122.56 in Himachal Pradesh. The indices of use of non-tax potential were notably higher than unity in Himachal Pradesh, Jammu and Kashmir, Haryana and Manipur. On the other hand, the indices were considerably lower than unity for the States of Bihar, Uttar Pradesh and West Bengal. For Punjab, the index of use of non-tax potential was a bit more than unity. However, in terms of ranking, the State further stepped down to the seventh place. Thus, although Punjab appeared to have realised the per capita non-tax potential to the desired extent, its actual *vis-a-vis* potential collections consistently dwindled.

Putting Tables 4.3 and 4.4 together, we may infer that the States of Manipur, Himachal Pradesh, Jammu and Kashmir and Haryana exploited the non-tax sources to the desired extent. Two developed States, Punjab and Maharashtra, realised the per capita non-tax revenue above the average figure but with respect to NSDP, there appeared some scope for additional resource mobilisation from non-tax sources.

For disaggregated analysis of non-tax revenue, we used the data from 1972-73 onwards. The data previous to 1972-73 were not comparable with the figures owing to change in the classification of the major components of non-tax revenue. While launching the new classification with effect from 1972-73, the Reserve Bank of India observed :

> "The existing classification of budgetary expenditure into various heads of accounts was primarily designed to ensure effective legislative control over Government expenditure. With the growth in public outlays and the diversification of Government functions, the emphasis has shifted from ensuring control over budget appropriations to monitoring and analysis of programmes and an assessment of the return from expenditure incurred. Also under the existing classification, there was no co-ordination between the plan heads of development and the heads of accounts; nor was the function-wise breakdown of Government expenditure brought out clearly. A 'Team on Reforms in the Structure of Budget and Accounts' constituted by the Government of India in 1969 to consider certain

matters relating to accounts and budget heads arising out of the recommendations of the Administrative Reforms Commission has suggested a revised classification which, among others, aims at overcoming these shortcomings of the existing system. Based on the recommendations of the Team, the Comptroller and Auditor General has prescribed a revised accounting classification for the Budgets of both Central and State Governments with effect from 1974-75. Revised estimates for 1973-74 have been recast on the same lines. Actuals for 1972-73 have also been presented in the revised form to the extent possible. In the case of revenue and capital receipts the aggregates according to the revised classification broadly conform with those of the earlier classification. However, due to regrouping and merger of certain items, some major heads on receipt side are not strictly comparable."[4]

The State's own non-tax revenue has been divided into five major sub-heads, *viz.* Interest receipts; Dividends; General services; Social and community services; and Economic services. Since the receipts from the dividends was very small, we clubbed it with the interest receipts.[5] Interest receipts include interest from departmental commercial undertakings; public sector undertakings; cultivators; local bodies; cooperative societies and others. Dividend receipts include dividend from public undertakings and investment.

Table 4.5 shows the percentage share of revenue from interest receipts and dividends in State's own non-tax revenue. For the three years' period 1973-74 through 1975-76, the overall percentage share of revenue from interest receipts and dividends was worked out to be 25.46. It ranged from 6.08 per cent in Assam to 45.76 per cent in Andhra Pradesh. The percentage share was more than all States' average in Andhra Pradesh (45.76 per cent), Gujarat (38.23 per cent), Orissa (35.32 per cent), Rajasthan (34.29 per cent), Uttar Pradesh (33.66 per cent) and Karnataka (32.43 per cent). In Punjab, the share of interest receipts and dividends (23.12 per cent) was a shade less than all State's average.

For the next three years' period, 1979-80 through 1981-82, the percentage share of interest receipts and dividends improved

TABLE 4.5 : **Percentage Share of Revenue from Interest Receipts and Dividends in State's Own Non-Tax Revenue**

State	*Three years' average share for 1973-74 through 1975-76*	*Three years' average share for 1979-80 through 1981-82*	*Growth rate (per cent)*	*Buoyancy coefficient*
Andhra Pradesh	45.76	55.11	15.09	1.427
Assam	6.08	1.16	7.75	0.719
Bihar	8.52	3.19	2.01	0.148
Gujarat	38.23	47.71	18.55	1.432
Haryana	27.29	32.43	15.52	1.231
Himachal Pradesh	6.37	3.24	7.56	0.999
Jammu & Kashmir	17.03	13.57	10.60	0.666
Karnataka	32.43	40.12	12.41	1.252
Kerala	17.98	11.70	3.19	0.419
Madhya Pradesh	16.11	20.23	18.96	1.585
Maharashtra	22.70	23.41	14.85	1.117
Manipur	8.49	2.89	—1.49	—0.161
Meghalaya	9.38	5.51	20.78	—
Nagaland	8.88	1.41	3.06	—
Orissa	35.32	7.14	—6.57	—0.916
Punjab	23.12	27.12	12.72	0.936
Rajasthan	34.29	30.58	13.86	1.075
Tamil Nadu	22.39	44.96	17.85	2.067
Tripura	24.00	2.48	—12.80	—1.033
Uttar Pradesh	33.66	33.46	8.48	0.588
West Bengal	16.58	11.71	12.98	1.248
All States	25.46	26.74	14.21	1.207

to 26.74 for all the States taken together. It was the maximum in Andhra Pradesh (55.11 per cent) and the minimum in Assam (1.16 per cent). In Andhra Pradesh, the revenue from interest receipts and dividends was more than half of the State's own non-tax receipts. The other States where the percentage contribution of this source was more than all States' average were Gujarat, Tamil Nadu, Karnataka, Uttar Pradesh, Haryana, Rajasthan and Punjab. The share of interest receipts and dividends had a positive change in the States of Andhra Pradesh, Gujarat, Haryana, Karnataka, Madhya Pradesh, Punjab and Tamil Nadu over the period under study. Whereas in Maharashtra and Uttar Pradesh, its share stayed put, in all other States, it registered some decline.

The growth rate of revenue from interest receipts and dividends for the period 1972-73 through 1982-83, amounted to 14.21 per cent for all the States taken together. The growth rates of revenue from this source were negative in three States, *viz.* Tripura, Orissa and Manipur. This meant that the revenue from interest receipts and dividends diminished even in absolute terms in these States. The growth rates in the remaining States varied between 2.01 per cent in Bihar and 20.78 per cent in Meghalaya. The growth rates were exceeded all States' average in Meghalaya (20.78 per cent), Madhya Pradesh (18.96 per cent), Gujarat (18.55 per cent), Tamil Nadu (17.85 per cent), Haryana (15.52 per cent), Andhra Pradesh (15.09 per cent) and Maharashtra (14.85 per cent). The buoyancy coefficient for all the States taken together worked out to 1.207, which meant that 1 per cent change in NSDP lead to more than 1 per cent change in revenue from interest receipts and dividends. The buoyancy coefficients were more than unity in the States of Tamil Nadu, Madhya Pradesh, Gujarat, Andhra Pradesh, Karnataka, West Bengal, Haryana, Maharashtra and Rajasthan. The buoyancy coeffieients in the States which registered negative growth rates *i.e.* Manipur, Orissa and Tripura were also negative. In Punjab, the growth rate and buoyancy coefficient accounted for 12.72 per cent and 0.936 respectively.

In order to examine the potentials for additional resource mobilisation from interest receipts and dividends, the effective rates were worked out and are given in Table 4.6. Taking Net State Domestic Product as the base, the average effective rate

TABLE 4.6 : **Effective Rates and Revenue Potentials for States' Interest Receipts and Dividends (based on NSDP)**

State	*1973-74 through 1975-76*						*1979-80 through 1981-82*					
	Revenue (Rs. lakhs)	*Revenue base (Rs. lakhs)*	*Effective rate (%)*	*Revenue potential (Rs. lakhs)*	*Index of use of revenue potential (col. 2/5)*	*Ranking (based on col. 6*	*Revenue (Rs. lakhs)*	*Revenue base (Rs. lakhs)*	*Effective rate (%)*	*Revenue potential (Rs. lakhs)*	*Index of use of revenue potential (col. 8/11)*	*Ranking (based on col. 12)*
1	*2*	*3*	*4*	*5*	*6*	*7*	*8*	*9*	*10*	*11*	*12*	*13*
Andhra Pradesh	4562.67	427166.67	1.07	2802.21	1.6282	3	12512.00	712710.67	1.76	5680.30	2.2027	1
Assam	103.67	122180.00	0.08	801.50	0.1293	18	141.33	240633.33	0.06	1917.85	0.0736	17
Bihar	412.00	386700.00	0.11	2536.75	0.1624	17	364.67	626700.00	0.06	4994.80	0.0730	18
Gujarat	2968.67	324833.33	0.91	2130.91	1.3931	7	8375.00	635526.33	1.32	5065.14	1.6535	4
Haryana	1471.67	144974.67	1.02	951.03	1.5474	5	3983.33	292093.00	1.36	2327.98	1.7111	3
Himachal Pradesh	112.67	40026.67	0.28	262.57	0.4291	14	166.67	64735.33	0.26	515.94	0.3230	13
Jammu & Kashmir	517.00	41650.66	1.24	273.23	1.8922	1	944.67	86717.33	1.09	691.14	1.3668	7
Karnataka	3940.00	320566.67	1.23	2102.92	1.8736	2	8333.67	497809.00	1.67	3967.53	2.1005	2

Kerala	944.00	196866.67	0.48	1291.45	0.7310	13	1772.67	345193.33	0.51	2751.19	0.6443	12
Madhya Pradesh	1658.00	344533.33	0.49	2260.14	0.7469	12	5850.00	557956.67	1.05	4446.91	1.3155	8
Maharashtra	4976.67	703800.00	0.64	4616.93	0.9696	9	10401.33	1399043.00	0.74	11150.37	0.9328	9
Manipur	18.33	9133.33	0.20	59.19	0.3060	15	34.33	14289.33	0.24	113.89	0.3014	15
Orissa	1532.67	167266.67	0.93	1097.27	1.4150	6	700.33	284472.33	0.25	2267.24	0.3089	14
Punjab	1224.00	220700.00	0.55	1447.79	0.8454	10	2820.00	471195.67	0.60	3755.43	0.7509	11
Rajasthan	2532.00	237133.33	1.07	1555.59	1.6277	4	5306.00	418944.67	1.27	3338.99	1.5891	5
Tamil Nadu	1911.67	367833.33	0.52	2412.99	0.7922	11	7468.00	606656.00	1.23	4835.05	1.5446	6
Uttar Pradesh	5413.67	679300.00	0.80	4456.21	1.2149	8	8887.00	1303872.30	0.68	10391.86	0.8552	10
West Bengal	915.33	501000.00	0.18	3286.56	0.2785	16	1693.33	821983.00	0.21	6551.20	0.2585	16
	Average effective rate = 0.656 per cent						Average effective rate = 0.797 per cent					

TABLE 4.7: **Effective Rates and Revenue Potentials for States' Interest Receipts and Dividends (based on population)**

State	1973-74 through 1975-76						1979-80 through 1981-82					
	Revenue (Rs. lakhs)	*Revenue base (Population in lakhs)*	*Effective rate (per capita)*	*Revenue potential (Rs. lakhs)*	*Index of use of revenue potential (col. 2/5)*	*Ranking (based on col. 6)*	*Revenue (Rs. lakhs)*	*Revenue base (Population in lakhs)*	*Effective rate (per capita)*	*Revenue potential (Rs. lakhs)*	*Index of use of revenue potential (col. 8/11)*	*Ranking (based on col. 12)*
1	*2*	*3*	*4*	*5*	*6*	*7*	*8*	*9*	*10*	*11*	*12*	*13*
Andhra Pradesh	4562.67	463.08	9.85	2963.71	1.5395	5	12512.00	524.56	23.85	6174.07	2.0265	3
Assam	103.67	160.45	0.65	1026.88	0.1010	18	141.33	187.15	0.76	2202.76	0.0642	17
Bihar	412.00	601.26	0.69	3848.06	0.1071	17	364.67	684.34	0.53	8054.68	0.0453	18
Gujarat	2268.67	287.33	10.33	1838.91	1.6144	4	8375.00	332.70	25.17	3915.88	2.1387	2
Haryana	1471.67	108.29	13.59	693.06	2.1234	1	3983.33	126.03	31.61	1483.37	2.6853	1
Himachal Pradesh	112.67	36.89	3.05	263.10	0.4772	14	166.67	41.91	3.98	493.28	0.3379	13

Jammu & Kashmir	517.00	49.92	10.36	319.49	1.6182	3	944.67	58.35	16.19	686.78	1.3755	7
Karnataka	3940.00	314.64	12.52	2013.70	1.9566	2	8333.67	362.73	22.97	4269.33	1.9520	4
Kerala	944.00	225.07	4.19	1440.45	0.6554	12	1772.67	250.13	7.09	2944.03	0.6021	12
Madhya Pradesh	1688.00	445.74	3.79	2852.74	0.5917	13	5850.00	510.25	11.46	6005.64	0.9741	10
Maharashtra	4476.67	538.52	8.31	3446.53	1.2989	8	10401.33	614.31	16.93	7230.43	1.4385	6
Manipur	18.33	11.67	1.57	74.69	0.2454	16	34.33	13.82	2.48	162.66	0.2111	16
Orissa	1552.67	231.91	6.70	1484.22	1.0461	9	700.33	258.93	2.70	3047.61	0.2298	15
Punjab	1224.00	144.53	8.47	924.99	1.3233	7	2820.00	164.36	17.16	1934.52	1.4577	5
Rajasthan	2532.00	280.73	9.02	1796.67	1.4093	6	5306.00	333.08	15.93	3920.35	1.3535	8
Tamil Nadu	1911.67	432.45	4.42	2767.68	0.6907	11	7468.00	476.33	15.68	5606.40	1.3320	9
Uttar Pradesh	5413.67	945.85	5.72	6053.44	0.8943	10	8887.00	1083.87	8.20	12757.15	0.6966	11
West Bengal	915.33	471.78	1.94	3019.39	0.3032	15	1693.33	534.63	3.17	6292.60	0.2691	14
	Average effective rate = Rs. 6.40 per capita						Average effective rate = Rs. 11.77 per capita					

was computed to be 0.656 per cent for the three years' period 1973-74 through 1975-76. The effective rate was the maximum in Jammu and Kashmir (1.24 per cent) and the minimum in Assam (0.08 per cent). The indices of use of revenue potential were significantly higher than unity in the States of Jammu and Kashmir, Karnataka, Andhra Pradesh, Rajasthan and Haryana. For Punjab, the index of use of revenue potential stood at 0.8454.

For the period 1979-80 through 1981-82, the average effective rate showed a slight increase to 0.797 per cent. The effective rate was the highest in Andhra Pradesh (1.76 per cent) and the lowest in Assam as well as Bihar (0.06 per cent). The indices of use of revenue potential were notably above unity in the States of Andhra Pradesh, Karnataka, Haryana, Gujarat, Rajasthan and Tamil Nadu. On the other hand, in Bihar, Assam, West Bengal, Manipur, Orissa and Himachal Pradesh, the indices of use of revenue potential were markedly below unity. It was interesting to find that whereas in Orissa and Uttar Pradesh the indices of use of revenue potential sank to less than unity, in the later period compared with the previous period (when the indices were more than unity), the reverse was the case with Tamil Nadu. In Punjab, the index of use of revenue potential further shrank to 0.7509 during this period.

As already stated, we have also taken population as the second variant for estimating the potential revenue. Table 4.7 is an attempt in this direction. The per capita average effective rate was calculated to be Rs. 6.40 for the three years' period 1973-74 through 1975-76. The per capita effective rate ranged between Rs. 13.59 in Haryana and Rs. 0.65 in Assam. The indices of use of revenue potential for interest receipts and dividends were higher than unity in the States of Haryana, Karnataka, Jammu and Kashmir, Gujarat, Addhra Pradesh, Rajasthan, Punjab, Maharashtra and Orissa. For the next three-year period, 1979-80 through 1981-82, the per capita average effective rate jumped up to Rs. 11.77. The per capita effective rate was the maximum in Haryana (Rs. 31.61) and the minimum in Bihar (Rs. 0.53). The indices of use of revenue potential were higher than unity in the States of Haryana, Gujarat, Andhra Pradesh, Karnataka, Punjab, Maharashtra, Jammu and Kashmir, Rajasthan and Tamil Nadu. Thus, in Punjab the index of use of revenue potential for interest receipts and dividends was less than unity when NSDP was taken as the base, but, more than unity when population was considered as the base.

Table 4.8 depicts the share of revenue from general services in State's own non-tax revenue. For the three years' period 1973-74 through 1975-76, the share of revenue from general services was worked out to be 10.75 per cent for all the States taken together. It had variations from 5.11 per cent in Jammu and Kashmir to 30.84 per cent in Meghalaya. Further, the share of revenue from general services was less than all States' average only in Jammu and Kashmir (5.11 per cent), Madhya Pradesh (6.18 per cent), Orissa (6.69 per cent), Andhra Pradesh (7.35 per cent), Himachal Pradesh (7.63 per cent), Uttar Pradesh (8.26 per cent), and Haryana (8.52 per cent). In all other States, it was more than all States' average.

TABLE 4.8 : **Percentage Share of Revenue from General Services in State's Own Non-Tax Revenue**

State	*Three years' average share for 1973-74 through 1975-76*	*Three years' average share for 1979-80 through 1981-82*	*Growth rate (per cent)*	*Buoyancy coefficient*
1	2	3	4	5
Andhra Pradesh	7.35	7.89	15.55	1.417
Assam	14.90	68.54	24.29	2.088
Bihar	11.75	9.05	10.44	1.229
Gujarat	10.98	7.86	9.89	0.727
Haryana	8.52	5.82	11.87	0.643
Himachal Pradesh	7.63	53.15	23.44	1.964
Jammu & Kashmir	5.11	5.80	9.26	0.772

(Contd.)

1	2	3	4	5
Karnataka	13.20	10.72	9.95	0.774
Kerala	14.50	36.11	19.91	2.155
Madhya Pradesh	6.18	5.26	10.29	1.022
Maharashtra	11.80	11.21	14.88	1.119
Manipur	12.26	83.73	23.32	3.111
Meghalaya	30.84	63.60	23.84	—
Nagaland	19.57	79.65	28.75	—
Orissa	6.69	26.85	17.27	2.024
Punjab	12.71	9.60	11.08	0.602
Rajasthan	12.68	24.52	23.08	1.657
Tamil Nadu	15.99	12.65	6.14	0.676
Tripura	13.68	67.80	46.66	3.298
Uttar Pradesh	8.26	12.29	13.97	0.729
West Bengal	15.10	24.15	17.60	2.130
All States	10.75	17.29	16.53	1.314

For the next three years' period, 1979-80 through 1981-82, the share of revenue from general services registered an upward trend to 17.29 per cent for all the States taken together. It was the maximum in Manipur (83.73 per cent) and the minimum in Madhya Pradesh (5.26 per cent). The share of general services in the non-tax revenue was more than 50 per cent in the States of Manipur (83.73 per cent), Nagaland (79.65 per cent), Assam (68.54 per cent), Tripura (67.80 per cent), Meghalaya (63.60 per cent) and Himachal Pradesh (53.15 per cent). On the other hand, its share was less than 10 per cent in the States of Madhya Pradesh (5.26 per cent), Jammu and Kashmir (5.80 per cent), Haryana (5.82 per cent), Gujarat (7.86 per cent), Andhra Pradesh (7.89 per cent), Bihar (9.05 per cent) and Punjab (9.60 per cent).

The overall growth rate of revenue from general services for the period 1972-73 through 1982-83 was computed to be 16.53 per cent per annum. The growth rate was the highest in Tripura

(46.66 per cent) and the lowest in Tamil Nadu (6.14 per cent). In Tripura, Nagaland, Assam, Meghalaya, Himachal Pradesh, Manipur, Rajasthan and Kerala, the growth rate crossed the overall average. In Punjab, the growth rate of revenue from general services came out to be 11.08 per cent. The buoyancy coefficient for all the States taken together was 1.314, which varied from 0.602 in Punjab to 3.298 in Tripura. The buoyancy coefficient was less than unity in the States of Punjab, Haryana, Tamil Nadu, Gujarat, Uttar Pradesh, Jammu and Kashmir and Karnataka. The buoyancy coefficient revealed that the revenue from general services was the least responsive to NSDP in Punjab.

Table 4.9 shows the effective rates of revenue from general services. During the three-year period 1973-74 through 1975-76, the average effective rate worked out to 0.312 per cent. The effective rate had a range from 0.14 per cent in Andhra Pradesh to 0.55 per cent in Karnataka. The indices of use of revenue potential were higher than unity in the States of Karnataka, Jammu and Kashmir, Rajasthan, Tamil Nadu, Kerala, Haryana, Himachal Pradesh and Maharashtra. In Punjab, the index of use of revenue potential was slightly less than unity (*i.e.* 0.9769). For the next three years' period, 1979-80 through 1981-82, the average effective rate moved up to 0.429 per cent. The effective rate was the maximum in Rajasthan (1.02 per cent) and the minimum in Bihar (0.17 per cent). The indices of use of revenue potential were above unity in the States of Rajasthan, Orissa, Assam, Himachal Pradesh, Jammu and Kashmir and Karnataka. In the States of Bihar and Punjab, the index of use of revenue potential was significantly below unity. This meant that in these two States there existed a comparatively large scope for additional resource mobilisation from general services. If Punjab had attained the average effective rate, it would have fetched additional resources to the tune of Rs. 1023 lakhs from general services.

Table 4.10 depicts the effective rates of revenue from general services taking population as the base. During the three years' period 1973-74 through 1975-76, the per capita average effective rate was Rs. 2.86. The per capita effective rate varied from Rs. 0.95 in Bihar to Rs. 5.58 in Karnataka. The indices of revenue potential were significantly more than unity in the States

TABLE 4.9: **Effective Rates and Revenue Potentials for States' General Services (based on NSDP)**

State	*1973-74 through 1975-76*						*1979-80 through 1981-82*					
	Revenue (Rs. lakhs)	*Revenue base (Rs.) lakhs)*	*Effective rate (%)*	*Revenue potential (Rs. lakhs)*	*Index of use of revenue potential (col. 2/5)*	*Ranking (based on col. 6)*	*Revenue (Rs.) lakhs)*	*Revenue base (Rs.) lakhs)*	*Effective rate (%)*	*Revenue potential (Rs. lakhs)*	*Index of use of revenue potential (col. 8/11)*	*Ranking (based on Col. 12)*
1	*2*	*3*	*4*	*5*	*6*	*7*	*8*	*9*	*10*	*11*	*12*	*13*
Andhra Pradesh	603.33	427166.67	0.14	1332.76	0.4527	18	1790.33	712710.67	0.25	3057.53	0.5855	13
Assam	233.33	122180.00	0.19	381.20	0.6121	14	1674.67	240633.33	0.70	1032.32	1.6222	3
Bihar	568.67	386700.00	0.15	1206.50	0.4713	16	1035.00	626700.00	0.17	2688.54	0.3850	18
Gujarat	852.67	324833.33	0.26	1013.48	0.8413	11	1379.00	635526.33	0.22	2726.41	0.5058	16
Haryana	511.00	144974.67	0.35	452.21	1.1300	6	716.33	292093.00	0.25	1253.08	0.5717	15
Himachal Pradesh	135.00	40026.77	0.34	124.88	1.0810	7	396.67	64735.33	0.61	277.71	1.4284	4
Jammu and Kashmir	200.33	41650.76	0.48	129.95	1.5416	2	403.33	86717.33	0.47	372.02	1.0842	5
Karnataka	1756.00	320566.67	0.55	1000.17	1.7557	1	2227.00	497809.00	0.45	2135.60	1.0428	6
Kerala	761.67	196866.67	0.39	614.22	1.2401	5	1292.97	345193.33	0.37	1480.88	0.8729	9

Madhya Pradesh	645.67	344533.33	0.19	1074.94	0.6007	15	1522.33	557956.67	0.27	2393.63	0.6360	12
Maharashtra	2328.00	703800.00	0.68	2195.86	1.0602	8	4981.00	1399043.00	0.36	6001.89	0.8299	10
Manipur	24.33	9133.33	0.27	28.50	0.8537	10	59.67	14289.33	0.42	61.30	0.9734	8
Orissa	330.00	167266.67	0.20	521.87	0.6323	12	2633.00	284472.33	0.93	1220.39	1.1575	2
Punjab	672.67	220700.00	0.30	688.58	0.9769	9	998.00	471195.67	0.21	2021.43	0.4937	17
Rajasthan	936.67	237133.33	0.39	739.86	1.2660	3	4254.33	418944.67	1.02	1797.27	2.3671	1
Tamil Nadu	1435.00	367833.33	0.39	1147.64	1.2504	4	2101.33	606656.00	0.35	2602.55	0.8074	11
Uttar Pradesh	1328.33	679300.00	0.20	2119.42	0.6267	13	3265.33	1303872.30	0.25	5593.61	0.5818	14
West Bengal	719.33	501000.00	0.14	1563.12	0.4602	17	3491.23	821983.00	0.42	3526.31	0.9901	7
	Average effective rate=0.312 per cent						Average effective rate=0.429 per cent					

TABLE 4.10: **Effective Rates and Revenue Potential for States' General Services (Based on Population)**

State	1973-74 through 1975-76						1979-80 through 1981-82					
	Revenue (Rs. lakhs)	*Revenue base (population in lakhs)*	*Effective rate (per capita)*	*Reveuue potential (Rs. lakhs)*	*Index of use of revenue potential (col. 2/5)*	*Ranking (based on col. 6)*	*Revenue (Rs. lakhs)*	*Revenue base (population in lakhs)*	*Effective rate (per capita)*	*Revenue potential (Rs. lakhs)*	*Index of use of revenue potential (col. 8/11)*	*Ranking (based on col. 12)*
1	2	3	4	5	6	7	8	9	10	11	12	13
Andhra Pradesh	603.33	463.03	1.30	1324.41	0.4555	17	1790.33	524.56	3.41	3189.32	0.5614	15
Assam	233.33	160.45	1.45	458.89	0.5085	13	1634.67	187.15	8.73	1137.87	1.4366	4
Bihar	568.67	601.45	0.95	1719.60	0.3307	18	1035.00	684.34	1.51	4160.79	0.2488	18
Gujarat	852.67	287.33	2.97	821.76	1.0376	10	1379.00	332.70	4.14	2022.82	0.6817	14
Haryana	511.00	108.29	4.72	309.71	1.6499	2	716.33	126.03	5.68	766.26	0.9348	10
Himachal Pradesh	135.00	36.89	3.66	105.51	1.2795	6	396.67	41.91	9.46	254.81	1.5567	3
Jammu and Kashmir	200.33	49.92	4.01	142.77	1.4032	5	403.33	58.35	6.91	354.77	1.1369	6
Karnataka	1756.00	314.64	5.58	899.87	1.9514	1	2227.00	362.73	6.14	2205.40	1.0098	8
Kerala	761.67	225.07	3.38	643.70	1.1833	7	1292.67	250.13	5.17	1520.79	0.8500	11

Madhya Pradesh	645.67	445.74	1.45	1274.82	0.5065	14	1522.33	510.25	2.98	3102.32	0.4907	17
Maha-rashtra	2328.00	538.52	4.32	1540.17	1.5115	4	4981.00	614.31	8.11	3735.00	1.3336	5
Manipur	24.33	11.67	2.08	33.78	0.7202	11	59.67	13.82	4.32	84.03	0.7101	13
Orissa	330.00	231.91	1.42	663.26	0.4975	15	2633.00	258.93	10.17	1574.29	1.6725	2
Punjab	672.67	144.53	4.65	413.36	1.6273	3	898.00	164.36	6.07	999.31	0.9987	9
Rajasthan	936.67	280.73	3.34	802.89	1.1666	8	4254.33	333.08	12.77	2025.13	2.1008	1
Tamil Nadu	1435.00	432.45	3.32	1236.81	1.1602	9	2101.33	476.33	4.41	2896.09	0.7256	12
Uttar Pradesh	1328.33	945.85	1.40	2705.13	0.4910	16	3265.33	1083.87	3.01	6589.93	0.4955	16
West Bengal	719.33	471.78	1.52	1349.29	0.5331	12	3491.33	534.63	6.53	3250.55	1.0741	7
	Average effective rate=Rs. 2.86 per capita						Average effective rate=Rs. 6.08 per capita					

of Karnataka, Haryana, Punjab and Maharashtra. On the other hand, these were markedly less than unity in the States of Bihar, Andhra Pradesh, Uttar Pradesh and Orissa. For the next three-year period, 1979-80 through 1981-82, the per capita average effective rate coursed upward to Rs 6.08. The per capita effective rate was the maximum in Rajasthan (Rs. 12.77) and the minimum in Bihar (Rs. 1.51). The indices of use of revenue potential were notably above unity in the States of Rajasthan, Orissa and Himachal Pradesh. On the other hand, these were significantly below unity in the States of Bihar, Madhya Pradesh and Uttar Pradesh. In Punjab, the index of use of revenue potential was marginally less than unity. Comparing the effective rates of Punjab for general services, based on NSDP and on population, there was visible some scope for additional resource mobilisation, particularly with respect to the former.

The share of revenue from social and community services in State's own non-tax revenue is given in Table 4.11. For the three years' period 1973-74 through 1975-76, the overall share of social and community services was 11.07 per cent and the share ranged from 2.45 per cent for Jammu and Kashmir to 22.48 per cent for West Bengal. The share of social and community services was more than the overall average in the States of West Bengal (22.48 per cent), Kerala (17.50 per cent), Tamil Nadu (16.01 per cent), Assam (14.51 per cent), Maharashtra (14.03 per cent), Rajasthan (13.49 per cent), Punjab (12.87 per cent), Tripura (12.13 per cent), Bihar (11.79 per cent), Andhra Pradesh (11.48 per cent) and Manipur, (11.32 per cent). For the next three years' average period, 1979-80 through 1981-82, the overall share of revenue from social and community services decreased to 9.25 per cent. It had variations from 1.19 per cent in Nagaland to 21.38 per cent in West Bengal. Putting these two periods together, the share of revenue from social and community services appeared to have improved only in the States of Gujarat, Karnataka, Orissa and Uttar Pradesh, whereas in all other States it had a downward trend.

The growth rate of revenue from social and community services was 12.93 per cent for all the States taken together and it varied between 2.73 per cent for Assam and 23.69 per cent for Meghalaya. The growth rate was more than the overall average in the States of Meghalaya (23.69 per cent), Nagaland (17.38 per

TABLE 4.11: **Percentage Share of Revenue from Social and Community Services in State's Own Non-Tax Revenue**

State	*Three years' average share for 1973-74 through 1975-76*	*Three years' average share for 1979-80 through 1981-82*	*Growth rate (per cent)*	*Buoyancy coefficient*
Andhra Pradesh	11.48	9.24	12.70	1.217
Assam	14.51	1.55	2.73	0.228
Bihar	11.79	10.00	16.83	1.501
Gujarat	10.89	11.01	16.61	1.233
Haryana	6.69	5.16	11.78	0.670
Himachal Pradesh	5.07	3.06	9.92	0.974
Jammu and Kashmir	2.45	2.32	12.84	0.851
Karnataka	6.12	6.69	10.98	0.610
Kerala	17.50	11.31	12.90	1.244
Madhya Pradesh	6.33	4.26	5.34	0.928
Maharashtra	14.03	9.92	12.25	0.937
Manipur	11.32	2.78	10.30	1.122
Meghalaya	9.22	3.26	23.69	—
Nagaland	3.62	1.19	17.38	—
Orissa	8.05	8.73	15.19	1.445
Punjab	12.87	10.12	8.57	0.581
Rajasthan	13.49	13.43	15.43	1.279
Tamil Nadu	16.01	13.15	7.61	0.685
Tripura	12.13	5.73	16.33	1.369
Uttar Pradesh	8.45	10.90	15.83	1.082
West Bengal	22.48	21.38	13.24	1.342
All States	11.07	9.25	12.93	1.003

TABLE 4.12 : **Effective Rates and Revenue Potentials for States' Social and Community Services (based on NSDP)**

State	1973-74 through 1975-76						1979-80 through 1981-82					
	Revenue (Rs. lakhs)	*Revenue base (Rs. lakhs)*	*Effective rate (%)*	*Revenue potential (Rs. lakhs)*	*Index of use of revenue potential (col. 2/5)*	*Ranking (based on (col. 6)*	*Revenue (Rs. lakhs)*	*Revenue base (Rs. lakhs)*	*Effective rate (%)*	*Revenue potential (Rs. lakhs)*	*Index of use of revenue potential (col. 8/11)*	*Ranking (based on col. 12)*
1	*2*	*3*	*4*	*5*	*6*	*7*	*8*	*9*	*10*	*11*	*12*	*13*
Andhra Pradesh	1149.67	427166.67	0.27	1149.67	1.0000	7	2097.67	712710.67	0.29	1995.59	1.0512	8
Assam	160.33	122180.00	0.13	329.89	0.4860	18	189.33	240633.33	0.08	673.77	0.2795	18
Bihar	570.67	386700.00	0.15	1044.09	0.5466	17	1143.00	626700.00	0.18	1754.76	0.6514	17
Gujarat	846.00	324833.33	0.26	877.05	0.9646	8	1932.00	635526.33	0.30	1779.47	1.0857	6
Haryana	401.00	144974.67	0.28	391.43	1.0244	6	634.33	292093.00	0.22	817.86	0.7756	15
Himachal Pradesh	89.67	40026.67	0.22	108.07	0.8297	13	157.33	64735.33	0.24	181.26	0.8680	10
Jammu & Kashmir	86.00	41650.67	0.21	112.46	0.7514	15	161.33	86717.33	0.19	242.81	0.6644	16

Karnataka	814.67	320566.67	0.25	865.53	0.9412	9	1389.33	497809.00	0.28	1389.53	1.0000	9
Kerala	919.67	196866.67	0.47	531.54	1.7302	1	1712.33	345193.33	0.50	966.54	1.7716	2
Madhya Pradesh	745.33	344533.33	0.22	930.24	0.8012	14	1231.00	557956.67	0.22	1562.28	0.7880	14
Maharashtra	2767.33	703800.00	0.39	1900.26	1.4563	3	4406.33	1399043.00	0.31	3917.32	1.1248	5
Manipur	20.67	9133.33	0.23	24.66	0.8382	12	33.00	14289.33	0.23	40.01	0.8248	11
Orissa	397.00	167266.67	0.24	451.62	0.8791	11	855.87	284472.33	0.30	796.52	1.0743	7
Punjab	681.33	220700.00	0.31	595.89	1.1434	5	1052.33	471195.67	0.22	1319.35	0.7976	12
Rajasthan	996.33	237133.33	0.42	640.26	1.5561	2	2330.00	418944.67	0.56	1173.05	1.9863	1
Tamil Nadu	1437.00	367833.33	0.39	993.15	1.4469	4	2184.33	606656.00	0.36	1698.64	1.2859	4
Uttar Pradesh	1359.00	679300.00	0.20	1834.31	0.7410	16	2894.87	1303872.30	0.22	3650.84	0.7929	13
West Bengal	1241.33	501000.00	0.25	1352.70	0.9177	10	3090.33	821983.00	0.38	2301.55	1.3427	3
	Average effective rate=0.270 per cent						Average effective rate=0.280 per cent					

TABLE 4.13 : **Effective Rates and Revenue Potentials for States' Social and Community Services (based on population)**

State	1973-74 through 1975-76						1979-80 through 1981-82					
	Revenue (Rs. lakhs)	Revenue base (population in lakhs)	Effective rate (per capita)	Revenue potential (Rs. lakhs)	Index of use of revenue potential (col. 2/5)	Ranking (based on col. 6)	Revenue (Rs. lakhs)	Revenue base (population in lakhs)	Effective rate (per capita)	Revenue potential (Rs. lakhs)	Index of use of revenue potential (col. (8/11)	Ranking (based on col. 12)
1	2	3	4	5	6	7	8	9	10	11	12	13
Andhra Pradesh	1149.67	463.08	2.48	1231.79	0.9333	10	2097.67	524.56	4.00	2040.54	1.0280	9
Assam	160.33	160.45	1.00	426.80	0.3757	17	188.33	187.15	1.01	728.01	0.2587	18
Bihar	570.67	601.26	0.95	1599.35	0.3568	18	1143.00	684.34	1.67	2662.08	0.4294	17
Gujarat	846.00	287.33	2.94	764.30	1.1069	7	1932.00	332.70	5.81	1294.20	1.4928	5
Haryana	401.00	108.29	3.70	288.05	1.3921	4	634.33	126.03	5.03	490.26	1.2939	7
Himachal Pradesh	89.67	36.89	2.43	98.13	0.9138	11	157.33	41.91	3.75	163.03	0.9650	11
Jammu & Kashmir	86.00	49.92	1.72	132.79	0.6476	13	161.33	58.35	2.76	226.98	0.7108	13

Karnataka	814.67	314.64	2.59	836.94	0.9734	9	1389.33	362.73	3.83	1411.02	0.9846	10
Kerala	919.67	225.07	4.09	598.69	1.5361	3	1712.33	250.13	6.85	973.01	1.7598	3
Madhya Pradesh	745.33	445.74	1.67	1185.67	0.6286	15	1231.00	50.25	2.41	1984.87	0.6202	15
Maharashtra	2767.33	538.52	5.14	1432.46	1.9318	1	4406.33	614.31	7.17	2389.67	1.8439	1
Manipur	20.67	11.67	1.77	31.04	0.6659	12	33.00	13.82	2.39	53.76	0.6138	16
Orissa	397.00	231.91	1.71	616.88	0.6436	14	855.67	258.93	3.30	1007.24	0.8495	12
Punjab	681.33	144.53	4.71	384.45	1.7722	2	1052.33	164.36	3.16	639.36	1.6459	4
Rajasthan	996.33	280.73	3.55	746.74	1.3342	5	2230.00	333.08	6.99	1295.68	1.7983	2
Tamil Nadu	1437.00	432.45	3.32	1150.32	1.2492	6	2184.33	476.33	4.59	1852.92	1.1789	8
Uttar Pradesh	1359.00	945.00	1.44	2515.96	0.5402	16	2894.67	1083.87	2.67	4216.25	0.6866	14
West Bengal	1241.33	471.78	2.63	1254.93	0.9892	8	3090.33	534.63	5.78	2079.71	1.4859	6
	Average effective rate=Rs. 2.66 per capita						Average effective rate=Rs. 3.89 per capita					

cent), Bihar (16.83 per cent), Gujarat (16.61 per cent), Tripura (16.33 per cent), Uttar Pradesh (15.83 per cent), Rajasthan (15.43 per cent), Orissa (15.19 per cent) and West Bengal (13.24 per cent). In Punjab, the growth rate was 8.57 per cent which was less than all States' average. The buoyancy coefficient for all the States together was 1.003, and it ranged from 0.228 in Assam to 1.501 in Bihar. In the States of Assam, Punjab, Karnataka, Haryana, Tamil Nadu, Jammu and Kashmir, Madhya Pradesh and Maharashtra, the buoyancy rate was less than unity.

Table 4.12 shows the effective rates of revenue from social and community services. For the three years' period, 1973-74 through 1975-76, the average effective rate was worked out to be 0.270 per cent. The effective rate had a range from 0.13 per cent in Assam to 0.47 per cent in Kerala. The indices of use of revenue potential were higher than unity in the States of Kerala, Rajasthan, Maharashtra, Tamil Nadu, Punjab and Haryana. For the next three years' period, 1979-80 through 1981-82, the average effective rate increased a little to 0.280 per cent. The effective rate was the highest in Rajasthan (0.56 per cent) and the lowest in Assam (0.08 per cent). The indices of use of revenue potential were higher than unity in the States of Rajasthan, Kerala, West Bengal, Tamil Nadu, Maharashtra, Gujarat, Orissa and Andhra Pradesh. In Punjab, the index of use of revenue potential (0.7976) was less than unity. This meant that had Punjab applied the average effective rate, it would have mobilised some additional resources from social and community services.

Table 4.13 shows the effective rates of revenue from social and community services, taking population as the base. For the three years' period, 1973-74 through 1975-76, the per capita average effective rate was computed to be Rs. 2.66. The per capita effective rate varied from Rs. 0.95 in Bihar to Rs. 5.14 in Maharashtra. The indices of use of revenue potential were significantly higher than unity in the States of Maharashtra, Punjab and Kerala. For the next three years' period, 1979-80 through 1981-82, the per capita average effective rate expanded to Rs. 3.89. The per capita effective rate ranged from Rs. 1.01 in Assam to Rs. 7.17 in Maharashtra. The indices of use of revenue potential were markedly above unity in the States of Maharashtra, Rajasthan, Kerala and Punjab. The States of Rajasthan and Kerala had the index of use of revenue potential notably lower than unity with respect to NSDP as well as population. Punjab had some scope to raise additional revenue from social and community services only if NSDP was considered as the base.

The revenue from economic services includes revenue from forests, industries, co-operation, royalty on minerals and minerals concession fee, multipurpose river project, agriculture, irrigation, navigation, drainage and flood control projects, power projects, road and water transport services, dairy development, animal husbandry, fisheries and others.

Table 4.14 shows the share of revenue from economic services in State's own non-tax revenue. For the three years' period, 1973-74 through 1975-76, the share of revenue from economic services was 52.72 per cent for all the States taken together. It had variations from 35.41 per cent in Andhra Pradesh to 80.93 per cent in Himachal Pradesh. The revenue from economic services was more than the overall average in the States of Himachal Pradesh (80.93 per cent), Jammu and Kashmir (75.41 per cent), Madhya Pradesh (71.38 per cent), Bihar (67.94 per cent), Manipur (67.93 per cent), Nagaland (67.93 per cent), Assam (64.50 per cent) and Haryana (57.50 per cent). In Punjab, the share of revenue from economic services (51.30 per cent) was a shade less than all States' average.

TABLE 4.14 : **Percentage Share of Revenue from Economic Services in State's Own Non-Tax Revenue**

State	*Three years' average share for 1973-74 through 1975-76*	*Three years' average share for 1979-80 through 1981-82*	*Growth rate (per cent)*	*Buoyancy coefficient*
1	2	3	4	5
Andhra Pradesh	35.41	27.76	10.58	0.940
Assam	64.50	28.75	19.77	1.372
Bihar	67.94	77.76	20.07	1.972
Gujarat	39.90	33.42	10.34	0.972

(*Contd.*)

1	2	3	4	5
Haryana	57.50	56.59	13.38	1.078
Himachal Pradesh	80.93	40.55	7.05	0.652
Jammu & Kashmir	75.41	78.31	11.07	0.968
Karnataka	48.25	42.57	7.06	0.783
Kerala	50.02	40.88	15.94	1.587
Madhya Pradesh	71.38	70.25	16.01	1.494
Maharashtra	51.47	55.46	25.91	1 718
Manipur	67.93	10.60	0.82	0.096
Meghalaya	50.56	27.63	19.79	—
Nagaland	67.93	17.75	19.81	—
Orissa	49.94	57.28	14.98	1.405
Punjab	51.30	53.16	14.05	1.090
Rajasthan	39.54	31.47	12.88	1.122
Tamil Nadu	45.61	29.24	5.74	0.373
Tripura	50.19	23.99	17.89	1.438
Uttar Pradesh	49.63	43.35	7.20	0.644
West Bengal	45.84	42.76	17.74	1.754
All States	52.72	46.72	11.97	1.096

For the next three years' period, 1979-80 through 1981-82, the overall share of revenue from economic services came down to 46.72 per cent. It was the maximum in Jammu and Kashmir (78.71 per cent) and the minimum in Manipur (10.60 per cent). Considering the two periods together, the percentage contribution of revenue from economic services registered an increase only in the States of Bihar, Jammu and Kashmir, Maharashtra, Orissa and Punjab. Further, the share of economic services was above 50 per cent of non-tax revenue in the States of Jammu and

Kashmir, Bihar, Madhya Pradesh, Orissa, Haryana, Maharashtra and Punjab.

The growth rate of revenue from economic services was 11.97 per cent per annum for all the States taken together. It ranged between 0.82 per cent in Manipur and 25.91 per cent in Maharashtra. In the States of Andhra Pradesh, Gujarat, Karnataka, Jammu and Kashmir, Manipur, Tamil Nadu and Uttar Pradesh, the growth rate was less than the overall average. In Punjab, the growth rate of revenue from economic services was calculated to be 14.05 per cent. The overall buoyancy rate was 1.096, which implied that 1 per cent change in NSDP led to slightly more than 1 per cent change in revenue from economic services. The buoyancy coefficient varied from 0.096 in Manipur to 1.972 in Bihar. It was less than unity in Manipur, Tamil Nadu, Uttar Pradesh, Himachal Pradesh, Karnataka, Andhra Pradesh and Gujarat. For Punjab, the buoyancy coefficient was 1.090, which was a bit less than the overall average.

Table 4.15 shows the effective rates of revenue from economic services, taking Net State Domestic Product as the base. The average effective rate amounted to 1.74 per cent. The effective rates varied between 0.51 per cent in West Bengal and 6.36 per cent in Jammu and Kashmir. The indices of use of revenue potential were higher than unity in the States of Jammu and Kashmir, Himachal Pradesh, Madhya Pradesh, Haryana and Karnataka. For the next three-year period, 1979-80 through 1981-82, the average effective rate increased to 1.85 per cent. The effective rate ranged from 0.75 per cent in West Bengal to 6.29 per cent in Jammu and Kashmir. The indices of use of revenue potential were above unity in the States of Jammu and Kashmir, Madhya Pradesh, Himachal Pradesh and Orissa. In Punjab, the index of use of revenue potential was 0.6343 only. This meant that if Punjab had attained the average effective rate, it would have mobilised additional resources from economic services to the extent of Rs. 3186 lakhs.

Table 4.16 depicts the effective rates of revenue from economic services with population as the base. For the period 1973-74 through 1975-76, the per capita average effective rate was Rs. 16.64 and per capita effective rate was the maximum in Jammu and Kashmir (Rs. 49.29), and the minimum in West Bengal (Rs. 5.37). The indices of use of revenue potential exceed-

TABLE 4.15: **Effective Rates and Revenue Potentials for States' Economic Services (based on NSDP)**

State	1973-74 through 1975-76						1979-80 through 1981-82					
	Revenue (Rs. lakhs)	*Revenue base (Rs. lakhs)*	*Effective rate (%)*	*Revenue potential (Rs. lakhs)*	*Index of use of revenue potential (col. 2/5)*	*Ranking (based on col. 6)*	*Revenue (Rs. lakhs)*	*Revenue base (Rs. lakhs)*	*Effective rate (%)*	*Revenue potential (Rs. lakhs)*	*Index of use of revenue potential (col. 8/11)*	*Ranking (based on col. 12)*
1	*2*	*3*	*4*	*5*	*6*	*7*	*8*	*9*	*10*	*11*	*12*	*13*
Andhra Pradesh	3544.00	427166.67	0.83	7432.70	0.4768	17	6304.00	712710.67	0.88	13178.02	0.4784	14
Assam	1099.33	122180.00	0.90	2125.93	0.5171	15	3498.67	240633.33	1.45	4449.31	0.7863	9
Bihar	3287.33	386700.00	0.85	6728.58	0.4886	16	8891.00	626700.00	1.42	11587.68	0.7673	10
Gujarat	3088.00	324833.33	0.95	5652.10	0.5463	14	5866.33	635526.33	0.92	11750.88	0.4992	13
Haryana	3447.00	144974.67	2.38	2522.56	1.3655	4	6962.33	292093.00	2.38	5400.80	1.2891	4
Himachal Pradesh	1431.00	40026.67	3.58	696.46	2.0547	2	2082.33	64735.33	3.22	1196.96	1.7396	3
Jammu & Kashmir	2647.67	41650.67	6.36	724.72	3.6534	1	5450.33	86717.33	6.29	1603.40	3.3992	1

Karnataka	6417.67	320566.67	2.00	5577.86	1.1506	5	8842.67	497809.00	1.78	9204.49	0.9607	7
Kerala	2627.00	196866.67	1.33	3425.48	0.7669	9	6192.33	345193.33	1.79	6382.62	0.9701	6
Madhya Pradesh	8402.33	344533.33	2.44	5994.88	1.4016	3	20315.67	557956.67	3.64	10316.62	1.9692	2
Maharashtra	10152.00	703800.00	1.44	12246.12	0.8290	8	24646.00	1399043.00	1.76	25868.31	0.9527	8
Manipur	144.00	9133.33	1.58	158.92	0.9061	6	125.67	14289.33	0.88	264.21	0.4756	16
Orissa	2463.33	167266.67	1.47	2910.44	0.8464	7	5615.67	284472.33	1.97	5259.89	1.0676	5
Punjab	2715.33	220700.00	1.23	3840.18	0.7071	11	5526.33	471195.67	1.17	8712.41	0.6343	12
Rajasthan	2919.67	237133.33	1.23	4126.12	0.7076	10	5460.67	418944.67	1.30	7746.29	0.7049	11
Tamil Nadu	4095.00	367833.33	1.11	6400.30	0.6398	13	4857.33	606656.00	0.80	11217.07	0.4330	17
Uttar Pradesh	7984.00	679300.00	1.18	11819.62	0.6755	12	11516.33	1303872.30	0.88	24108.60	0.4777	15
West Bengal	2531.67	501000.00	0.51	8717.40	0.2904	18	6180.33	821983.00	0.75	15198.47	0.4066	18
	Average effective rate = 1.74 per cent						Average effective rate = 1.85 per cent					

TABLE 4.16: **Effective Rates and Revenue Potentials for States' Economic Services (based on Population)**

State	1973-74 through 1975-76						1979-80 through 1981-82					
	Revenue (Rs. lakhs)	*Revenue base (population in lakhs)*	*Effective rate (per capita)*	*Revenue potential (Rs. lakhs)*	*Index of use of revenue potential (col. 2/5)*	*Ranking (based on col.6)*	*Revenue (Rs. lakhs)*	*Revenue base (population in lakhs)*	*Effective rate (per capita)*	*Revenue potential (Rs. lakhs)*	*Index of use of revenue potential (col. 8/11)*	*Ranking (based on col. 12)*
1	*2*	*3*	*4*	*5*	*6*	*7*	*8*	*9*	*10*	*11*	*12*	*13*
Andhra Pradesh	3544.00	463.08	7.65	7705.65	0.4599	15	6304.00	524.56	12.02	15154.54	0.4160	14
Assam	1099.33	160.45	6.85	2669.89	0.4118	16	3498.67	187.15	18.69	5406.76	0.6471	10
Bihar	3287.33	601.26	5.47	10004.97	0.3286	17	8891.00	684.34	12.99	19770.58	0.4497	13
Gujarat	3088.00	287.33	10.75	4781.17	0.6459	10	5866.33	332.70	17.63	9611.70	0.6103	11
Haryana	3447.00	108.29	31.83	1801.95	1.9129	3	6962.33	126.03	55.24	3641.01	1.9122	2
Himachal Pradesh	1431.00	36.89	38.79	613.85	2.3312	2	2082.33	41.91	49.69	1210.78	1.7198	3
Jammu & Kashmir	2647.67	49.92	53.04	830.67	3.1874	1	5450.33	58.35	93.41	1685.73	3.2332	1
Karnataka	6417.67	314.64	20.40	5235.61	1.2258	4	8842.67	362.73	24.38	10479.27	0.8438	8
Kerala	2627.00	225.07	11.67	3745.16	0.7014	9	6192.33	250.13	24.76	7226.26	0.8569	7

Madhya Pradesh	8402.33	445.74	18.85	7417.11	1.1328	6	20315.67	510.25	39.82	14741.12	1.3782	5
Maharashtra	10152.00	538.52	18.85	8960.97	1.1329	5	24646.00	614.31	40.12	17747.42	1.3887	4
Manipur	144.00	11.67	12.33	194.19	0.7415	8	125.67	13.82	9.09	399.26	0.3148	18
Orissa	2463.33	231.91	10.62	3858.98	0.6383	11	5615.67	258.93	21.69	7480.49	0.7507	9
Punjab	2715.33	144.53	18.79	2404.98	1.1290	7	5526.33	164.36	33.62	4748.36	1.1638	6
Rajasthan	2919.67	280.73	10.40	4671.35	0.6250	12	5460.67	333.08	16.39	9622.68	0.5675	12
Tamil Nadu	4095.00	432.45	9.47	7195.97	0.5691	13	4857.33	476.33	10.20	13761.17	0.3530	17
Uttar Pradesh	7984.00	945.85	8.44	15738.94	0.5073	14	11516.33	1083.87	10.63	31313.00	0.3678	16
West Bengal	2531.67	471.78	5.37	7850.42	0.3225	18	6180.33	534.63	11.56	15445.46	0.4001	15
	Average effective rate = Rs. 16.64 per capita						Average effective rate = Rs. 28.89 per capita					

ed unity in the States of Jammu and Kashmir, Himachal Pradesh, Haryana, Karnataka, Maharashtra, Madhya Pradesh and Punjab. For the next three-year period, 1979-80 through 1981-82, the per capita average effective rate pushed forward to Rs. 28.89. The per capita effective rate ranged from Rs. 9.09 in Manipur to Rs. 93.41 in Jammu and Kashmir. The indices of use of revenue potential were higher than unity in the States of Jammu and Kashmir, Haryana, Himachal Pradesh, Maharashtra, Madhya Pradesh and Punjab.

From the above analysis, two contradictory conclusions emerge. One, considering NSDP as the base for non-tax sources, there appeared to be some scope for additional resource mobilisation. However, when population was taken as the base *i.e.* considering per capita non-tax revenue, there appeared to be no possibility of mobilising additional resources. Thus, the answer to the question whether additional resources could be mobilised from non-tax sources or not, depends upon how one views the role of non-tax sources. If non-tax revenues from social and community services, general services and interest receipts are meant only for the service of the people, apparently Punjab could not go beyond the level it had already reached. However, if the objective of administering such services is also to mobilise some resources, the State could go a little further to mobilise additional resources because of the fact that the per capita income of Punjab is the highest. Further, even from the viewpoint of per capita non-tax revenue, there is some scope for mobilising additional resources, particularly from the economic services which are administered partly on commercial basis.

State Lotteries

The lottery scheme, introduced by various State Governments since 1968, has gained considerable importance among people of all walks of life in the country. A popular interest in the lottery scheme has been created by the fact that an individual has to invest only a nominal amount to expect a big sum as the prize and the State's involvement in the scheme is sufficient guarantee that wins the confidence of the people. The States are now vying with one another in offering ever bigger and more tempting sums as prizes.

Lotteries have now come to constitute an important source

of non-tax revenue for the State governments. In the past few years, the share of lotteries in non-tax revenue registered a sharp increase. Tables 4.17A and 4.17B examine the growth of revenue from State lotteries and their percentage share in States' own non-tax revenue respectively. For the States, which are running lottery schemes, the overall share of lottery to States' non-tax revenue was 2.45 per cent in 1968-69 and it increased to 2.79 per cent in 1982-83. In 1968-69, the percentage contribution of lotteries was the maximum in Kerala (7.60 per cent) and the minimum in West Bengal (0.33 per cent). In Haryana also the contribution of lottery was significant *i.e.*, 4.15 per cent. During 1982-83, the share of State letteries varied from 0.49 per cent in Madhya Pradesh to 20.10 per cent in Himachal Pradesh. Further, the contribution of State lotteries was more than all States' average in the case of Himachal Pradesh (20.10 per cent), Uttar Pradesh (6.79 per cent), Kerala (5.23 per cent), Tamil Nadu (5.22 per cent), Haryana (4.27 per cent), Punjab (4.19 per cent), Maharashtra (3.50 per cent) and Karnataka (2.99 per cent). The contribution of State lotteries in Punjab, though not very significant during the years 1972-73 through 1979-80, has lately picked up and now it is 4 to 5 per cent of States' own non-tax revenue.

The overall revenue from State lotteries mounted at a rate of 10.35 per cent per annum during the study period. The growth rate was the maximum in West Bengal (32.11 per cent) and the minimum in Karnataka (5.52 per cent). For Tamil Nadu, though the growth rate was worked out to be negative *i.e.* —0.17 per cent, its contribution to State's non-tax revenue was notable. The growth rate of revenue from State lottery was more than 20 per cent in the States of West Bengal, Himachal Pradesh, Uttar Pradesh and Punjab. Keeping in view the various constraints of mobilising resources through additional taxation, the system of raising resources through lotteries should be considered a significant one.

However, it should be mentioned that the system of raising resources through State lotteries is slightly different from that of tax and non-tax sources. State lotteries have been started primarily to collect additional revenue for the States. So what is important is the net contribution of lotteries to the State's exchequer *i.e.* what is left after paying prizes to the winners and

TABLE 4.17A : Revenue from State Lotteries

(*Rupees lakhs*)

State	*Year*															
	1968-69	*1969-70*	*1970-71*	*1971-72*	*1972-73*	*1973-74*	*1974-75*	*1975-76*	*1976-77*	*1977-78*	*1978-79*	*1979-80*	*1980-81*	*1981-82*	*1982-83*	*Growth rate (per cent)*
Andhra Pradesh	—	—	—	—	—	—	20	13	—	—	—	—	21	207	156	—
Assam	—	19	—	33	23	18	20	20	22	27	—	24	—	—	90	8.10
Bihar	—	8	97	80	—	—	85	—	11	—	—	—	—	—	—	—
Gujarat	—	—	—	—	—	—	—	—	—	—	—	—	—	270	676	—
Haryana	68	—	—	—	—	—	86	82	87	101	146	122	115	288	683	13.88
Himachal Pradesh	—	—	—	21	8	—	—	—	—	—	22	43	49	136	773	28.10
Jammu & Kashmir	—	15	—	20	—	—	—	—	—	—	—	—	—	—	—	—
Karnataka	—	207	686	558	361	216	192	207	241	345	426	488	512	705	795	5.52
Kerala	181	257	254	187	167	175	189	204	280	347	379	312	374	438	609	7.36
Madhya Pradesh	—	36	83	88	55	66	113	65	96	81	105	159	188	166	194	10.52

Maharashtra	131	860	610	733	560	520	603	897	1347	1098	1225	1267	1477	1932	2050	13.46
Nagaland	—	—	—	—	14	5	18	22	20	24	—	—	—	—	—	—
Orissa	—	8	23	—	—	—	—	—	—	—	—	—	—	—	—	—
Punjab	78	307	265	85	32	47	34	42	57	53	85	119	116	280	1017	25.37
Rajasthan	34	80	103	156	88	75	74	89	100	40	—	57	190	309	287	8.21
Tamil Nadu	—	705	850	711	—	—	257	185	337	389	499	462	488	733	874	—0.17
Uttar Pradesh	29	193	137	59	48	104	84	250	447	421	587	447	756	767	2547	27.59
West Bengal	12	78	38	15	10	36	61	108	258	295	468	441	468	442	386	32.11
All States	533	2773	3146	2736	1368	1262	1836	2184	3303	3221	3942	3941	4754	6673	11133	10.35

TABLE 4.17B : **Percentage Share of Revenue from State Lotteries in the States' Own Non-Tax Revenue**

State	*Year*														
	1968-69	*1969-70*	*1970-71*	*1971-72*	*1972-73*	*1973-74*	*1974-75*	*1975-76*	*1976-77*	*1977-78*	*1978-79*	*1979-80*	*1980-81*	*1981-82*	*1982-83*
Andhra Pradesh	—	—	—	—	—	—	0.21	0.12	—	—	—	—	0.09	0.79	0.60
Assam	—	1.91	—	5.33	1.46	1.13	1.62	0.88	0.82	0.66		0.55	—	—	1.22
Bihar	—	0.39	5.11	4.70	—	—	2.20	—	0.18	—	—	—	—	—	—
Gujarat	—	—	—	—	—	—	—	—	—	—	—	—	—	1.43	2.76
Haryana	4.15	—	—	—	—	—	1.56	1.27	1.11	1.29	1.56	1.09	0.96	2.08	4.27
Himachal Pradesh	—	—	—	3.16	0.52	—	—	—	—	—	0.93	1.93	0.48	4.42	20.10
Jammu and Kashmir	—	1.62	—	2.43	—	—	—	—	—	—	—	—	—	—	—
Karnataka	—	3.36	15.03	15.09	3.80	1.83	1.53	1.33	1.55	2.37	2.33	2.75	2.54	2.89	2.99
Kerala	7.60	11.03	10.87	5.43	4.77	4.43	3.43	3.24	4.13	4.30	4.12	2.56	3.74	1.89	5.23
Madhya Pradesh	—	0.70	1.62	1.50	0.57	0.74	0.96	0.45	0.57	0.46	0.50	0.63	0.71	0.47	0.49
Maharashtra	1.92	12.50	9.30	9.96	7.09	3.54	3.75	3.55	4.44	3.41	3.33	3.22	3.38	3.84	3.50
Nagaland	—	—	—	—	8.28	2.78	9.09	9.57	6.62	7.19	—	—	—	—	—
Orissa	—	0.84	1.12	—	—	—	—	—	—	—	—	—	—	—	—
Punjab	0.41	8.97	7.73	4.58	0.75	1.02	0.67	0.68	0.73	0.69	0.69	1.03	1.25	4.26	4.19

Rajasthan	1.82	3.77	4.86	7.56	1.58	1.41	1.05	0.91	0.88	0.38	—	0.39	0.96	1.76	1.22
Tamil Nadu	—	13.62	17.25	11.16	—	—	2.85	2.07	3.37	3.52	4.07	3.79	2.10	5.09	5.22
Uttar Pradesh	0.44	2.69	1.77	0.83	0.34	0.67	0.53	1.46	2.16	2.24	2.70	1.72	3.11	2.61	6.79
West Bengal	0.33	2.44	2.10	0.81	0.26	0.81	1.10	1.64	3.51	3.34	4.61	3.18	3.01	3.17	2.34
All States which run lotteries	2.45	4.56	5.53	4.80	1.37	1.10	1.41	1.39	1.81	1.67	1.75	1.59	1.47	2.03	2.79

TABLE 4.18: **Gross and Net Receipts from State Lotteries**

(*Rupees lakhs*)

State	*1978-79*				*1979-80*				*1980-81*			
	Gross receipts	*Expenditure*	*Net receipts*	*Expenditure as percentage of gross receipt*	*Gross receipts*	*Expenditure*	*Net receipts*	*Expenditure as percentage of gross receipt*	*Gross receipts*	*Expendi ture*	*Net receipts*	*Expenditure as percentage of gross receipt*
Andhra Pradesh	—	—	—	—	—	—	—	—	21	23	—2	109.52
Assam	—	—	—	—	24	30	—6	125.00	—	—	—	—
Gujarat	—	—	—	—	—	—	—	—	—	—	—	—
Haryana	146	120	26	82.19	112	115	7	94.26	115	146	—31	126.96
Himachal Pradesh	22	7	15	31.82	43	30	13	69.77	49	37	12	75.51
Karnataka	426	286	140	67.14	488	320	168	65.57	512	366	146	71.48
Kerala	379	200	179	52.77	312	176	136	56.41	374	230	144	61.50
Madhya Pradesh	105	77	28	73.33	159	128	31	80.50	188	163	25	86.70

Maharashtra	1225	782	443	63.84	1267	901	366	71.11	1477	1017	460	68.86
Punjab	85	79	6	92.94	119	113	6	94.96	116	116	0	100.00
Rajasthan	—	—	—	—	57	11	46	19.30	190	115	75	60.53
Tamil Nadu	499	294	205	58.92	462	270	192	58.44	488	246	242	50.41
Uttar Pradesh	587	650	—63	110.73	447	335	112	74.94	756	876	—120	115.87
West Bengal	468	250	228	51.28	441	289	152	65.53	468	270	198	57.68
All States	3942	2735	1207	69.38	3941	2718	1223	68.97	4754	3605	1149	75.83

(*Contd.*)

State	1981-82				1982-83			
	Gross receipts	Expenditure	Net receipts	Expenditure as percentage of gross receipts	Gross receipts	Expenditure	Net receipts	Expenditure as percentage of gross receipts
Andhra Pradesh	207	218	—11	105.31	156	223	—67	142.95
Assam	—	—	—	—	90	35	55	38.89
Gujarat	270	130	140	48.15	676	488	188	72.19
Haryana	288	257	31	89.24	683	572	111	83.75
Himachal Pradesh	136	100	36	73.53	773	709	64	91.72
Karnataka	705	512	193	72.62	795	562	233	70.69
Kerala	438	272	166	62.10	609	356	253	58.46
Madhya Pradesh	166	146	20	87.95	194	171	23	88.14
Maharashtra	1932	1318	614	68.22	2050	1421	629	69.32
Punjab	280	261	19	93.21	1017	913	104	89.77
Rajasthan	309	189	120	61.17	287	201	86	70.03
Tamil Nadu	733	405	328	55.25	874	581	293	66.48
Uttar Pradesh	767	776	—9	101.17	2547	1074	1473	42.17
West Bengal	442	295	147	66.74	386	285	101	73.83
All States	6673	4879	1794	73.12	11137	7591	3546	68.16

commission to the agents and incurring pertinent administrative expenses. Table 4.18 is an attempt to assess this net contribution. The period covered is from 1978-79 to 1982-83 because we could obtain the relevant data only for these years. The gross receipts from State lotteries for all the States taken together were estimated to be Rs. 3,942 lakhs in 1978-79. The total expenditure on State lotteries including the prize money was Rs. 2,735 lakhs, which formed 69.38 per cent of the total revenue. State-wise, the highest gross revenue collected from State lotteries was in Maharashtra (Rs. 1,225 lakhs) and the lowest in Himachal Pradesh (Rs. 22 lakhs). The highest expenditure on State lotteries was found in the case of Uttar Pradesh, which incurred even a loss of 10.33 per cent. Expenditure on a draw being almost fixed, the State perhaps could not sell the requisite number of tickets to earn a net surplus. For other States, the expenditure ranged from 31.82 per cent in Himachal Pradesh to 92.94 per cent in Punjab. As for the net proceeds from State lotteries, it was found that Maharashtra (Rs. 443 lakhs) topped the list and was followed by West Bengal (Rs. 228 lakhs).

During 1982-83, the gross receipts from State lotteries for all the States taken together were Rs. 11,137 lakhs and total expenditure thereof was Rs. 7,591 lakhs *i.e.* 68.16 per cent of the total gross revenue. Thus, for every Rs. 100 paid by the society, only Rs. 32 reached the State exchequer. The highest collection from State lottery was Rs. 2,547 lakhs in Uttar Pradesh, followed by Rs. 2,050 lakhs in Maharashtra. The minimum collection (Rs. 90 lakhs) was found in the case of Assam. The highest expenditure on the conduct of lotteries was found in the case of Andhra Pradesh, which actually incurred a loss, the expenditure being 42.95 per cent more than the gross receipts from the lotteries. In respect of the remaining States, the expenditure varied between 38.89 per cent in Assam and 91.72 per cent in Himachal Pradesh. With respect to the net receipts from State lotteries, it was observed that Uttar Pradesh (Rs. 1473 lakhs) topped the list, followed by Maharashtra (Rs. 629 lakhs). It should be mentioned that apart from net receipts by State Governments from the State lotteries, the Union Government also earns income tax on prize money.

As well known, the State lotteries were started in order to

obtain more funds for economic development. Since the expenditure incurred is much more than what the State is getting, the society appears to be paying too high a price for obtaining these funds. Thus, there is a need to bring down the expenditure on lotteries, particularly the administrative costs, to make them a useful source of revenue.

In respect of Punjab, it was observed that at the time of the present study, the State has been running three lotteries, *viz.* Shubh Lakshmi, Punjab Raffle Weekly Lottery and Ashta Lakshmi. In each lottery scheme, the ticket costs one rupee. The commission paid to the agent is 20 per cent of the face value of the tickets. In addition, the agents also get bonus on the prized tickets. Ashta Lakshmi is a fortnightly lottery and the draw is held on the 5th and the 20th of each month. For this lottery, 30 lakh tickets are printed. The first prize is Rs. 4 lakhs and there are three second and three third prizes each of the value of Rs. 50,000 and Rs. 10,000 respectively. Other prizes vary from Rs. 5 to Rs. 500. In all 96,307 prizes, amounting to Rs. 15.40 lakhs, are offered under Ashta Lakshmi lottery scheme.

Shubh Lakshmi and Punjab Raffle are weekly lotteries, and their draws are held on each Friday and Wednesday respectively. Under Shubh Lakshmi lottery scheme, 21 lakh tickets are printed. There are three first and three second prizes each of the value of Rs. 1 lakh and Rs. 10,000 respectively. Other prizes vary between Rs. 10 and Rs. 1,000 and in all 25,416 prizes, involving an amount of Rs. 10.65 lakhs, are offered. But in the Punjab Raffle Weekly Lottery only 9 lakh tickets are printed. The values of the first and second prizes are Rs. 1 lakh and Rs. 10,000 respectively, there being only one first and only one second prize. Other prizes vary from Rs. 3 to Rs. 1000 and in all 1,00,016 prizes, working out to Rs. 5.39 lakhs, are offered under the scheme.

Table 4.19 explains the number of draws held, gross receipts and net receipts from State lotteries in Punjab. In this State, the lottery scheme was introduced in July 1968. Up to March 1969, only 3 draws were held. Between 1969-70 and 1980-81, the number of draws was decided in an ad-hoc manner and the number varied from 6 in 1972-73 to 18 in 1980-81. In 1981-82, the State Government launched the weekly lottery scheme, thereby increasing the number of draws to 56. In 1982-83, the number of draws held further rose to 104. In 1968-69, the gross sales from State lotteries accounted for Rs. 77.67 lakhs, out of which the State incurred Rs. 31.17 lakhs on prizes, commission, printing, publicity and establishment charges. This gave a net profit of Rs. 46.50 lakhs. From the 104 draws held in 1982-83, the gross sales and net profits amounted to Rs. 1,017.13 lakhs and Rs. 103.81 lakhs respectively.

Table 4.19 also shows the percentage share of different items of expenditure and net receipts in respect of State lotteries in Punjab. In 1968-69, the total expenditure on State lotteries constituted 40.18 per cent of gross receipts from State lotteries, thereby ensuring a net receipt of 59.82 per cent. However, over the period, the expenditure on State lotteries swelled disproportionately. For example, in 1982-83, as much as 89.79 per cent of gross receipts was spent on different items which left a net profit of 10.21 per cent. More than 50 per cent of the gross receipts was paid as prize money and about 30 per cent was paid as commission and bonus to the agents. In the intervening period *i.e.* from 1974-75 to 1981-82, the net contribution of State lotteries was hardly significant, so much so that even in some years (1980-81) the State incurred net losses on the lottery scheme. In 1980-81, the State suffered losses due to poor sale of tickets. The declining trend in the net proceeds from State lotteries could primarily be explained in terms of consistent increase in prize money, commission and bonus paid to the agents.

To sum up, we may say that out of the non-tax sources, the transfer from the Union Government in terms of grants-in-aid and other contributions is more significant in relatively less developed States. In certain developed States like Punjab and Maharashtra, although these realised the per capita non-tax revenue above the all States' average figure, in relation to NSDP, there is still some scope for additional resource mobilisation. Punjab can mobilise additional resources from general services, social and community services and economic services. The significance of State lotteries as a source of public revenue appears to lie not in the amount of money collected but in the fact that it is a novel attempt by the State governments to mobilise additional resources in order to finance their public expenditure programme.

TABLE 4.19: **Gross Receipts and Net Receipts from State Lotteries in Punjab**

(*Rs. lakhs*)

Year	*No. of draws*	*Gross receipts*	*Prizes paid*	*Commission*	*Other expenditure**	*Total expenditure*	*Net profit*
1968-69	3	77.57	5.37	22.89	2.91	31.17	46.40
		(100.00)	(6.92)	(29.51)	(3.75)	(40.18)	(59.82)
1969-70	10	307.28	63.05	98.09	13.26	174.40	132.88
		(100.00)	(20.52)	(31.92)	(4.32)	(56.76)	(43.24)
1970-71	18	265.22	90.38	77.05	22.02	189.45	75.77
		(100.00)	(34.08)	(29.05)	(8.30)	(71.43)	(28.57)
1971-72	7	84.79	39.94	27.79	11.72	79.45	5.34
		(100.00)	(47.10)	(32.78)	(13.82)	(93.70)	(6.30)
1972-73	6	32.37	9.93	10.75	6.34	27.02	5.35
		(100.00)	(30.68)	(33.21)	(19.59)	(83.48)	(16.52)
1973-74	8	47.37	15.96	14.32	7.57	37.85	9.52
		(100.00)	(33.69)	(30.23)	(15.98)	(79.90)	(20.10)
1974-75	9	33.71	14.45	10.19	8.30	32.94	0.77
		(100.00)	(42.87)	(30.23)	(24.62)	(97.72)	(2.28)

1975-76	11	42.00	18.94	13.55	8.54	41.03	0.97
		(100.00)	(45.10)	(32.26)	(20.33)	(97.69)	(2.3')
1976-77	12	56.76	26.47	18.01	10.39	54.87	1.89
		(100.00)	(46.63)	(31.73)	(18.31)	(96.67)	(3.33)
1977-78	9	53.43	21.73	16.83	11.05	49.61	3.82
		(100.00)	(40.67)	(31.50)	(20.68)	(92.85)	(7.15)
1978-79	16	84.86	32.57	31.22	15.45	79.24	5.62
		(100.00)	(38.38)	(36.79)	(18.21)	(93.28)	(6.62)
1979-80	17	119.17	55.71	37.77	19.10	112.58	6.59
		(100.00)	(46.75)	(31.69)	(16.03)	(94.47)	(5.53)
1980-81	12	115.96	62.26	33.86	19.86	115.98	—0.02
		(100.00)	(53.69)	(29.20)	(17.13)	(100.02)	(—0.02)
1981-82	56	280.34	151.45	76.95	32.32	260.72	19.62
		(100.00)	(54.02)	(27.45)	(11.53)	(93.00)	(7.00)
1982-83	104	1017.13	570.08	273.99	69.25	913.32	103.81
		(100.00)	(56.05)	(26.94)	(6.81)	(89.79)	(10.21)

Note : Figures in brackets are percentages to gross receipts.

* Includes expenditure on printing, publicity, establishment charges and miscellaneous.

Notes and References

1. Government of Punjab, *Report of the Taxation Enquiry and Resources Committee, Punjab*, (1971), p. 102.
2. *Ibid.*, p. 103.
3. Reserve Bank of India, *Reserve Bank of India Bulletin*, May 1974 pp. 883-84.
4. The proportion of dividends to total receipts (interest+dividends), never exceeded 4.06 per cent.

5

EVOLUTION AND ECONOMIC SIGNIFICANCE OF STATE LOTTERIES

Gambling is a basic human instinct. It is also very much a part of our tradition and recognised as such by Hindu mythology, which projects Yudhishtra (who gambled away his kingdom as well as his wife Draupati) as the greatest of the ancient gamblers. Though banned by government, gambling still forms an important part of Diwali celebrations, and it continues to flourish surreptitiously through matka, satta, tambola, races and in a variety of other forms.[1]

Lottery is a variant of gambling. The institution of lottery is very ancient. In line with human psychology, considering the important role that chance plays in life, Western countries introduced a new alternative to gambling called State lotteries. These were run on humanitarian considerations and as a means of raising funds for public good. State lotteries were also intended to serve as an alternative to private gambling run on unfair lines by unscrupulous individuals.[2]

Lottery is a scheme for distribution of prizes determined by chance. Invented by the Romans, it was used by Augustus, Nero and other Roman emperors to finance building projects and to augment imperial revenues. During the middle ages, merchants in Italy used lottery procedure to dispose of their unsaleable goods. Soon it spread from Italy and Holland to France, Germany, Spain and Australia. Governments began to exercise the right of supervisory regulations with a view to protect the public against fraudulent transactions and subsequently themselves ran lotteries.[3]

The first lottery was held in Holland. Whereas some encyclopaedias mention Germany, other Italy as the land of origin of State lottery. The respective dates are said to be 1521 and 1530. As gathered from a recently published account, the first official lottery was held in Utrecht in Netherlands in 1444. In steady succession, thereafter, other Dutch towns followed suit.[4]

There are plenty of fifteenth century records to show how each municipality used the lottery to solve its individuals problems. Stakes and prizes varied widely, especially in the early stages of the game. In many cases, the prizes consisted of varying sums of money, or of objects in gold and silver, but sometimes an annuity was issued as the first prize, or, as in the case of Utrecht in 1454, the top winner was offered a public office—the post of the town auctioneer. The revenues from lotteries were earmarked for a variety of purposes, most often to fill the municipal coffers. But at least one town used it to build fortifications, and then there was the prime example of the city of Den Bosch (Boss). It added a steeple to its beautiful Gothic cathedral by assiduously saving up lottery funds.[5]

A.V. Rangachari considers that the first money lottery was established in France during 1530 for the benefit of the State. Lottery was introduced in England by Queen Elizabeth in 1569 and it was utilized as a source of State's income until 1826. Venice, the cradle of State lotteries, instituted the first known government monopoly of lotteries which yielded considerable revenue. The USSR in its war with Germany used lottery for war financing. A ticket was issued to the purchaser of a war bond and prizes were as high as 1 lakh roubles. The real home of State lottery, however, was Australia, where lotteries were conducted under government sponsorship for financing public purpose.[6]

Thus, in the early 15th and 16th centuries, European countries floated their own lottery schemes of different types to fulfil their needs and to raise additional resources for national development programmes. Holland, Italy, France, Denmark, Sweden, Poland, Germany, USA, Burma were pioneers in this line. They introduced their lotteries and accumulated considerable funds for social welfare schemes.[7]

An outstanding feature of modern State lottery is the scrupulous honesty with which it is conducted. The Irish Hospitals sweep-stakes were the biggest lottery in the world till

1940 when the lottery was suspended on account of war. Its average annual income was more than £5 million, of which nearly one quarter was retained for the benefit of hospitals and the remainder was returned in prizes.[8]

EL Gordo, the first prize of the Christmas draw in Spain's national lottery, is said to be the richest in the world. In 1983, the lottery was the biggest, showering 53 billion pesetas—$334 million–in 10,419 prizes. The top prize EL Gordo totalled 11.5 billion pesetas. Each full ticket costs 25,000 pesetas, and is divisible into 10 parts. These parts are often shared by various persons. For weeks they sub-divide like atoms as friends, neighbours and clients buy or are given a participation that may be as low as a single peseta.[9]

When government lotteries came into existence, some countries used goods as prizes. In the twentieth century, Denmark had a lottery for agriculture, which paid in commodity prizes; Israel's State lottery offers flats as winnings; the Ghana government organises car raffles. Lotteries in communist countries are especially liberal with winnings in kind; these range from books and sewing machines to cars and plots of land—the most popular prizes being journeys abroad.

The mechanics of lottery is very simple. Tickets bearing different numbers are placed on sale and a date is set for the draw. On that date, a device is set up wherein the duplicates of all the tickets sold are placed in a drum or wheel from which winning numbers are drawn at random. From the money realised by the sale of tickets, the proprietors of the lottery deduct some amount for expenses and profits, the remainder is paid to the holders of tickets corresponding to the numbers drawn.

The hope of winning is based on the peculiar law of valuation according to which the subjective valuation of a potential prize does not diminish proportionately with the probability coefficient but tends to remain larger than the value of the prize and the coefficient. Thus, with equal probability values, the small chance of winning a large sum is valued more than a large chance of winning a small sum. Further, the time interval between the purchase of lottery tickets and the expected date of draw also influences the decision of an individual to buy a ticket. The lesser the interval of time between the purchase of the ticket and the draw, the greater the influence of gambling spirit.[10]

Adam Smith describes gamblers as conceited men, who are presumptuous enough to believe in their fortune being greater than that of their neighbours, overvalue their chances of gain, and undervalue their chances of loss. Gambling presupposes a belief in luck. Undoubtedly many gamblers are so irrationally minded as to think that they possess gifts of luck that their brethren do not share. But it does not follow that gambling necessarily goes with a player's faith in such a metaphysical attitude. Even a rational person, too, participates in gambling ventures without thinking that the chances of winning are greater for him than for any other player. Adam Singh claims that the lottery business is nourished by the vain hope of gaining some of the great prizes.[11] Friedman and Savage ignore the Adam Smith approach and, conceding that large prizes can be won, stress the arithmetical improbability. They find it perplexing that there are people who willingly make investments that are more likely to result in a loss than in a high yield.[12]

In India, too, the lotteries have their own historical background. It was for the first time in 1850 that the Governor of Madras presidency started a provincial lottery for the welfare of the people. Out of the net income derived from the sale of tickets, he financed the construction of modern building like Victoria Hall, Rippon Building, Government museum and various theatre halls. In Goa, a government-controlled institution called *Provedoria de Associonia Publica* ran lotteries till the time of liberation of Goa from the Portuguese. This public institution used to earn a net profit of Rs. 15 lakhs a year which was utilized to help various humanitarian causes such as running hospitals and providing medical aid besides giving doles to the poor and offering scholarships to the deserving students to enable them to prosecute higher studies.[13] In Calcutta, lottery was introduced for the improvement of the metropolitan town.

In India, lotteries were often organised by philanthropic societies for a long time to raise funds for their social welfare activities. After independence and particularly after the economic development initiated by the Five Year Plans, the private sector has been using lotteries to promote sale of goods and services. In the 1960's, faced with the problem of raising additional revenue for the Fourth Five Year Plan, and for meeting the evergrowing normal expenditure needs, the State governments started running their own lotteries. The Government of Kerala was the first to introduce the lottery in January 1968, followed by Punjab, Madras and other States.

We have tried to arrange the States in chronological order with respect to the adoption of State lottery scheme:

State/Union Territory	*Year of adoption of lottery scheme*
Kerala	January, 1968
Punjab	July, 1968
Tamil Nadu	August, 1968
Haryana	September, 1968
Rajasthan	December, 1968
Uttar Pradesh	December, 1968
West Bengal	January, 1969
Maharashtra	April, 1969
Madhya Pradesh	July, 1969
Assam	September, 1969
Jammu and Kashmir	September, 1969
Karnataka	October, 1969
Delhi	December, 1969
Bihar	January, 1970

Some other States and Union Territories also started their own lotteries after January, 1970.

The lottery scheme as a source of revenue is specifically mentioned in the Union list of the Constitution of India, though betting and gambling are included in the State list. Since lottery is a variant of gambling, the States can run lotteries but only with the approval of the Union Government, as it enjoys the power to regulate lotteries run by the States, State lotteries do not require any legislative approval for their floatation. The authority for the purpose is the finance department of the State concerned. The rules and regulations are usually in the form of notification issued by the State Government.

At a time when people were complaining of back-breaking

taxes, it seemed a good idea to cash in on man's get-rich-quick desire and his gambling instinct to raise resources for development mainly. Several States in the beginning earmarked the profits for specific projects; later on almost all of them added these to the general revenues of the States. Kerala set aside the money for public health and agriculture, Delhi for low cost housing and UP for medical facilities. In Tamil Nadu, besides medical facilities, the other purposes for which the money was utilised were construction of elementary school buildings and slum clearance.

When the State lotteries were launched in the late sixties, several people, including C. Rajagopalachari (First Indian Governor General of India), were conscientious objectors to the government's participation in gambling. Rajaji, based his strong oppositton to State lotteries on two solid grounds. First, it is against all canons of morality that the State should exploit the cupidity of poor people by offering huge amounts as prizes for a rupee or two; an act which is morally wrong does not become right because the government wants money. Secondly, State lottery tends to induce people to become lazy; instead of earning their bread by the sweat of their brow, they start trusting to their luck for getting their living.[14]

The evils of lotteries have been pointed out clearly by many men in our country but the State governments seem in no mood to listen to them. The issue expectedly remains unresolved and somewhat controversial even today. The lotteries, however, have continued to enjoy the fancy of the State governments and undeterred by the objections raised by a small minority, they have been competing with one another in lottery running. They justify the lotteries on the ground that these are needful for undertaking nation-building activities such as education and public health.

The lottery schemes, introduced by various State governments since 1968 have gained considerable importance among people of all walks of life. The lottery tickets of various State governments are now selling like hot cakes throughout the country. They are available not only in every nook and corner of cities and towns but even in remote villages. Quite a number of people are earning money through selling the lottery tickets on a commission basis. A popular interest in the lottery scheme has been created by the fact that an individual has to invest only a nominal amount to get a big sum as the prize and the lottery being a State enterprise, people place reliance on it.

The main objective of State lotteries is to raise revenue for financing developmental and welfare activities which would otherwise suffer for want of resources. Against this background, it is relevant to examine the economic merits and demerits of State lotteries as an alternative as well as additional source of revenue.

There are two normal measures for mobilising revenue. One is taxation, as far as possible progressive taxation, and second, public borrowing. Apparently, we have reached the limits in both the directions. The public is unwilling to bear the burden of additional taxes. In any case, the people will not pay any more taxes willingly unless there is evidence that the government is taking steps to stop all wasteful expenditure. With rising cost of living, the general public has little margin to save for lending it to the government. In any event, unless prices show any sign of stability, people would be unwilling to contribute to public borrowing because they apprehend that by the time the loan matures after 10 or 15 years, the value of the rupee might be greatly reduced. Moreover, those who have money and are generally the main beneficiaries of development cannot be taxed any more, because they wield great influence with the government administration. They are in a position to save and lend to the government but are loth to do so because they are keen to plough back their savings into their own industry and business.

Compared to the raising of resources by the State Government through borrowing, both by floating public loans and by introducing small savings schemes, the lottery scheme is better in the sense that it does not involve interest liabilities and repayment of loans. At the same time, the State lotteries act as a method of diverting to the government the purchasing power in varying amounts from the consumers indulging in wasteful expenditure and from savers who would like to keep their savings idle.

In contrast with the method of overdrafts from the Reserve Bank of India by the State governments, the lottery scheme definitely enjoys the advantage of not creating additional purchasing power in the hands of the government in an inflationary situation.

Vis-a-vis the grants and loans from the Government of India, the lottery scheme possesses certain advantages. Except in the case of general unconditional grants, specific grants have to be used for specified projects. The terms of execution of the projects are mostly dictated by the Government of India; whether the State governments want to foster those projects or not, matters little. No such compulsion is there in the case of revenue raised by lotteries Loans from the Government of India carry the responsibility of repayment of principal as well as interest and sometimes commitment of utilisation for some specific purpose. Consequently, grants and loans from the Government of India ultimately limit the autonomy of the State Government.

As compared to taxation, the lottery scheme has certain advantages as well as disadvantages. First of all, whereas taxation in any case compels people to give up the control over a part of their income, expenditure or wealth, the lottery scheme has the advantage of inducing the people to divert voluntarily a part of their purchasing power. Secondly, taxation does not confer any immediate direct reward while the lottery scheme offers the bait of prospective prizes. Thirdly, taxation, being compulsory, may operate arbitrarily without regard to the convenience of the taxpayer, whereas the lottery scheme, being voluntary avoids this inconvenience.

On the other hand, the lottery scheme being voluntary may not serve as a permanent source of revenue for long as compared to taxation. In the long run, people's enthusiasm to purchase lottery tickets may be dampened when they start feeling that it is not a desirable way of getting rich as it is a variant of gambling which involves risk and uncertainty. So, the response may dwindle, with the result that the operation of lottery scheme might become uneconomic. The costs of administration may actually exceed the revenue yield. One may argue that this may happen even in the case of a new tax or a bad tax. But the chances of making a tax productive are higher than those of making the lottery scheme productive.

Secondly, in addition to raising revenue, taxation also fulfils certain other social objectives like reducing inequalities of income and wealth. But, it is not possible to use the lottery scheme to achieve this objective. Taxation, being compulsory, can be made steeply progressive. But the lottery scheme, being voluntary, cannot be made progressive in that way. On the other hand, the lottery scheme involves the participation of poor people who pool their poverty to make a few rich overnight while the rich continue to be rich. Even if the State governments utilise the net revenue from lotteries for providing welfare amenities in a planned way to the poor and the needy, the lottery scheme is still an inefficient fiscal tool to achieve this social objective.

Furthermore, the State governments have been running their lotteries in urban areas although there is no bar on rural people participating in it. So, urban people have been increasingly participating in the State lotteries. This trend may continue even if the lotteries are popularised in rural areas. The rural people are prone to suspect this method of becoming rich quickly and since sentiments die hard, they may hesitate to invest their savings in this unconventional method of getting rich. If this happens, it will have two implications. One is that the urban people will have to buy the lottery tickets and bear the cost of development activities in the State. The urban people have already been bearing a relatively heavy tax burden and their contribution to the lottery funds makes their total contribution still bigger than the contribution of the rural people. The second implication which follows from the first is that the rural sector, which is not taxed in proportion to its relative tax-paying ability as compared to the urban sector, would again escape the obligation of payment under the lottery scheme of raising revenue.

It may be added that the lottery scheme ensures a substantive income to the Union Government also. It is only in lottery trade where every winning ticket automatically entitles the Union revenue department to its share. Presently lottery business alone is contributing about Rs. 54 crores annually by way of taxes deducted at source.[15]

Generating self-employment opportunities is another merit of the lotteries. Even at the end of 35 years of economic development, the problem of unemployment in the country has not been solved. Indeed, there is a growing feeling that over the years the problem has become all the more acute. The State lotteries have provided employment to a large number of educated and not-so-educated. Hundreds of poor students have found new media of income by selling lottery tickets for pursuing their studies.

In brief, lotteries may be supported from the following angles of vision :

(i) It is an effective method of raising additional resources.
(ii) State lottery, if at all considered a form of taxation, may be treated as voluntary taxation.
(iii) State lotteries can generate employment by engaging agents and retail-sellers.
(iv) Another benefit of the lottery scheme may be that it can cut down gambling to some extent.

Lotteries should be regarded as a simple game of chance and luck. And here the loser is sacrificing a very small amount of money in an anticipation of getting rich overnight. Even the loser would not feel the pinch so much if he is convinced that the income from lotteries will ultimately be utilised for development purposes of the State.

It may be of some interest to see how and in what form the lotteries are run by various States in the country today. Lotteries operated by various State governments may be broadly classified into three categories, *viz.* weekly, monthly and bumper draws. Maharashtra has even started daily draws which are becoming increasingly popular. The prices of tickets normally range between 50 paise and one rupee for the weekly, one rupee to two rupees for the monthly, and two rupees to five hundred rupees for the bumper draws. To start with, lotteries were confined to the geographical boundaries of the sponsoring States. Their instant popularity, however, resulted in their being marketed on a national scale. States are now vying with one another in offering ever bigger and more tempting sums as prizes. The sizes of the first and other prizes vary from State to State. Even the central services like armed forces and para military forces have also joined the fray with bumper offers running into crores of rupees. The Central Reserve Police Force announced what it called "the world's biggest draw" in October 1983; it printed 60 lakh tickets, each costing Rs. 10. The first prize was Rs. 2 crore. Other lottery organisers have got into the race to create "crorepatis" (multi-millionaires). The Deaf and Blind offered double the prize of the CRPF for tickets costing only half as much. The mountain State of Himachal Pradesh promised a 'Himalayan Prize' of

Rs. 2.02 crore to its winner. The lucky winners, however, do not always get everything the advertisement promises. A third of the prize money goes to the tax collector and up to another quarter towards sellers' bonuses and organisers' expenses.

There are three types of lotteries going on : those organized by State governments; those organised by private agents for State governments; and those organised by private agents for the so-called charitable institutions. The extent of government control on the conduct of the lottery diminishes gradually in that order. In India, most of the States appoint private agencies as wholesalers and State stockists and they, in turn, appoint agents and sub-agents. Certain States simply lend their names to private firms or individuals who offer the maximum stipulated amount to the States. Such firms or agencies make their own arrangements for printing and selling the lottery tickets. Once an authorised agent lifts the stock of lottery tickets, it is deemed to be sold and he is allowed a fixed commission. Now, it is the turn of such authorised agents to sell the tickets to the public for the face value. If he has any tickets unsold on or before the date of draw, he will be a loser to that extent since the tickets will have no value thereafter.

The commission paid to the agents for the sale of lottery tickets also varies from State to State and ranges between 20 per cent and 30 per cent of the face value of the ticket. In addition, the agents selling the maximum number of tickets and those selling prize-winning tickets get a special commission or bonus.

The numbers and amounts of prizes for each lottery scheme are separately determined and announced. Each ticket is entitled to only one prize, the highest that is drawn against it. The prize amount generally should be claimed within 30 days and in case of dispute the legal jurisdiction is the State which issues the ticket. The date of draw is indicated on the tickets and the draw is held in public on the appointed day under the supervision of a committee. The procedure for the draw is generally to draw discs from drums (the number of drums would vary with the number of letters and digits on the tickets).

However, it is not always the poor who buy lottery tickets for getting rich quick. There is bulk buying of tickets by the wealthy who use lotteries to get rid of 'black' money. It is also suspected that people with (black) money regularly buy up prize-winning tickets at a premium, thus, converting their black money into white money.

Recently the Union Government has evolved a variant of lottery scheme which while stimulating savings by the small man, gives him an added incentive to keep his deposits intact, at least, for a period of six months. The post office savings bank draw stipulates that anyone seeking to participate in the draw should have opened a savings account with the post office and maintained a balance of at least Rs. 200 for a minimum period of six consecutive months. The account numbers of all such qualifying participants go in for the draw and handsome cash prizes are offered.[16]

Thus, we may summarise that in spite of shortcomings of the lottery scheme, it is going to stay as a source for raising revenue. However, as far as possible, the various lottery schemes or their variants, should be so operated that maximum benefits accrue to the poor. How is the lottery scheme operated in Punjab? What is the socio-economic background of persons buying the lottery tickets? What is the impact of the State lottery on different income groups of the population? It is to these questions that the following two chapters are addressed.

Notes and References

1. Faridi, Javed "The Lure of State Lotteries". *The Hindustan Times*, October 12, 1980, Magazine Section 1.
2. Dikshit, D.V., "Evolution and Growth of State Lotteries", *The Times of India*, February 7, 1979.
3. Rangachari, A.V., "Economics of State Lotteries", *Southern Economic Review*, Vol. 1, No. 4, June 1972, p. 385.
4. Raghvachari, T.N.S., "The Lottery Craze", *Swarajya*, Vol. 20, No. 8, August 23, 1975, p. 9.
5. *Ibid.*, p. 9.
6. Rangachari, A.V., *op. cit.*, p. 383.
7. Dikshit, D.V., *op. cit.*
8. Rangachari, A.V., *op. cit.*, p. 383.
9. The Times of India, "Lottery becomes the Spaniard's Santa", *The Times of India*, January 1, 1984.
10. Rangachari, A.V., *op. cit.*, p. 385.

11. Smith, Adam, *The Wealth of Nations* (New York, Random House, Inc. 1937), p. 108.
12. Rangachari, A.V., *op. cit.*, p. 386.
13. Thimmaiah, G., "State Lottery Scheme", *AICC Economic Review*, March 15, 1969.
14. Rajagopalachari, C., "State Raffles for Revenue", *Swarajya*, Vol. XIII, No. 9, August 31, 1968, pp. 1-2.
15. Khurana, Iqbal Chand, "Indian Lottery—A Social Commitment", *Indian Express*, July 11, 1985, p. 8.
16. The scheme is intended to be terminated with effect from December 1986.

6

STATE LOTTERIES—PARTICIPANT AND NON-PARTICIPANT HOUSEHOLDS

The impact of State lotteries in Punjab may be studied by comparing people who buy lottery tickets with those who do not, hereinafter called participants and non-participants. Keeping in mind convenience and resource constraints, Patiala City was chosen to collect the relevant data from participant and non-participant households.[1] For the purpose of sampling a complete list of wards in the city was obtained from the office of the Municipal Committee. The information provided revealed that the city had 35 wards. In consultation with the Municipal authorities, we classified these wards as 'residential', 'commercial' and 'industrial' depending on their predominant characteristics. In all, there were 13 residential, 21 commercial and 1 industrial wards. Of the 13 residential wards, 7 were selected at random. And from each selected ward a list of 250 households was prepared to identify the participant and non-participant households. In addition, there were 12 squatter settlements in the city, comprising about 800 households. A listing of 250 such households was also done to identify participants and non-participants. Thus, in all 2000 households were listed, out of which 1120 (56 per cent) were found to be participants and 880 (44 per cent) non-participants. A random sample of 250 households (140 participant and 110 non-participant) was chosen from different localities on the probability proportion of the participant and non-participant households in different localities.[2] Each household was approached personally to explain the purpose of enquiry and to solicit information on the basis of a questionnaire

(Appendix I). In what follows the general characteristics of the participant and non-participant households have been compared.

A caste-wise analysis of the participant households (Table 6.1) showed that Khatris were 30 per cent and Aggarwals 19.29 per cent. Another 14.29 per cent each belonged to Brahmin and Scheduled Castes. It was observed from the data that the percentages of Khatris, Backward castes, Bazigars and Scheduled Castes in the participant households were more than their percentages in the non-participant households. It was interesting to find that there were 8 households of Bazigar caste in the sample and all of them were participating in the lottery. Out of 23 households of Scheduled Castes in the sample, 20 were participating. Similarly, in the case of Backward castes, 10 out of 16 households in the sample were participating in the lottery. The percentage of the non-participating households was higher than that of the participant households in the case of Brahmins, Aggarwals, Jat Sikhs and Muslims. From the above we may infer that the incidence of State lotteries was usually more among the lower castes.

TABLE 6.1 : **Caste-wise Distribution of the Selected Households**

Caste	*Participant households*	*Non-participant households*	*Total households*
Brahmin	20 (14.29)	19 (17.19)	39 (15.60)
Aggarwal (Bania)	27 (19.29)	32 (29.09)	59 (23.60)
Jat Sikh/Bhatia	12 (8.57)	20 (18.18)	32 (12.80)
Khatri/Arora	42 (30.00)	26 (23.64)	68 (27.20)
Rajput	1 (0.71)	2 (1.82)	3 (1.20)
Muslim	0 (0.00)	2 (1.82)	2 (0.80)
Backward castes	10 (7.14)	6 (5.45)	16 (6.40)
Bazigar	8 (5.71)	0 (0.00)	8 (3.20)
Scheduled Castes	20 (14.29)	3 (2.73)	23 (9.20)
Total	140 (100.00)	110 (100.00)	250 (100.00)

(Figures in brackets are percentages.)

Religion-wise distribution of the participant and non-participant households (Table 6.2) revealed that Hindus participated more in State lotteries than Sikhs. It was interesting to observe that all the three Christian households were participating in the lottery, whereas the two households belonging to Muslims did not participate in State lotteries at all.

TABLE 6.2: **Religion-wise Distribution of the Selected Households**

Religious group	*Participant households*	*Non-participant households*	*Total households*
Hindus	98(70.00)	65(59.09)	163(65.20)
Sikhs	39(27.86)	43(39.09)	82(32.80)
Christians	3(2.14)	0(0.00)	3(1.20)
Muslims	0(0.00)	2(1.82)	2(0.80)
Total	140(100.00)	110(100.00)	250(100.00)

(Figures in brackets are pecentages.)

Table 6.3 depicts the type of accommodation of the selected households. The data reveal that two-thirds of households covered by the survey owned accommodation and one-third, rented it. It was found that the proportion of households living in rented accommodation was higher for the participant households (35.71 per cent) than for the non-participant households (31.82 per cent). The average value of the owned accommodation worked out to Rs. 1.17 lakhs and it was more for the non-participant households (Rs. 1.27 lakhs) than for the participant households (Rs. 1.10 lakhs).

The data in Table 6.4 show that the proportions of pucca, semi-pucca and katcha households were 87.60 per cent, 8.00 per cent and 4.40 per cent respectively. Comparing the houses of participants and non-participants, we observed that the proportion of households having pucca houses was less for participants (82.86 per cent) than for non-participants (93.64 per cent). Further, it was noted that whereas 7.85 per cent of the participant households had katcha houses, there was no such non-participant

TABLE 6.3: **Accommodation-wise Distribution of the Selected Households**

Type of accommodation	*Participant households*	*Non-participant households*	*Total households*
Owned	90(64.29)	75 (68.18)	165(66.00)
Rented	50(35.71)	35 (31.82)	85 (34.00)
Total	140(100.0)	110(100.0)	250(100.0)
Average value of owned accommodation (Rs. lakhs)	1.10	1.27	1.17

(Figures in brackets are percentages.)

households. The proportion of the participant households having semi-pucca houses was also higher than that of the non-participant households. Thus, the instinct to improve the housing accommodation might be one of the factors inducing the people to participate in State lotteries and thereby bear its incidence.

TABLE 6.4: **Distribution of the Selected Households by Type of House**

Type of house	*Participant households*	*Non-participant households*	*Total households*
Pucca	116(82.86)	103(93.64)	219(87.60)
Semi-pucca	13(9.29)	7(6.36)	20(8.00)
Katcha	11(7.85)	—	11(4.40)
Total	140(100.0)	100(100.0)	250(100.0)

(Figures in brackets are percentages.)

It was found (Table 6.5) that 1198 persons constituted the households covered in the survey; out of them 565 were females

(47.17 per cent). The sex-ratio or the proportion of females per thousand males was lower among the non-participant households than among the participant households. Thus, the presence of relatively more number of females in a family might be the cause of a household going in for the lottery scheme.

Table 6.5: **Population-wise Distribution of the Selected Households**

Population	*Participant households*	*Non-participant households*	*Total households*
Male	336(51.93)	297(53.90)	633(52.83)
Female	311(48.07)	254(46.10)	565(47.17)
Total	647(100.0)	551(100.0)	1198(100.0)
Sex ratio	926	855	893

(Figures in brackets are percentages.)

$$\text{Sex-ratio} = \frac{\text{Number of females}}{\text{Number of males}} \times 1000$$

The data in Table 6.6 point out that out of 250 selected households, 190 were nuclear families (76.00 per cent), 53 joint families (21.20 per cent) and only 7 single person families (2.80 per cent). The proportion of nuclear families was higher among the participant households (80.00 per cent) than among the non-participant households (70.91 per cent). But in the case of joint families, the position was reverse. The proportion of joint families was more among the non-participant households (26.36 per cent) than among the participant households (17.14 per cent). The proportion of single person families was almost the same in both the cases. This analysis leads us to the conclusion that perhaps the nuclear families were more interested in windfall gains than the joint families where the number of earners was expected to be comparatively large.

Considering that the size of the family is another characteristic closely related with the type of family, the number of members in each family in the selected households was also

TABLE 6.6: **Distribution of the Selected Households by Type of Family**

Type of family	*Participant households*	*Non-participant households*	*Total households*
Nuclear	112 (80.00)	78 (70.91)	190 (76.00)
Joint	94 (17.14)	29 (26.36)	53 (21.20)
Single person	4 (2.86)	3 (2.73)	7 (2.80)
Total	140(100.0)	110(100.0)	250(100.0)

(Figures in brackets are percentages.)

examined and given in Table 6.7. The data indicated that 67.20 per cent of the selected households were of medium size comprising 4-6 members, 19.20 per cent of small size comprising 1-3 members and 13.60 per cent of large size comprising 7-9 members. The proportions of small and medium families were higher among the participant households than among the non-participant households. However, in the case of large families the position was reverse. The proportion of large families was more in the case of non-participants (20.00 per cent) than in the case of participants (8.57 per cent). Further, the average size of household

TABLE 6.7: **Distribution of the Selected Households by Size of Households**

Size of household (persons)	*Participant households*	*Non-participant households*	*Total households*
1—3 (small)	29 (20.71)	19 (17.27)	48 (19.20)
4—6 (medium)	99 (70.72)	69 (62.73)	158 (67.20)
7—9 (large)	12 (8.57)	22 (20.00)	34 (13.60)
Total	140 (100.0)	110 (100.0)	250 (100.0)
Average size of household	4.62	5.01	4.79

(Figures in brackets are percentages.)

was smaller in the case of participants (4.62 persons) than in the case of non-participants (5.01 persons). This appears to corroborate the earlier conclusion that the participant households were generally nuclear in whose case the size of the family might be comparatively small.

The age-wise distribution of the population of the selected households (Table 6.8) brought out that an overwhelming majority was below the age of 50 years (83.22 per cent). Those below the age of 30 years accounted for 46.41 per cent while those below the age of 15 years were 18.45 per cent. Further, the proportion of the population below the age of 30 years was more among the participant households (52.09 per cent) than among the non-participant households (39.75 per cent). The reverse was the case with the population above the age of 30 years. The proportion of the population below the age of 15 years was much higher for the participant households (24.11 per cent) than for the non-participant households (11.80 per cent). Thus, we may conclude that the population of the participant households generally belonged to the younger age group where the participants might be interested in fortuitous gains for education and marriages of their children.

TABLE 6.8 : **Age-wise Distribution of the Population of the Selected Households**

Age (in years)	*Participant households*	*Non-participant households*	*Total households*
Up to 14	156 (24.11)	65 (11.80)	221 (18.45)
15—29	181 (27.98)	154 (27.95)	335 (27.96)
30—49	212 (32.77)	229 (41.56)	441 (36.81)
50—59	92 (14.22)	80 (14.52)	172 (14.36)
60+	6 (0.92)	23 (4.17)	29 (2.42)
Total	647 (100.0)	551 (100.0)	1198 (100.0)

(Figures in brackets are percentages.)

The marital status of the population of the selected households (Table 6.9) revealed that 46.24 per cent were married, 51.42 per cent unmarried and only 2.34 per cent widow/widower. Comparing the participant and non-participant persons, it was found that the proportions of unmarried (52.09 per cent) and widow/widower (2.47 per cent) among participants were higher than those among non-participants in which case these proportions were 50.64 per cent and 2.17 per cent respectively.

TABLE 6.9 : **Distribution of the Population of the Selected Households by Marital Status**

Marital status	*Participant households*	*Non-participant households*	*Total households*
Married	294 (45.44)	260 (47.19)	554 (46.24)
Unmarried	337 (52.09)	279 (50.64)	616 (51.42)
Widow/ Widower	16 (2.47)	12 (2.17)	28 (2.34)
Total	647 (100.0)	551 (100.0)	1198 (100.0)

(Figures in brackets are percentages.)

It is clear from the data contained in Table 6.10 that the proportion of the population below the age of 4 years was 7.09 per cent. Further, this proportion was higher among participants (8.19 per cent) than among non-participants (5.80 per cent). It was also evident that the proportion of the population with no formal education was much more in the case of participants (15.30 per cent) than in the case of non-participants (6.72 per cent). Up to middle standard also, the proportion was significantly higher for participants (25.04 per cent) than for non-participants (14.16 per cent). But beyond the middle standard, the position was reverse. The proportion of the population with education beyond middle was much lower among the participant households (45.59 per cent) than among the non-participant households (70.24 per cent). Thus, we may conclude that the level of education among the population of the participant households was generally lower than that among the non-participant households.

TABLE 6.10 : **Distribution of the Population of Selected Households by Educational Level**

Educational level	*Participant households*	*Non-participant households*	*Total households*
(No formal education)	99 (15.30)	37 (6.72)	136 (11.35)
Up to primary standard	87 (13.45)	33 (5.99)	120 (10.02)
Beyond primary but up to middle standard	75 (11.59)	45 (8.17)	120 (10.02)
Beyond middle but up to matric/higher secondary standard	97 (14.99)	108 (19.60)	205 (17.11)
Beyond matric/higher secondary standard	198 (30.60)	279 (50.64)	477 (39.82)
Technical Education			
Below graduation	17 (2.63)	15 (2.72)	32 (2.67)
Graduation	21 (3.25)	2 (0.36)	23 (1.92)
(Population below age of 4 years)	53 (8.19)	32 (5.80)	85 (7.09)
Total	647 (100.0)	551 (100.0)	1198 (100.0)

(Figures in brackets are percentages.)

The data in Table 6.11 show the population of the sampled households by their activity status. It may be observed that 31.55 per cent of the population of the sampled households was employed and 5.76 per cent unemployed. About one-third (30.97 per cent) comprised students and about one-fourth (22.12 per cent) was engaged in housekeeping. Another 8.68 per cent consisted of dependents *i.e.* children, old persons and those who were unable to work. A negligible proportion (0.92 per cent) lived on rent, pension, dividends and interest. Comparing the participant and non-participant households, it was noted that the proportion of the employed was higher among participants than among non-participants. Reverse was the case with the unemployed. It may be added that although the proportion of the employed population of the sampled households was higher for participants than for non-participants, the employed were generally engaged in low-paid occupation.[3]

TABLE 6.11 : **Distribution of the Population of the Selected Households by Activity Status**

Activity Status	*Participant households*	*Non-participant households*	*Total households*
Employed	208 (32.15)	170 (30.85)	378 (31.55)
Unemployed	24 (3.71)	45 (8.17)	69 (5.76)
Housekeeper	144 (22.26)	121 (21.96)	265 (22.12)
Student	201 (31.07)	170 (30.85)	371 (30.97)
Unable to work (child, old, sick, etc.)	68 (10.51)	36 (6.54)	104 (8.68)
Living on rent, dividends, interest and pension	2 (0.30)	9 (1.63)	11 (0.92)
Total	647 (100.0)	551 (100.0)	1198 (100.0)

(Figures in brackets are percentages.)

The data in Table 6.12 bring to light that a very high proportion (71.16 per cent) of the employed workers in the sample consisted of wage/salary earners. The remaining comprised own-account workers (22.49 per cent), unpaid family workers (5.03 per cent) and employers (only 1 32 per cent). It was interesting to find that all the employers in the sample were non-participants. Further, own-account workers were participating in State lotteries more than any other category of workers.

TABLE 6.12 : **Distribution of the Employed Workers of the Selected Households by Employment Status**

Employment status	*Participant households*	*Non-participant households*	*Total households*
Employer	—	5 (2.94)	5 (1.32)
Own-account worker	61 (29.32)	24 (14.12)	85 (22.49)
Wage/salary-earner	139 (66.83)	130 (76.47)	269 (71.16)
Unpaid family worker	8 (3.85)	11 (6.47)	19 (5.03)
Total	208 (100.0)	170 (100.0)	378 (100.0)

(Figures in brackets are percentages.)

Occupations of employed workers of the selected households are given in Table 6.13. According to the breakdown, 28.84 per cent of the workers were self-employed and the remaining (71.16 per cent) were wage/salary-earners. Among the self-employed, shop-keepers (12.44 per cent) were the most important, followed by street hawkers (3.71 per cent), commission agents (2.38 per cent) and persons engaged in small-scale industry (2.12 per cent). Among the wage workers, the relatively important were : clerks (22.49 per cent), school teachers (10.32 per cent), supervisory staff (9.52 per cent), and university/college teachers (6.61 per cent). The proportion of self-employed workers was higher among the participant households (33.16 per cent) than among the non-participant

TABLE 6.13 : **Distribution of the Employed Workers of Selected Households by Occupation Status**

Occupation status	*Participant households*	*Non-participant households*	*Total households*
1	*2*	*3*	*4*
Self-employed	69 (33.16)	40 (23.53)	109 (28.84)
Advocate	5 (2.40)	—	5 (1.32)
Doctor (Practising)	3 (1.44)	4 (2.35)	7 (1.85)
Commission Agent	5 (2.40)	4 (2.35)	9 (2.38)
Cultivator	1 (0.48)	4 (2.35)	5 (1.32)
Flour mill-owner	—	2 (1.18)	2 (0.53)
Truck-owner	—	1 (0.59)	1 (0.26)
Small-scale industrialist	5 (2.40)	3 (1.76)	8 (2.12)
Shop-keeper	28 (13.46)	19 (11.18)	47 (12.44)
Street-hawker	11 (5.29)	3 (1.76)	14 (3.71)
Rickshaw-puller	6 (2.89)	—	6 (1.59)
Chhajj-maker	1 (0.48)	—	1 (0.26)
Waste-product collector	4 (1.92)	—	4 (1.06)
Wage/salary-earner	139 (66.84)	130 (76.47)	269 (71.16)
University/college teacher	11 (5.29)	14 (8.24)	25 (6.61)
School teacher	13 (6.25)	26 (15.29)	39 (10.32)
Doctor/engineer	7 (3.37)	8 (4.71)	15 (3.97)

(*Contd.*)

1	2	3	4
Bank Officer	9 (4.33)	13 (7.65)	22 (5.82)
Supervisory staff	14 (6.73)	22 (12.94)	36 (9.52)
Clerk	45 (21.63)	40 (23.53)	85 (22.49)
Peon	17 (8.17)	1 (0.59)	18 (4.76)
Sweeper	4 (1.92)	—	4 (1.06)
Shop attendant	3 (1.44)	2 (1.18)	5 (1.32)
Others	16 (7.69)	4 (2.35)	20 (5.29)
Total	208 (100 0)	170 (100.0)	378 (100.0)

(Figures in brackets are percentages.)

households (23.53 per cent). There were two flour mill-owners and one truck-owner in the sample, they did not participate in the State lotteries at all. On the other hand, all the advocates (5), Chhajj-makers (1) and rickshaw pullers (6) were participating in State lotteries. The proportion of street-hawkers and shop-owners belonging to the participant households was higher than the proportion of those belonging to the non-participant households. Further, as already stated, the proportion of wage-earners was higher among the non-participant households (76.47 per cent) than among the participant households (66.84 per cent). The breakdown of the wage-earners showed that in the case of peons, sweepers, and shop attendants, the proportion of the participants was higher than that of the non-participants. But in the case of university/college teachers, school teachers, bank officers and supervisory staff, the proportion was comparatively high for non-participants. Thus, we may infer that the incidence of State lotteries was higher among the workers of lower categories like peons, sweepers, street hawkers and small shop-keepers. Workers like advocates in possession of some black money were also extensively participating in State lotteries.

Having found that persons participating in State lotteries, were mostly engaged in low-paid jobs, it was thought necessary to identify the income groups to which the participants belonged.

The relevant data are presented in Table 6.14. The per capita income of the sampled households was computed to be Rs. 472.25 per month. The distribution of households according to per capita income pointed out that 55.60 per cent were receiving less than Rs. 500 per month, these included 10 per cent receiving less than Rs. 200. Only 7.20 per cent of the households had per capita income more than Rs. 1000. Comparing the per capita income of the participant and non-participant households, it was found that

TABLE 6.14 : **Distribution of the Selected Households by Per Capita Income**

Per capita income (Rs. per month)	*Participant households*	*Non-participant households*	*Total households*
0—100	5 (3.57)	—	5 (2.00)
101—200	19 (13.57)	1 (0.91)	20 (8.00)
201—300	18 (12.86)	16 (14.55)	34 (13.60)
301—400	28 (20.00)	17 (15.45)	45 (18.00)
401—500	17 (12.14)	18 (16.36)	35 (14.00)
501—600	15 (10.77)	16 (14.55)	31 (12.40)
601—700	13 (9.29)	14 (12.73)	27 (10.80)
701—800	8 (5.71)	7 (6.36)	15 (6.00)
801—900	4 (2.86)	10 (9.09)	14 (5.60)
901—1000	1 (0.71)	5 (4.55)	6 (2.40)
1000+	12 (8.57)	6 (5.45)	18 (7.20)
Total	140 (100.0)	110 (100.0)	250 (100.0)
Average per capita income (Rs. per month)	432.02	519.48	472.25

(Figures in brackets are percentages.)

the latter had higher per capita income (Rs. 519.48) than the former (Rs. 432.02). It was interesting to observe that only one household from non-participants had per capita income below Rs. 200, whereas 17.14 per cent of particpants had income bleow Rs. 200. The percentage of households with per capita income between Rs. 300 and Rs. 500 was almost the same for both participants and non-participants. The percentage of households with per capita income between Rs. 500 and Rs. 1000 was significantly higher for non-participants (47.28) than for participants (29.28). However, in the case of largest income group, the proportion of participant households (8.57 per cent) was found to be more than that of non-participants (5.45 per cent).

An attempt was also made to examine the relationship between poverty and incidence of State lotteries. With this end in view the following Table 6.15, showing the number of selected households below and above the poverty line,[4] was prepared. It was found that all the households below the poverty line were participating in State lotteries.

TABLE 6.15 : **Distribution of Selected Households Below and Above the Poverty line (Rs. 134.03)**

Below/above poverty line	*Participant households*	*Non-participant households*	*Total households*
Below poverty line	15	—	15
Above poverty line	125	110	235
Total	140	110	250

Finally, in order to identify the reasons for not participating in State lotteries, non-participants were specifically questioned and the relevant responses were tabulated (Table 6.16). As many as 47.27 per cent of the respondents stated that they considered lottery a form of gambling and unethical. About 23 per cent of the respondents had no interest in lottery. The other reasons mentioned by the non-participant respondents were : wastage of money (19.09 per cent); idea never occurred (10.91 per cent); lottery prizes are unearned money (7.27 per cent), method of draw not fair (5.45 per cent). Nine respondents gave no specific reasons for not participating in State lotteries.

TABLE 6.16 : **Reasons for Not Participating in State Lotteries**

Reason	*Number of respondents*	*Per cent*
Idea never occurred	12	10.91
Lottery is gambling/ unethical	52	47.27
No interest in lottery	25	22.73
Participating in lottery a bad habit	5	4.55
Lottery prizes are unearned money for the hard working	8	7.27
Wastage of money	21	19.09
Method of draw not fair	6	5.45
Chance of fraud in prize disbursement	2	1.82
No specific reason	9	8.18

From the above, we may conclude that the incidence of State lotteries was more among the lower castes, low-educated groups and low-income persons. Further, the incidence of State lotteries was rather high among workers of lower categories like peons, sweepers, street hawkers and small shop-owners. Persons possessing black money were also found to be paticipating in State lotteries.

NOTES AND REFERENCES

1. A household whose any member purchased a State lottery ticket at any time was identified as participant.
2. The numbers of the participant and non-participant households, listed as well as selected, in different wards are given in Appendix II.
3. For example, see page 224.
4. The economists have suggested various norms for the estimation of minimum consumption requirements. In the present study, the calorie norms estimated for Punjab by K.L. Dutta has been used. His estimates are based on the Perspective Planning Division estimates. The calories intake for Punjab (2095 calories per person per day) works out to be Rs. 61.10 per capita per month for urban areas at 1973-74 prices. When computed at 1984-85 prices, the estimate works out to Rs. 134.03

7

STATE LOTTERIES—CHARACTERISTICS AND VIEWS OF PARTICIPANT PERSONS

The lottery scheme, introduced by various State Governments in 1968, has gained considerable importance among people of all walks of life in the country. State lotteries are little different from gambling, presumably because of the fact that here an individual is required to invest only a nominal amount to get a big sum as the prize. Further, the proceeds of the lotteries are invariably used for welfare schemes approved by the government. But how do the buyers of lottery tickets view this form of resource mobilisation? Do they consider the lottery scheme another variant of gambling? Are they satisfied with the operation of the scheme? Do they want the scheme to be continued? If yes, in what form? In order to get answers to these and many other questions, the views of participants were recorded and analysed. In the present chapter, the characteristics and views of such persons have been discussed.

Among 140 selected households who participated in State lotteries, we could identify 162 persons who had ever actually purchased lottery tickets, hereinafter called participant persons. In order to study the characteristics and views of such persons, they were personally interviewed.

Table 7.1 depicts the distribution of households by number of participant persons. The table shows that in most of the cases (85 per cent of households) only one member in the household was participating in State lotteries. In some cases (14.29 per cent) even two participants per household were found. The average number of participant persons per household worked out to 1.16. It may also be mentioned that in many cases the participants were observed to have purchased the lottery tickets even in the names of other members of their family.

TABLE 7.1 : **Distribution of Households by Number of Participant Persons**

Number of participant person/ persons	*Number of households*	*Per cent*
One	119	85.00
Two	20	14.29
Three	1	0.71
Total	140	100.00
Average number of participant persons per household	1.16	

A sex-wise distribution of participants in lotteries (Table 7.2) showed that 88.89 per cent were males and only 11.11 per cent females. An analysis of the marital status of the participant persons (Table 7.3) revealed that 71.60 per cent were married, 24.69 per cent unmarried and only 3.71 per cent widow/widower. This meant that married persons were more interested in making quick money.

TABLE 7.2: **Distribution of Participant Persons by Sex**

Sex	*Number of participant persons*	*Per cent*
Male	144	88.89
Female	18	11.11
Total	162	100.00

TABLE 7.3 : **Distribution of Participant Persons by Marital Status**

Marital status	*Number of participant persons*	*Per cent*
Married	116	71.60
Unmarried	40	24.69
Widow/widower	6	3.71
Total	162	100.00

Age-wise distribution of participant persons (Table 7.4) indicated that 37.65 per cent belonged to 15-29 years age group and 48.15 per cent to 30-49 years age group. Only 14.20 per cent were above 50 years of age. This indicated that perhaps aged people were not interested in the purchase of lottery tickets and the scheme was popular only in the middle age group.

TABLE 7.4 : **Age-wise Distribution of Participant Persons**

Age (in years)	*Number of participant persons*	*Per cent*
15—29	61	37.65
30—49	78	48.15
50—59	20	12.35
60+	3	1.85
Total	162	100.00

The data on educational level (Table 7.5) brought out that 13.58 per cent of the participant persons had no formal education and 2.47 per cent had education up to primary standard. The proportion of the participant persons having education beyond middle standard but up to matric/higher secondary standard was 17.28 per cent, and 48.15 per cent of the participant persons had education beyond matric/higher secondary standard. 10.50 per cent of the participant persons had some technical education. It was inferred that education did not appear to have any dampening effect on participation in State lotteries.

TABLE 7.5 : **Distribution of Participant Persons by Educational Level**

Educational level	*Number of participant persons*	*Per cent*
(No formal education)	22	13.58
Upto primary standard	4	2.47
Beyond primary but upto middle standard	13	8.02
Beyond middle but upto matric/higher secondary standard	28	17.28
Beyond matric/higher secondary standard	78	48.15
Technical education		
Below graduation	8	4.94
Graduation	9	5.56
Total	162	100.00

The data in Table 7.6 depict the activity status of the participant persons. An overwhelming majority of the participant persons (83.95 per cent) was employed and only one person was found to be unemployed. The proportions of housekeeping and student participants were observed to be 4.94 per cent and 10.49 per cent respectively.

The occupation of the employed participant persons (Table 7.7) showed that the majority *i.e.* 72.79 per cent consisted of wage/salary-earners. Only 27.21 per cent were self-employed. Among the self-employed, shopkeepers (13.23 per cent) were the most important, followed by street hawkers (5.15 per cent), and

TABLE 7.6 : **Distribution of Participant Persons by Activity Status**

Activity Status	*Number of participant persons*	*Per cent*
Employed	136	83.95
Unemployed	1	0.62
Housekeeper	8	4.94
Student	17	10.49
Total	162	100.00

rickshaw pullers and waste product collectors (2.94 per cent each). Among the wage/salary-earners, the relatively important participants in State lotteries were : clerks (27.94 per cent), university/college teachers (7.35 per cent), school teachers (7.35 per cent) and supervisory staff (7.35 per cent). Further, 8.83 per cent were lower class employees *i.e.* peons and sweepers.

TABLE 7.7 : **Distribution of the Employed Participant Persons by Occupation Status**

Occupation status	*Number of participant persons*	*Per cent*
1	*2*	*3*
Self-employed		
Shopkeeper	18	13.23
Chhajj-maker	1	0.74
Rickshaw-puller	4	2.94
Small scale industrialist	3	2.21
Street hawker	7	5.15
Waste product collector	4	2.94
Total self-employed	37	27.21

(*Contd.*)

1	2	3
Wage/salary-earners		
University/college teachers	10	7.35
School teacher	10	7.35
Doctor/engineer	2	1.47
Bank officer	8	5.88
Supervisory staff	10	7.35
Clerk	38	27.94
Peon/chowkidar	9	6.62
Sweeper	3	2.21
Shop attendant	2	1.47
Others	7	5.15
Total wage/salary-earners	99	72.79
Grand total	136	100.00

It is generally believed that the incidence of State lotteries is the highest among the poor. Hence, it may be of some interest to study the monthly income of participant persons. Table 7.8 is an

TABLE 7.8 : **Distribution of Employed Participant Persons by Income Level**

Monthly income (Rupees)	*Number of participant persons*	*Per cent*
0-500	21	15.44
501-1000	40	29.41
1001-1500	36	26.47
1501-2000	17	12.50
2001-2500	12	8.82
2501-3000	6	4.41
3001-4000	3	2.21
4001-5000	—	—
5000+	1	0.74
Total	136	100.00

attempt in this direction. Out of the 136 employed participant persons, 15.44 per cent belonged to the income group of less than Rs. 500 per month. The maximum number of participant persons (29.41 per cent) was found in the case of Rs. 501-1000 income group and as we moved along the higher income brackets the proportion of participant persons declined successively. However, there was one participant person who earned more than Rs. 5000 per month. Thus, the propensity to purchase lottery tickets appeared to be higher in the case of lower income groups.

In order to study the relative importance of different media of disseminating the knowledge about State lotteries, the distribution of participant persons by source of information was prepared (Table 7.9). It was revealed that the informal sources like relatives and friends played a key-role in initiating the persons into participation in State lotteries. Lottery stalls, too, were inducing people to buy lottery tickets. Although radio and television did not play much role to popularise the lottery scheme, newspapers were doing rather commendable job in this regard.

TABLE 7.9 : **Distribution of Participant Persons by Sources of Information for Buying Lottery Tickets**

Source	*Number of participant persons*	*Per cent*
Newspaper	31	19.14
Radio/television	4	2.47
Relative/friend	68	41.98
Lottery hawker	9	5.55
Lottery stall	50	30.86
Total	162	100.00

Out of 162 participant persons who had ever participated in State lotteries, 27 were found to have discontinued the purchase of lottery tickets. These persons were further approached in order to elicit the reasons why they had discontinued. The reasons are recorded in Table 7.10. Most of the participant persons who had discontinued purchasing the lottery tickets were disillusioned by not having won any prize. Some considered lottery to be a variant of gambling, hence unethical. Increasing frauds and sale of duplicate tickets also discouraged some participants. It may be mentioned here that most of the participant persons recorded more than one reason for giving up participation in State lotteries.

TABLE 7.10 : **Distribution of Participant Persons by Reason for Discontinuing Participation**

Reason	*Number of participant persons (Total 27)*	*Per cent*
Did not get any prize	20	74.70
Consider lottery a form of gambling	19	70.37
No spare money for purchase of tickets	1	3.70
Do not find lottery beneficial	1	3.70
Increase in fraud cases and sale of duplicate tickets	7	25.93

The average monthly expenditure on State lotteries was computed to be Rs. 6.97 (Table 7.11) and a majority of the participant persons were spending hardly Rs. 5 per month on the purchase of lottery tickets. Thus, the lottery scheme is a convenient way which involves a negligible cost to get rich overnight.

Most of the participant persons were purchasing lottery tickets with a face value of a rupee or two. Only 40 participant persons (29.63 per cent) purchased lottery tickets of higher denominations. Table 7.12 depicts distribution of the participant persons by price of tickets of higher denominations. The data revealed that a vast majority of these participant persons (80.00 per cent) were purchasing lottery tickets worth Rs. 10. Only one

TABLE 7.11 : **Distribution of Participant Persons by Average Monthly Expenditure on State Lotteries**

Average monthly expenditure on State lotteries (Rupees)	*Number of participant persons*	*Per cent*
Below 2	48	35.56
3—5	56	41.48
6—10	21	15.56
11—15	4	2.96
16—20	5	3.70
20+	1	0.74
Total	135	100.00
Average expenditure (Rs.)	6.97	

person each purchased lottery tickets worth Rs. 50, Rs. 100, and Rs. 500. Thus, from the viewpoints of these participants, lottery tickets worth Rs. 10 seemed to be the appropriate price which they could easily afford.

In order to examine general awareness of the participant persons about the lottery scheme, data regarding their knowledge

TABLE 7.12 : **Distribution of Participant Persons by Price of Tickets of Higher Denomination**

Price of ticket (Rs.)	*Number of participant persons*	*Per cent*
5	2	5.00
10	32	80.00
20	3	7.50
50	1	2.50
100	1	2.50
500	1	2.50
Total	40	100.00

about the winners of prizes (worth Rs. 1000 or more) were obtained and recorded in Table 7.13. It was noted that only (32.72 per cent)

TABLE 7.13 : **Distribution of Participant Persons by their Knowledge about Prize-winners**

Knowledge about prize-winners	*Number of participant persons*	*Per cent*
Yes	53	32.72
No	109	67.28
Total	162	100.00

of the participant persons were aware of the prize-winners. And 52.83 per cent (Table 7.14) of the known prize-winners were either members of the households of participant persons or their relatives.

TABLE 7.14: **Distribution of Knowledgeable Participant Persons by their Relationship with Prize-winners**

Relationship with Prize-winner	*Number of knowledgeable participant persons*	*Per cent*
Self/member of own family	15	28.30
Relative	13	24.53
Friend	10	18.87
Neighbour/acquaintance	15	28.30
Total	53	100.00

As revealed in Table 7.15, the majority (45.28 per cent) of known prize-winners had won Rs. 10,000/- prize, followed by those (35.84 per cent) with Rs. 1000/- prize. About 13.21 per cent won

Rs. 1 lakh prize. In order to examine the use pattern of prize-money, the relevant data are given in Table 7.16. The data revealed that about one-fourth of the prize-winners spent the prize-money on construction of house and 39.62 per cent on household goods. Further, 13.21 per cent each utilised the money for establishing new business and for marriage ceremonies. While two prize-winners used the money to repay debt, another deposited the amount in a bank. Further, 13.21 per cent of the participant persons had no knowledge about the purposes for which the prize-winners had used the money.

TABLE 7.15: **Distribution of Lottery Prize-winners by Amount of Prize**

Amount of prize (Rupees)	*Number of prize-winners*	*Per cent*
1,000	19	35.84
10,000	24	45.28
25,000	1	1.89
50,000	1	1.89
1 lakh	7	13.21
2 lakh	1	1.89
Total	53	100.00

TABLE 7.16: **Distribution of Lottery Prize-winners by Use Pattern of Prize-money**

Use pattern	*Number of prize-winners (Total 53)*	*Per cent*
House construction	13	24.53
Marriage	7	13.21
Household goods	21	39.62
Establishment of new business	7	13.21
Deposit in the bank	1	1.80
Debt repayment	2	3.77
Not known	7	13.21

It was interesting to know that the actual use pattern of prize-money almost corresponded to the purpose of the participant person behind going in for the lottery. (Table 7.17)

TABLE 7.17: **Distribution of Participant Persons by Purpose behind Going in for Lottery**

Purpose	*Number of participant persons (Total 135)*	*Per cent*
House construction	84	62.22
Marriage	30	22.92
Household goods	57	42.22
Establishment of new business	61	45.19
Deposit in the bank	65	48.15
Debt repayment	4	2.96
Children's education	39	28.89
Help to relatives/friends	15	11.11
No fore-thought	5	3.70

In order to test the gambling instinct in the participant persons, they were asked to record their knowledge about other relevant gambling games. Such data are presented in Table 7.18. It was observed that only 11.73 per cent of participant persons did not have any knowledge about other gambling games. Further, the degree of their participation (defined as a ratio between the participant persons with knowledge about gambling game to those who actually participate) was the highest in *Satta* (matka system), followed by cards game (flash), Tambola, and *Satta* (bull and bear) in that order.

TABLE 7.18: **Distribution of Participant Persons by Their Knowledge about Gambling Games and Their Actual Participation**

Name of game	*Number of participant persons with knowledge*		*Actual participation*	*Proportion of (4) to (2)*
	Number (Total 162)	*Per cent*	*(Total 72)*	
1	*2*	*3*	*4*	*5*
Tambola	65	40.12	21	35.31
Satta (matka system)	56	34.57	27	48.21
Satta (bull and bear)	25	15.43	8	32.00
Shatranj	71	43.83	3	5.64
Cards game (flash)	134	82.72	55	41.04
Rope game (batti system)	25	15.43	—	—
Games through machines	66	40.74	2	3.03
No knowledge	19	11.73	—	—

It may be added that although there were some participant persons who did not indulge in other gambling games, some of them participated in more than one gambling game. 72 out of 162 participant persons indulged in other gambling games. The gains made or losses incurred by such individuals during the year preceding the survey (*i.e.* 1984-85) are given in Table (7.19). On the whole, gambling appeared to be a losing game. The number of losers was more than that of the gainers. This was particularly true in the case of gains/losses involving relatively large amounts.

The gambling instinct of the participant persons was further revealed by the fact that the majority (72.22 per cent) considered the lottery scheme also a gambling game (Table 7.20).

In order to streamline the lottery scheme, the participant persons were specifically asked to record their opinions about the appropriate price of the lottery ticket, time interval of various

TABLE 7.19: **Distribution of Participant Persons Participating in Other Gambling Games also by Amount of Gain/ Loss during the Year Preceding the Survey (1984-85)**

Amount	*Gain*		*Loss*	
(Rs.)	*Number of participant persons*	*Per cent*	*Number of participant persons*	*Per cent*
5-50	13	46.43	20	50.00
51-100	6	21.43	9	22.50
101-200	5	17.86	2	5.00
201-300	—	—	2	5.00
301-400	1	3.57	1	2.50
401-500	2	7.14	3	7.50
501-1000	1	3.57	3	7.50
Total	28 (38.88)	100.00	40 (55.56)	100.00
Neither gain nor loss		4 (5.56)		

TABLE 7.20: **Distribution of Participant Persons Considering Lottery Gambling**

Consider Lottery gambling	*Number of participant persons*	*Per cent*
Yes	117	72.22
No	45	27.78
Total	162	100.00

draws, the quantum of prize money which the government should offer, etc. Table 7.21 and Table 7.22 are attempts in this direction.

It was observed that a majority of the participant persons favoured lottery tickets of lower denominations (up to Rs. 2) and a large number of prizes, may be of small amount. It may be due to the fact that they found a high chance of winning a prize if a host of prizes were offered.

From the above discussion, we could infer that a majority of the respondents were in favour of State lotteries. Most of the participant persons possessed the gambling instinct and they

TABLE 7.21: **Distribution of Participant Persons by Opinion regarding Value of Lottery Tickets**

Value of lottery ticket (Rs.)	*Number of participant persons*	*Per cent*
Up to Rs. 1	57	32.19
Up to Rs. 2	78	48.15
Up to Rs. 5	16	9.88
Up to Rs. 10	10	6.17
Up to Rs. 20	—	—
Up to Rs. 50	—	—
Up to Rs. 100	1	0.61
Total	162	100.00

TABLE 7.22: **Distribution of the Participant Persons by Opinion regarding Optimum Number and Size of Prizes**

Optimum	*Number of Participant persons*	*Per cent*
A large number of small prizes	97	59.88
A small number of bumper prizes	42	25.92
A combination of both	23	14.20
Total	162	100.00

considered lottery scheme as a variant of gambling. The majority were in favour of lottery tickets of lower denominations. They also preferred a large number of small prizes to a small number of bumper prizes. It may be because they believed that their chances of winning a prize were high if a large number of prizes were offered. Some of the participants also complained of malpractices in the existing lottery scheme. They suggested that the draw should be held at a fixed time on the appointed day and the sale of tickets should be stopped one week before the date of draw to avoid the sale of tickets even after the draw. They also complained about the sale of duplicate tickets. In many cases, it was found that the prizes of smaller amount (say less than Rs. 100), which had to be collected straight from the commission agents, were seldom paid in cash. Commission agents, on the other hand, compelled the prize-winners to buy the lottery tickets of equivalent amount. In view of these facts, it is suggested that computers should be increasingly used for the lottery draw. A strict vigilance should be exercised to check the sale of duplicate tickets. As far as possible, the maximum amount of prizes offered by the different States/agencies should be uniformally fixed by the Union Government.

8

SUMMARY AND CONCLUSIONS

Problems of taxation in developing countries have been receiving special and increasing attention in recent years. Much of the theoretical and applied work has been focused on the task of constructing a productive and equitable tax system, suited to the peculiar economic and social conditions prevailing in various developing countries. In chalking out a development plan or a stabilisation programme, a major question that always arises is how much tax revenue a country can reasonably expect to raise and from what sources.

India being a federal country, the State Governments have an exclusive Constitutional right over several sources of public revenue. In addition, the States receive funds from the Union Government as grants and also share a few taxes levied by the latter. The financial dependence of the States on the Union Government has been lately on the increase. It is felt that the resources available to the States under present dispensation are not adequate for meeting their requirements. However, it is generally believed that to a large extent the financial problems of the States arise on account of lack of efforts on their own part to raise resources and almost all the States in India possess untapped resource potentials. The expenditure on development programmes has been mounting day by day. In the recent past, it has been suggested that public expenditure must be restrained and unproductive expenditure eliminated. Several economy measures have been explored in order to cut down public expenditure. But they have turned out to be politically infeasible. On the other hand, the governments cannot raise any more resources through taxation or borrowing. How should then the finances be raised for meeting soaring and unrestrainable public expenditure ? And, how can this be done without inconveniencing the people ? To the extent that the non-tax receipts can be augmented, the need for placing an additional burden of tax on the people can be obviated. State lotteries, neglected so far, appear to be one such source. In the 1960s, faced with the problem of raising additional revenue for the Fourth Five Year Plan and for meeting the ever-growing needs of normal expenditure, the State Governments started running their own lotteries.

In the present study, an attempt has been made to examine the scope of additional resource mobilisation in Punjab both from tax and non-tax sources. In particular, State lotteries as a source of non-tax revenue and their economic implications have been brought under sharp focus. However, the specific objectives of the study are :

(i) to work out the untapped potential for mobilising additional resources in Punjab through the existing tax and non-tax structure;
(ii) to study the scope of imposing additional tax and non-tax levies;
(iii) to examine the role of State lotteries as a source of revenue;
(iv) to analyse the socio-economic background of persons participating in the State lotteries; and
(v) to work out the incidence of State lotteries on different income groups.

The study has been based both on primary and secondary sources of data. To work out the scope of raising additional resources through the existing and new tax and non-tax levies, the data have been culled from various issues of the *Reserve Bank of India Bulletin*, *Report on Currency and Finance*, *Statistical Abstract of Punjab*, and State Budgets of the Punjab Government. The data on State lotteries in Punjab regarding gross receipts, prizes, commission, bonus to agents and other expenditure have been collected from the Directorate of Punjab State Lotteries. Besides, the study has also made use of the

Census data. To examine the impact of State lotteries, primary data from 250 randomly selected households (140 participants and 110-non-participants) have been gathered. Apart from calculation of simple percentages and averages, an attempt has been made to study the relative importance of different tax and non-tax sources by computing their compound growth rates and buoyancy coefficients. In order to review the intensity of use of various potential bases of tax and non-tax sources in different States, relevant representative approach has been made use of. The study covers a period of 16 years, 1967-68 through 1982-83. In major part of the study, a comparative analysis of three sub-periods, *viz.* 1967-68 through 1969-70, 1973-74 through 1975-76, and 1979-80 through 1981-82, has been made. For this purpose, simple average was used.

The main findings of the study are as follows :

(i) The overall percentage share of States' own tax and non-tax revenue to total revenue (*i.e.* including the transfer from the Union Government) was found to be 54.12 during the three years' period of 1967-68 through 1969-70. During the period 1973-74 through 1975-76, this percentage share rose to 64.02. But it declined to 60.96 during 1979-80 through 1981-82, implying that the States had to depend on the Union Government to the tune of 39.04 per cent of their total revenue. During all the periods, in States like Punjab, Haryana, Maharashtra, Gujarat, Karnataka and Tamil Nadu, the percentage share of State's own revenue exceeded the all States' average.

Some of the relatively underdeveloped States like Himachal Pradesh, Jammu and Kashmir, Manipur, Meghalaya, Nagaland, Orissa, Rajasthan and Tripura raised a lower proportion of revenue through their own tax sources than some of the relatively developed States like Andhra Pradesh, Gujarat, Maharashtra, Punjab and West Bengal.

(ii) In each State, the total revenue (tax and non-tax) grew at a much higher rate than the Net State Domestic Product (NSDP). Examining overall States' own tax and non-tax sources, it was interesting to observe that States' own non-tax revenue increased at a higher rate (16.92 per cent) than States' own tax revenue (15.93 per cent). However, in the case of Punjab, it was the reverse.

The buoyancy coefficient of States' own total revenue (1.444) for all the States taken together was slightly higher than that of the total revenue (1.434). The buoyancy coefficient of State's own total revenue varied from 1.207 for Punjab to 2.745 for Manipur. Comparing overall States' own tax and non-tax revenues, we found that the buoyancy coefficient was slightly more for non-tax revenue (1.536) than for tax revenue (1.407). This was true even of individual States except Gujarat, Karnataka, Punjab, Tamil Nadu, Tripura and Uttar Pradesh, indicating that in these States a positive change in NSDP led to a greater increase in State's tax revenue than that in State's non-tax revenue.

(iii) Almost during the entire period under study, the States of Gujarat, Haryana, Himachal Pradesh, Maharashtra, Punjab, and West Bengal were found to be relatively well off in terms of per capita income. The per capita income as well as per capita State tax was the highest in Punjab throughout the period.

Taxable capacity is usually measured by the ratio of per capita tax revenue to per capita income. Under progressive tax structure, a State with relatively high per capita income is also expected to bear a comparatively high tax burden. The tax-income ratios were generally low in the States with high per capita incomes, *viz*. Punjab, Haryana, and Maharashtra. This fact showed that these States were not putting in adequate efforts for raising revenue commensurate with their taxable capacities.

Throughout the period of our study, there was no tendency for the indices of effective tax rate for different States to cluster round the average, indicating thereby that there were perceptible disparities in their performance in tax field. It may also be mentioned that whereas Punjab was the richest State in terms of per capita income, it did not apply the highest effective rate for its tax revenue. This means that if Punjab had applied a little higher effective rate, as desired under progressivity, it would have mobilised more additional resources.

(iv) Minimisation of the cost of tax collection may also be an important objective of budgetary policy in the States. The per unit cost of tax collection diminished significantly in the States of Gujarat, Punjab, Uttar Pradesh and West Bengal over the period under examination. It was a happy sign that for all the States taken together, the cost of tax collection grew at a lower rate (11.16 per cent) than States' own tax revenue (rate 15.93 per cent). This also applied to the individual States except Manipur, Meghalaya and Tripura. Punjab, too, was favourably placed in this regard.

(v) So far, we have described the aggregate tax structure; now we examine the individual taxes, taking up agricultural income tax first. This tax is in operation in a few States, *viz.* Assam, Bihar, Karnataka, Kerala, Maharashtra, Orissa, Tamil Nadu, Tripura and West Bengal. It became a provincial subject as a consequence of Government of India Act, 1935. Its contribution to State's tax revenue was hardly 1-3 per cent in most of the States except Assam. Its average growth rate, however, was quite high (*i.e.* 13.28 per cent per annum). And the growth rate ranged from 7.01 per cent for West Bengal to 24.51 per cent for Tripura while Bihar and Orissa recorded negative growth rates.

(vi) Land revenue is an old tax on land which has become inelastic owing to the non-revision of its assessment. The overall share of land revenue in States' own tax revenue has been on the decline, yet the amount collected in absolute term has been increasing at the rate of 4.95 per cent per annum. Further, the percentage share of land revenue was less than the all States' average in the States of Haryana, Himachal Pradesh, Kerala, Maharashtra, Meghalaya, Nagaland, Orissa, Punjab, Tamil Nadu and West Bengal during the whole period under study. The buoyancy coefficient was less than unity in all the States except Orissa.

The effective rates of agricultural income tax and land revenue put together fell over the period under focus in all the States. Further, the actual rates in Punjab, Haryana, Himachal Pradesh and Jammu and Kashmir were considerably lower than the average effective rate, meaning thereby that there existed tax potential in these States. The case of Punjab is particularly interesting because in spite of being a predominantly agrarian State, it has been levying land revenue and surcharge on cash crops only, whose contribution to State's tax structure has been dwindling progressively. Land revenue is levied at a flat rate in money terms and it has not changed for a number of years. Pending fresh land settlements, a surcharge on land revenue could be levied in the State on a sliding scale.

(vii) The overall share of profession tax to States' own tax revenue was found to be showing consistently upward movement over the study period. For individual States, it was true only in the case of Assam, Kerala, Maharashtra, Meghalaya, Nagaland and Tripura. The other States either discontinued this tax or were found to be relying less and less on this tax as a source of revenue. The average growth rate of profession tax was found to be 24.90 per cent per annum and the buoyancy coefficient revealed that this tax was highly buoyant as a source of revenue.

The effective rates of profession tax revealed that barring Maharashtra, Karnataka, Tripura, West Bengal and Gujarat, the States were not earnestly exploiting this source of revenue. For all the States taken together, the total yield during the period 1979-80 through 1981-82 was only Rs. 6264 lakhs. Had all the States imposed this tax at an average effective rate of say 1 per cent, the total yield would have been as much as Rs. 23609 lakhs. Punjab, too, could have added another Rs. 1335 lakhs to its coffers if it had imposed profession tax.

(viii) The percentage share of stamp duty and registration fee went down in every State, apart from Rajasthan and Uttar Pradesh, over the period under review. Further, the growth rate of revenue from this tax was the highest for Himachal Pradesh (21.31 per cent) and the lowest for Bihar (6.37 per cent). Buoyancy coefficients, though these followed the pattern of growth rates, were more than unity for the States of Himachal Pradesh, Uttar Pradesh, Tripura, Madhya Pradesh, Karnataka, Kerala, Rajasthan, Orissa, Punjab, Gujarat, Andhra Pradesh and West Bengal.

Only four States, *viz.* Punjab, Tamil Nadu, Kerala, and Haryana, had indices of use of tax potential of stamp duty and registration fee significantly higher than unity. Although in relation to NSDP these States availed themselves of this source rather intensively yet the relative importance of this tax was on the decrease.

(ix) The percentage share of sales tax to State's own tax revenue has been improving over the period under study in all the States, Meghalaya excepted. The States with more than 50 per cent share of sales tax were generally those wherein the contribution of non-agricultural sector to NSDP was relatively high. The overall growth rate of sales tax revenue was 17.66 per cent and the rate varied between 10.40 per cent for Tripura and 31.32 per cent for Nagaland. In Punjab, the growth rate of sales tax (17.11 per cent) was less than that of all States. The important role which sales tax has come to play in the States' fiscal structure is because of its productivity. The buoyancy coefficient of sales tax for all the States taken together was 1.558. Notwithstanding the fact that in the case of States like Tripura (1.023), Assam (1.029), Punjab (1.313) and Maharashtra (1.331) the buoyancy coefficients were considerably less than all States' coefficient, these were more than unity.

The indices of use of tax potential were markedly higher than unity in the States of Tamil Nadu, Kerala, and Haryana throughout the period of our study. After reaching the unitary limit in the earlier two periods (1967-68 through 1969-70 and 1973-74 through 1975-76), the index of use of tax potential came down to less than unity in Punjab during the latest period (1979-80 through 1981-82). Perhaps Punjab could not have a high effective rate owing to the growth of agricultural sector at a relatively fast rate. By applying the average effective rate, Punjab could have gathered additional revenue to the tune of Rs. 832 lakhs per annum.

(x) The percentage contribution of State excise duty to State's own tax revenue consistently improved in the States of Andhra Pradesh, Karnataka, Kerala, Maharashtra, Manipur, Meghalaya and Tamil Nadu. In Punjab, however, the share of State excise duty had a downward trend from 31.01 per cent to 27.28 per cent during the study period. The implication is that state excise duty, though the second largest source of State tax revenue in Punjab, has been losing its importance.

The growth rate of state excise duty for all the States taken together worked out to 15.86 per cent. It was the highest for Meghalaya (38.06 per cent) and the lowest for Bihar (3.98 per cent). In Punjab, the growth rate was less than the all States' average. The overall buoyancy coefficient was computed to be 1.380 and the coefficient ranged between 0.397 for Bihar and 2.423 for Manipur. For Punjab, the buoyancy coefficient, although less than the all States' average, was higher than unity.

In order to arrive at the effective rates of State excise duty, we employed two variants. First, total consumption of liquor from 1973-74 through 1975-76 was chosen as the potential base, and this was kept constant for the period under probe. In the second variant, we assumed per capita consumption of liquor to be constant throughout the same period of analysis, and multiplying it with the respective population, we calculated the total consumption figures.

Under the first variant, the average effective rate for the period 1967-68 through 1969-70, amounted to Rs. 9.49 per London Proof Litre (L.P.L.). For the latest period, *i.e.* 1979-80 through 1981-82, the average effective rate shot up to Rs. 44.65 per L.P.L. During this period, the indices of use of tax potential were above unity only in the case of Kerala, Punjab, Haryana and Andhra Pradesh.

Taking the second variant, the average effective rate was Rs. 18.11 per L.P.L. for the period 1967-68 through 1969-70. For the three years' period, 1979-80 through 1981-82, the average effective rate swelled to Rs. 24.38 per L.P.L. For Kerala, Andhra Pradesh, Haryana, Punjab and Madhya Pradesh, the indices of use of tax potential were higher than unity. Thus, the relative results were not much different with the two variants.

(xi) The percentage contribution of motor vehicles tax had an upward course in the case of Bihar, Haryana, Madhya Pradesh, Manipur, Nagaland and Punjab, whereas for other States it had a downward swing over the period under study. The overall growth rate accounted for 14.18 per cent per annum. The growth rate had a range from 7.57 per cent in Assam to 25.99 per cent in Himachal Pradesh. For Punjab, the rate was 21.49 per cent. The buoyancy coefficient of motor vehicles tax was found to be 1.261 for all the States taken together and the coefficient varied between 0.671 for Assam and 2.406 for Himachal Pradesh. It was below unity only in two States, Assam and Maharashtra.

For the three years' average period, 1967-68 through 1969-70, the States of Uttar Pradesh, Jammu and Kashmir, Assam, Rajasthan and Orissa, recorded the indices of use of motor vehicles tax potential higher than unity. During the last three years' period, 1979-80 through 1981-82, the indices were more than unity in the States of Orissa, Jammu and Kashmir, Haryana, Assam and Karnataka. Punjab, with an index of 0.5887, was at the 14th place. Thus, the motor vehicles tax was another tax which was less than optimally exploited in Punjab. If the State had attained the index of use of tax potential equal to unity, additional revenue of the order of Rs. 860 lakhs per annum could have been reaped.

(xii) In the case of passengers and goods tax, the percentage share coursed upward in all the States except Assam, Gujarat, Himachal Pradesh, Karnataka and Maharashtra during the study period. For all the States taken together, its growth rate was reckoned up to be 16.65 per cent per annum and it ranged from 10.66 per cent in Assam to 36.33 per cent in Haryana. Punjab (15.43 per cent) had a growth rate lower than the all States' average. The overall buoyancy coefficient of passengers and goods tax was estimated as 1.454 and the coefficient varied between 0.690 for Maharashtra and 2.450 for West Bengal. The buoyancy coefficient in Punjab (1.197) was more than unity, yet it fell short of the all States' average.

For the three years' period, 1967-68 through 1969-70, the overall effective rate for passengers and goods tax was Rs. 1640.55 per vehicle and the rate ranged between Rs. 90.23 per vehicle for Jammu and Kashmir and Rs. 5374.04 per vehicle for Haryana. For the period 1979-80 through 1981-82, the average effective rate jumped up to Rs. 7138.05 per vehicle. Haryana, with an effective rate of Rs. 23685.42 per vehicle, again occupied the topmost position. Assam had the lowest effective rate of Rs. 771.06 per vehicle. Throughout the period under study, Punjab was at the second place as far as the index of use of tax potential was concerned. Naturally, the State appeared to have no scope for raising additional revenue from passengers and goods tax.

(xiii) For the three years' average period 1967-68 through 1969-70, the share of electricity duty was 4.44 per cent for all the States taken together and it registered variation from 0.02 per cent for Andhra Pradesh to 8.71 per cent for Orissa. For the period 1979-80 through 1981-82, its overall share dipped to 3.35 per cent. Orissa and Andhra Pradesh, with 12.96 per cent and 0.05 per cent shares, continued to occupy the uppermost and the lowermost positions respectively. In Orissa, Gujarat, Haryana, Maharashtra, Madhya Pradesh, Punjab, Manipur and Bihar, the percentage share of electricity duty was more than the all States' average.

The growth rate of electricity duty was 13.36 per cent per annum for all the States taken together. The overall buoyancy coefficient was calculated to be 1.158. The positive buoyancy coefficient varied from 0.677 in West Bengal to 2.279 in Himachal Pradesh. The buoyancy coefficient was more than unity in all the States except West Bengal, Bihar and Maharashtra. For Punjab, the growth rate and buoyancy coefficient were higher than the all States' average.

For the three years' period, 1967-68 through 1969-70, the average effective rate for electricity duty was worked out to be 1.41 paise per unit. It had a range from 0.01 paise per unit for Andhra Pradesh to 2.20 paise per unit for Maharashtra. For the period 1979-80 through 1981-82, the average effective rate of electricity duty upswung to 2.81 paise per unit. While Andhra Pradesh continued to be at the bottom, the top spot was claimed by Orissa. Andhra Pradesh and Tamil Nadu did not levy electricity duty on the total consumption of electricity but imposed enhanced electricity tariff. The effective rates were comparatively low in the States of Assam, Uttar Pradesh, Himachal Pradesh and Rajasthan. In Punjab, in spite of above-unity index of use of tax potential for electricity duty, the agricultural sector paid less duty than the non-agricultural sector. Had Punjab levied electricity duty equivalent to Haryana, it would have realised Rs. 720 lakhs as additional revenue.

(xiv) The percentage contribution of entertainment tax to States' own tax revenue slid down in the States' of Bihar, Himachal Pradesh, Kerala, Maharashtra, Manipur, Meghalaya, Nagaland and Tripura over the period of our study. For all the States taken together, the growth rate was 17.80 per cent per annum. Kerala was the only State which experienced a negative growth rate. For the other States, growth rates had variations from 9.30 per cent for Bihar to 31.07 per cent for Tamil Nadu. The overall buoyancy coefficient amounted to 1.631 and the coefficient varied between 0.888 for Assam and 2.775 for Tripura, leaving aside Kerala which had a negative buoyancy coefficient. Punjab registered a buoyancy coefficient of 1.291 which, however, was less than the all States' average.

Total seating capacity, measured in terms of number of seats in cinemas, was considered to be an appropriate potential base for entertainment tax. In order to find out the effective rates, we applied two alternatives. One, we assumed the seating capacity of 1973-74 through 1975-76 to be true for the other periods also. Two, assuming that the cinemas were mostly located in urban areas, we adjusted the seating capacity with the changes in urban population of a State. Comparing the two alternatives, we found that the relative positions of different States did not alter. Throughout the period under examination, the indices of use of tax potential, with both the alternatives, were significantly higher than unity in the case of Haryana, Maharashtra, Punjab, Rajasthan and Uttar Pradesh. Obviously, there did not exist much possibility for adding revenue through this tax in these States

(xv) Apart from taxes, a State can also mobilise additional resources from non-tax sources. Two types of non-tax sources are available to the States. One is the transfer from the Union Government in the form of grants-in-aid and other contributions. The other, which is more relevant from the viewpoint of resource mobilisation, is the administrative and commercial revenue from States' own sources. The percentage share of grants-in-aid and other contributions made by the Union Government to States' non-tax revenue was generally more in the relatively underdeveloped States than in the developed States. Further, the States of Andhra Pradesh, Assam, Gujarat, Haryana, Karnataka, Kerala, Maharashtra, Punjab and Rajasthan, consistently banked more and more on their own sources so far as the non-tax revenue was concerned.

For all the States taken together, the growth rate of grants-in-aid and other contributions (14.85 per cent) was less than that of States' own non-tax revenue (16.92 per cent). Barring Bihar, Tamil Nadu and Uttar Pradesh, this phenomenon was true of even individual States. The buoyancy coefficients followed the pattern of growth rates.

(xvi) Like tax revenue, the average effective rates for different kinds of non-tax sources were calculated and applied to the corresponding potential bases so as to work out the prospects for additional resource mobilisation. Two bases, NSDP and population, were tried.

For the period 1967-68 through 1969-70, the average effective rate for States' own non-tax sources, taking NSDP as the base, was computed to be 1.93 per cent. The effective rate varied from 0.95 per cent in Andhra Pradesh to 4.33 per cent in Jammu and Kashmir. Punjab stood seventh in order of ranking. For the period 1979-80 through 1981-82, the average effective rate increased to 4.17 per cent. The effective rate was the maximum in Manipur (8.30 per cent) and the minimum in West Bengal (1.76 per cent). During this period, Punjab was pushed almost to the lowest rank.

With population as the base, the indices of use of non-tax potential were higher than unity in the case of Jammu and Kashmir, Punjab, Haryana, Karnataka and Maharashtra for the period 1967-68 through 1969-70. For the period 1979-80 through 1981-82, these indices were above unity in the case of Himachal Pradesh, Jammu and Kashmir, Haryana and Manipur. Putting the two alternatives together, we could say that the States of Manipur, Himachal Pradesh, Jammu and Kashmir and Haryana explored their own non-tax sources to the desired extent. Two developed States, Punjab and Maharashtra, realised per capita non-tax revenue above the average figure, yet with respect to NSDP, there appeared some scope for additional resource mobilisation.

(xvii) As for disaggregated analysis of non-tax sources, comparable data were available only for the period 1972-73 through 1982-83. It was found that the percentage share of interest receipts and dividends rose in the States of Andhra Pradesh, Gujarat, Haryana, Karnataka, Madhya Pradesh, and Tamil Nadu. The overall growth rate of revenue from interest receipts and dividends amounted to 14.21 per cent. In three States, Tripura, Orissa and Manipur, the growth rates were negative. For the remaining States, the rates ranged from 2.01 per cent (Bihar) to 20.78 per cent (Meghalaya). The buoyancy coefficient for all the States taken together was 1.207. In Punjab, the growth rate and buoyancy coefficient were 12.72 per cent and 0.936 respectively.

Taking NSDP as the base, the indices of use of revenue potential for interest receipts and dividends from 1973-74 through 1975-76 markedly overstepped unity in Jammu and Kashmir, Karnataka, Andhra Pradesh, Rajasthan and Haryana. For the period 1979-80 through 1981-82, the States where the indices were above unity were Andhra Pradesh, Karnataka, Haryana, Gujarat, Rajasthan and Tamil Nadu.

Considering population base, the indices of use of revenue potential were more than unity in the States of Haryana, Karnataka, Jammu and Kashmir, Gujarat, Andhra Pradesh,

Rajasthan, Punjab and Maharashtra for both the periods under study. Thus, Punjab provided an interesting case where the index of use of revenue potential for interest receipts and dividends was less than unity when NSDP was chosen as the base but it was more than unity when population was taken as the base.

(xviii) The share of revenue from general services was found to have increased in the case of Assam, Himachal Pradesh, Kerala, Manipur, Meghalaya, Nagaland, Orissa, Rajasthan and West Bengal. The overall growth rate of revenue from general services was 16.53 per cent per annum. In Punjab, the growth rate of revenue from general services turned out to be 11.08 per cent. The buoyancy coefficient for all the States taken together was 1.314. The coefficient varied between 0.602 in Punjab and 3.298 in Tripura. The buoyancy coefficient pointed out that the revenue from general services was least responsive to NSDP in Punjab.

Taking NSDP as the base, the indices of use of revenue potential for general services from 1973-74 through 1975-76 were higher than unity in Karnataka, Jammu and Kashmlr, Rajasthan, Tamil Nadu, Kerala, Haryana, Himachal Pradesh and Maharashtra. For the next period, 1979-80 through 1981-82, the indices exceeded unity in the States of Rajasthan, Orissa, Assam, Himachal Pradesh, Jammu and Kashmir and Karnataka. In Punjab, the index of use of revenue potential (0.4937) was notably less than unity.

With population as the base, the indices of use of revenue potential during the period 1973-74 through 1975-76 were higher than unity in the States of Karnataka, Haryana, Punjab and Maharashtra. For the period 1979-80 through 1981-82, these indices were significantly higher than unity in the States of Rajasthan, Orissa and Himachal Pradesh.

(xix) The share of revenue from social and community services stepped up only in the States of Gujarat, Karnataka, Orissa and Uttar Pradesh, whereas in all other States it stepped down over the period under analysis. The overall growth rate of revenue from social and community services was 12.93 per cent and the rate ranged from 2.73 per cent for Assam to 23.69 per cent for Meghalaya. The buoyancy coefficient for all the States taken together was 1.003, and it varied from 0.228 in Assam to 1.501 in Bihar. For Punjab, the growth rate (8.57 per cent) as well as the buoyancy coefficient (0.581) was less than the all States' average.

Under NSDP base, the indices of use of revenue potential for social and community services from 1973-74 through 1975-76, went beyond unity in the States of Kerala, Rajasthan, Maharashtra, Tamil Nadu, Punjab and Haryana. For the period 1979-80 through 1981-82, the States where the indices were markedly above unity were Rajasthan and Kerala.

When population was the base, the indices of use of revenue potential were notably more than unity in the States of Maharashtra, Punjab and Kerala for both the periods under our study. Thus, Punjab could gain added revenue through social and community services only with NSDP as the base.

(xx) An increase in the percentage contribution of revenue from economic services was observed only in the States of Bihar, Jammu and Kashmir, Maharashtra, Orissa and Punjab. For all the States taken together, the growth rate was 11.97 per cent and the rate varied from 0.82 per cent in Manipur to 25.91 per cent in Maharashtra. The overall buoyancy coefficient was 1.096; the coefficient had a range of 0.096 (Manipur) to 1.972 (Bihar). For Punjab, the growth rate and buoyancy coefficient were 14.05 per cent and 1.090 respectively.

Taking NSDP as the base, the indices of use of revenue potential for economic services during the period 1973-74 through 1975-76 exceeded unity in the States of Jammu and Kashmir, Himachal Pradesh, Madhya Pradesh, Haryana and Karnataka. For the period 1979-80 through 1981-82, the indices were above unity in Jammu and Kashmir, Madhya Pradesh, Himachal Pradesh and Orissa.

With population as the base, the indices of use of revenue potential were more than unity in the States of Jammu and Kashmir, Himachal Pradesh, Haryana, Karnataka, Maharashtra, Madhya Pradesh and Punjab. For the next period *i.e.* 1979-80 through 1981-82, the indices of use of revenue potential overstepped unity in the States of Jammu and Kashmir, Haryana, Himachal Pradesh, Maharashtra, Madhya Pradesh and Punjab. Thus, in Punjab there was some possibility of raising additional revenue from economic services if NSDP was considered the base. Had Punjab attained the average effective rate, it could have utilised this source for additional resources to the extent of Rs. 3186 lakhs.

(xxi) Now we discuss specifically the State lottery scheme as a source of non-tax revenue. The scheme which has been introduced by various State Governments since 1968, has gained considerable importance among people of all walks of life in the country. For the States running lottery schemes, the average share of lotteries to States' non-tax revenue was 2.45 per cent in 1968-69; it expanded to 2.79 per cent in 1982-83. In certain States like Himachal Pradesh, its share went up as high as 20 per cent of non-tax revenue. The contribution of State lotteries in Punjab, though not very significant during the years 1972-73 through 1979-80, has lately picked up and now it is about 4-5 per cent of State's own non-tax revenue.

The revenue from State lotteries grew at a rate of 10.35 per cent per annum during the study period. The growth rate was the maximum in West Bengal (32.11 per cent) and the minimum in Karnataka (5.52 per cent). In certain other States, *viz.* Himachal Pradesh, Uttar Pradesh and Punjab, the growth rate was more than 20 per cent. Keeping in view the various constraints in mobilising resources through additional tax and non-tax sources, the method of raising resources through lotteries should be considered a significant one.

(xxii) Considering the fact that the lottery scheme was introduced primarily to collect additional revenue for the States, what is important is the net contribution of lotteries to the State exchequer, *i.e.* what is left after paying prizes to the winners and commission to the agents, and incurring related administrative expenses. For all the States taken together, the gross receipts from State lotteries were estimated to be Rs. 3942 lakhs against the total expenditure of Rs. 2735 lakhs in 1978-79. During 1982-83, the gross receipts zoomed up to Rs. 11137 lakhs against the total expenditure of Rs. 7591 lakhs. Thus, expenditure in relation to gross receipts appeared to have slightly diminished from 68.38 per cent to 68.16 per cent. The highest expenditure on the conduct of lotteries was observed in the case of Andhra Pradesh which actually incurred a loss of 42.95 per cent. In respect of the remaining States, the expenditure ranged between 38.89 per cent in Assam and 91.72 per cent in Himachal Pradesh.

(xxiii) In Punjab, the lottery scheme was introduced in July

1968. In 1968-69, the scheme yielded gross receipts of Rs. 77.67 lakhs against an expenditure of Rs. 31.17 lakhs. This gave a net profit of Rs. 46.50 lakhs which formed 59.82 per cent of the gross receipts. However, over the period, the expenditure on State lotteries mounted disproportionately. In 1982-83, the gross receipts and expenditure constituted Rs. 1017.13 lakhs and Rs. 913.32 lakhs respectively. This left a meagre net profit of 10.21 per cent. The downward trend in the net proceeds from State lotteries could be explained in terms of ever-increasing prize money and commission and bonus paid to the agents.

(xxiv) In order to examine the socio-economic implications of State lotteries in general and distributional implications in particular, primary data from participants and non-participants were collected. An analysis of the data showed that the proportion of the participant households was more amongst the lower castes than amongst the upper castes. A religion-wise comparison of the participant and non-participant households revealed that the Hindus participate more in State lotteries than the Sikhs.

(xxv) An examination of the type of accommodation indicated that the proportion of households living in rented accommodation was more for the participant households (35.71 per cent) than for the non-participant households (31.82 per cent). Further, the proportion of households living in pucca houses was less for participants (82.86 per cent) than for non-participant (93.64 per cent). Whereas 7.85 per cent of the participant households had katcha houses, there was no such non-participant households. The average value of the owned house was more for non-participants (1.27 lakhs) than for participants (Rs. 1.10 lakhs). Thus, the instinct to improve the housing accommodation may be one of the factors inducing people to participate in State lotteries.

(xxvi) The sex ratio was lower among the non-participant households than among the participant households. The presence of a relatively large number of females in a family might be the cause of a household going in for the lottery scheme.

(xxvii) The proportion of nuclear families was higher among the participant households (80.00 per cent) than among the non-participant households (70.91 per cent), but in the case of joint families, it was the other way round. Perhaps the nuclear families were more interested in windfall gains than the joint families where the number of earners was expected to be comparatively large.

(xxviii) The proportion of the population below the age of 30 years was more among the participant household (52.09 per cent) than among the non-participant households (46.41 per cent). We may say that the population of the participant households generally belonged to younger age groups where the participants might be interested in fortuitous gains for education and marriages of their children.

(xxix) Comparing the marital status of the population, it was noticed that the proportions of both unmarried and widow/widower persons were higher among the participant households than among the non-participant households.

(xxx) It was revealed that the proportion of the population with no formal education was more in the case of participants (15.30 per cent) than in the case of non-participants (6.72 per cent). The same was true of the population with education up to middle standard. We could, therefore, infer that the level of education was generally lower among participants than among non-participants.

(xxxi) It was also observed that the proportion of employed persons was higher among participants than among non-participants. The reverse was the case with unemployed persons. The data on employment status revealed that all the employers in the sample were non-participants. And it was only in the case of own-account workers that a relatively high proportion of participants was observed. For all other categories of workers, *viz.* wage/salary-earners and unpaid family workers, proportion of non-participants was more than that of participants.

A breakdown of the employed workers showed that the incidence of State lotteries was relatively high among the workers in low-income categories like peons, sweepers, street hawkers and small shop-owners. Workers like advocates, basking in some black money to some extent, were also extensively participating in State lotteries.

(xxxii) Per capita income of the participant households (Rs. 432.02) was found out to be less than that of non-participant households (Rs. 519.48). Further, whereas the proportion of households with per capita income below Rs. 200 per month was more among participants than among non-participants, it was reverse in the case of households with per capita income of Rs. 501-Rs. 1000. However, for the topmost income groups (*i.e.* households with per capita income of more than Rs. 1000 per month), the proportion of participants was more than that of non-participants.

(xxxiii) Further, the majority of non-participants considered it a form of gambling, hence unethical, to participate in State lotteries.

(xxxiv) Out of the 140 participant households consisting of 1198 persons, we could identify 162 respondents who had actually participated in State lotteries. The average number of participant persons per household worked out to 1.16. From a majority of the families (85 per cent), only one person per family participated in State lotteries. The participating persons were approached in order to record their views on the operation of existing lottery scheme. Most of these participants had a propensity towards gambling, they considered lottery to be a variant of gambling and therefore liked the scheme.

(xxxv) The bulk of these participant persons were in favour of lottery tickets of lower denomination and preferred a large number of small prizes to a handful of bumper prizes. May be they found a high chance of winning a prize in a host of prizes.

(xxxvi) Some of the participants complained of malpractices in the current lottery schemes. They suggested that the draw should be held at a fixed time on the appointed day and the sale of tickets should be stopped one week before the date of draw to avoid the sale of tickets even after the draw. They grumbled about the sale of duplicate tickets, too.

(xxxvii) In many cases it was observed that small prizes (say less than Rs. 100), which were required to be collected from the commission agents direct, were seldom paid in cash. Commission agents coaxed and coerced the prize-winners to purchase prize-amounts, worth of lottery tickets.

From the above study, it may be concluded that most of the States made half-hearted tax efforts during the period under study. The percentage of tax to per capita income was generally low in the States with relatively high per capita income, *viz.* Punjab, Haryana and Maharashtra. In other words, the burden of State taxes in these States was comparatively light. This indicates that Punjab did not put in adequate efforts for raising revenue commensurate with the taxable capacity of the State. Punjab is the richest State in terms of per capita income but it does not apply the highest effective rate for tax revenue. Normally, the taxable capacity in a State with per capita income higher than that of an average State is also expected to be higher. This means that if Punjab applies somewhat higher tax rates, as progressivity demands, it can mobilise some additional resources from its own tax sources, particularly from profession tax, sales tax, motor vehicles tax, electricity duty, surcharge on land revenue and agricultural income tax. Although Punjab collected more per capita non-tax revenue than the all States' average, yet in relation to NSDP, there exists some scope for further resource mobilisation. Punjab can add to its resources from general services, social and community services, and economic services. The significance of State lotteries as a source of public revenue appears to lie not in the amount of money collected, but in the novelty of attempt by the State governments to find the wherewithal for their expenditure programmes.

The incidence of State lotteries has been found to be higher among the low castes, low-educated groups and low-income strata. Such persons are generally employed as peons, sweepers, street hawkers, and small shop-owners, who mostly tend to gamble. In order to make the lottery scheme a success, it is suggested that there should be a host of small prizes rather than a handful of bumper prizes. It is observed that most of the participants like lottery tickets of low denominations. Therefore, as far as possible, the maximum price of lottery tickets and the amounts of prizes offered by different States/agencies should be controlled and uniformally fixed by the Union Government.

APPENDIX—I

QUESTIONNAIRE

SOME ASPECTS OF RAISING ADDITIONAL RESOURCES IN PUNJAB—A CASE STUDY OF STATE LOTTERIES

A. Identification particulars

1. Name of the locality ————————
2. Serial Number of the household ————————
3. Name and address of the household head ————————
4. Name of the respondent ————————
5. Relationship of the respondent with the head of the household ————————
6. To which State do you belong ? ————————
7. (a) Whether belongs to the
   (i) Scheduled Castes Yes/No
   (ii) Scheduled Tribes Yes/No
   (iii) Backward classes Yes/No

   (b) Caste ————

   (c) Religion ————

8. (a) Type of residential accommodation
   (i) Owned
   (ii) Rented
   (iii) Sharing on temporary basis

(iv) Free from the employer

(v) Other (specify)

If rented, rent paid Rs.——p.m.

(b) Facilities available in the house :

Electricity	Yes/No
Water	Tap/Handpump/Street tap/Street handpump/ well

(c) Type of house — Pucca/Semi Pucca/ Katcha/other (specify)

(i) Number of living rooms ——————

(ii) Covered area of the house ——————

(iii) Approximate value of the house Rs. ————

9. Whether you or any member of your family purchase lottery tickets ? Yes/No

(a) If yes, name of the member(s) who purchase the lottery tickets

1. ——————
2. ——————
3. ——————
4. ——————

(b) If no,

(i) Do you know about the existence of lotteries ? Yes/No

(ii) What are the reasons for not purchasing the lottery tickets ?

1. ——————
2. ——————
3. ——————

10. Household income (per month) Rs.————

B. Household particulars

Sr. No.	*Name of the members*	*Relationship with the head of the household*	*Age*	*Sex*	*Marital* status*	*Education***

*1. Married
2. Unmarried
3. Widower/widow
4. Divorced
5. Separated

***General Education*

1. No formal education
2. Primary
3. Middle
4. Matric/Higher Secondary
5. Graduate and above
6. Technical education :
   (a) Less than graduates
   (b) Graduate and above

*Main*** activity*	*If employed*		*Income (Rs. per month)*	*Have you ever purchased a lottery ticket ?*
	*Employment status*****	*Nature of employment******		
				Yes/No

***1. Employed
2. Unemployed (seeking, available and wanting work)
3. House-keeping
4. Student
5. Unable to work (child, old, crippled, ill, etc.)
6. Persons living on rents, dividends, interest payments, pensions, remittances, etc.
7. Other (specify)

****1. Employer
2. Own account worker
3. Unpaid family workers
4. Wage or salary earner
5. Contract worker
6. Any other (specify)

*****1. Regular full time
2. Regular part-time
3. Casual
4. Seasonal
5. Contractual
6. Other (specify)

C. Ask these questions when the answer to the question number 9 in block A is yes

	1	2	3
1. Have you ever purchased a lottery ticket ?	______	______	______
If yes	Yes/No	Yes/No	Yes/No
(a) When did you purchase lottery tickets for the first time ?	______	______	______
(b) Who introduced you to lottery ?	(i) Newspapers (ii) Radio/TV (iii) Relatives/ friends (iv) Lottery Stall (v) Other (specify)	(i) Newspapers (ii) Radio/TV (iii) Relatives/ friends (iv) Lottery Stall (v) Other (specify)	(i) Newspapers (ii) Radio/TV (iii) Relatives/ friends (iv) Lottery Stall (v) Other (specify)
(c) Are you still purchasing the lottery tickets ?	Yes/No	Yes/No	Yes/No
If yes, (i) Do you purchase lottery tickets ?	(i) Weekly (ii) Fortnightly (iii) Monthly (iv) Casually	(i) Weekly (ii) Fortnightly (iii) Monthly (iv) Casually	(i) Weekly (ii) Fortnightly (iii) Monthly (iv) Casually

(ii) Frequency	(i) Regular (ii) Irregular (iii) Casual	(i) Regular (ii) Irregular (iii) Casual	(i) Regular (ii) Irregular (iii) Casual
(iii) Number of tickets bought per month and expenditure incurred	No. of tickets—— Exp.———	No. of tickets—— Exp.———	No. of tickets—— Exp.———
(iv) Price of the ticket usually purchased	Re. 1 Rs. 2 Rs. 5 Rs. 10 Rs. 20 Rs. 50 Rs. 100 Rs. 500	Re. 1 Rs. 2 Rs. 5 Rs. 10 Rs. 20 Rs. 50 Rs. 100 Rs. 500	Re. 1 Rs. 2 Rs. 5 Rs. 10 Rs. 20 Rs. 50 Rs. 100 Rs. 500
(v) Have you ever purchased lottery tickets of higher denominations ?	Rs. 10 Rs. 20 Rs. 50 Rs. 100 Rs. 500	Rs. 10 Rs. 20 Rs. 50 Rs. 100 Rs. 500	Rs. 5 Rs. 10 Rs. 20 Rs. 50 Rs. 100 Rs. 500

2. If not purchasing lottery ticket now,

(a) when did you stop it ?	———	———	———
(b) Why did you stop it ? (give reasons)	1. ——— 2. ———	1.——— 2.———	1.——— 2.———
(c) What was your average monthly expenditure on lotteries ?	———	———	———

3. Amount spent on lottery tickets during the last month/year (Rs.)	1		2		3	
	Month	Year	Month	Year	Month	Year
On Punjab State Lotteries	___	___	___	___	___	___
On other State(s) lotteries	___	___	___	___	___	___

4. Do you know anyone who ever got a lottery prize ?	Yes/No	Yes/No	Yes/No
If yes,			
Name of the winner	___	___	___
Relationship with him	___	___	___
Date of draw, if known	___	___	___
Price of ticket	___	___	___
Amout of prize	___	___	___
Actual amount received after all the deductions	___	___	___

What are the items on which the money received was spent

Name of the items	*Amount spent*	*Name of the items*	*Amount spent*

5. Do you know about the following games :	Yes/No	Yes/No	Yes/No
(i) Tambola	___	___	___

(ii) Satta (Matka system)	———		———		———	
(iii) Satta (Bull and Bear or speculation)	———		———		———	
(iv) Shatranj	———		———		———	
(v) Playing card game (Flash)	———		———		———	
(vi) Rope game (batti system)	———		———		———	
(vii) Game through machines	———		———		———	
(viii) Any other (specify)	———		———		———	
6. Have you or any other member of your family ever engaged in any of the above games	Yes/No		Yes/No		Yes/No	
If yes,						
(a) Name of the member	———		———		———	
(b) Name of the game	1. 2.		1. 2.		1. 2.	
(c) Frequency	(i) Regular (ii) Irregular (iii) Casual		(i) Regular (ii) Irregular (iii) Casual		(i) Regular (ii) Irregular (iii) Casual	
(d) Gain/loss incurred in the last month/year (Rs.)	*Gain*	*Loss*	*Gain*	*Loss*	*Gain*	*Loss*
Last month	———	———	———	———	———	———
Last year	———	———	———	———	———	———

	1	2	3
(e) Total gain/loss incurred ever since the game was played (Rs.)	——— ———	——— ———	——— ———
(f) For how long participated in that game ?	———————	———————	———————
7. Do you consider lottery a form of gambling ?	Yes/No	Yes/No	Yes/No
8. In your opinion what should be the duration of lottery draw ?	(i) Daily (ii) Weekly (iii) Fortnightly (iv) Monthly (v) Any other (specify)	(i) Daily (ii) Weekly (iii) Fortnightly (iv) Monthly (v) Any other (specify)	(i) Daily (ii) Weekly (iii) Fortnightly (iv) Monthly (v) Any other (specify)
9. What should be the value of lottery tickets ?	Re. 1 Rs. 2 Rs. 5 Rs. 10 Rs. 20 Rs. 50 Rs. 100 Rs. 500	Re. 1 Rs. 2 Rs. 5 Rs. 10 Rs. 20 Rs. 50 Rs. 100 Rs. 500	Re. 1 Rs. 2 Rs. 5 Rs. 10 Rs. 20 Rs. 50 Rs. 100 Rs. 500
10. Are you in favour of lotteries of			
(i) Large number of small prizes	Yes/No	Yes/No	Yes/No
(ii) Small number of bumper prizes	Yes/No	Yes/No	Yes/No
(iii) A combination of both	Yes/No	Yes/No	Yes/No

11. Do you like that State lotteries should continue	Yes/No	Yes/No	Yes/No
If yes, why ? (give reasons)	1. ————	1. ————	1. ————
	2. ————	2. ————	2. ————
If no, why ? (give reasons)	1. ————	1. ————	1. ————
	2. ————	2. ————	2. ————
12. From where do you purchase lottery tickets ?	(i) Lottery stall (ii) Lottery hawker (iii) Any other (specify)	(i) Lottery stall (ii) Lottery hawker (iii) Any other (specify)	(i) Lottery stall (ii) Lottery hawker (iii) Any other (specify)
13. If you get a bumber draw (of more than Rs. 1 lakh), what would you do with that money ?			
(i) Improve living	————	————	————
(ii) Buy land	————	————	————
(iii) Construct a house	————	————	————
(iv) Start new enterprise	————	————	————
(v) Educate children	————	————	————
(vi) Marriage of children	————	————	————
(vii) Pay off debts	————	————	————

(viii) Help relatives/friends	______	______	______
(ix) Deposit in the bank	______	______	______
(x) No thought is yet given	______	______	______
(xi) Any other (specify)	______	______	______
14. Do you encourage other members of your family to buy lottery tickets ?	Yes/No	Yes/No	Yes/No
15. (a) Do you think that the method of drawing State lottery is fair ?	Yes/No	Yes/No	Yes/No
(b) If no, what are the malpractices ?	1. 2. 3.	1. 2. 3.	1. 2. 3.
(c) What in your opinion should be done to improve the method of draw ?	1. 2.	1. 2.	1. 2.
16. (a) Do you think that the sellers of lottery ticket (commission agents) are fair in their dealings ?	Yes/No	Yes/No	Yes/No
(b) If no, what are the malpractices adopted by them ?	1. 2. 3.	1. 2. 3.	1. 2. 3.

APPENDIX-II

Selection of Households in Selected Wards/Localities

Ward number/ locality	*Number of households listed*		*Number of households selected*	
	Participant	*Non-participant*	*Participant*	*Non-participant*
2	150	100	19	12
5	160	90	20	11
7	140	110	17	14
8	125	125	16	16
10	100	150	12	19
18	135	115	17	14
25	145	105	18	13
Squatter localities	165	85	21	11
Total	1120	880	140	110

BIBLIOGRAPHY

Acharya, G.N., "Ganapati Wins All Lotteries," *Mainstream*, Vol. 9, Nos. 1-3, 1970.

Ahmed, Mahfooz, "Cost of Tax Collection in India," *Economic and Political Weekly*, Vol. III, No. 17, February 17, 1968.

Aiyar, S. Narayan, "Socialism and Heavy Taxation", *Swarajya*, Vol. 11, No. 18, October 29, 1966.

Anantharaman, M.A., "Socialist Lotteries," *Commerce*, February 5, 1972.

Ansari, M.M., "Resource Mobilisation through Taxation", *Yojana*, Vol. XXVIII, No. 16, September 16-30, 1984.

Ammannaya, Keshava, "Economics of State Lotteries", *Mysore Economic Review*, Vol. 55, No. 2, February 1970.

Bahl, Roy W., "A Regression Approach to Tax Effort and Tax Ratio Analysis", *IMF Staff Papers*, Vol. XVIII, No. 3, 1971.

——, "A Representative Tax System Approach to Measuring Tax Effort in Developing Countries", *IMF Staff Papers*, Vol. XIX, No. 1, 1972.

Baliga, B. Vittal, "Code of Conduct for Lotteries", *The Economic Times*, June 18, 1970.

Bapat, L. G., "The Economics of State Lotteries", *Swarajya*, Vol. 16, No. 30, January 22, 1972.

——, "Tax on State Lotteries", *Eastern Economist*, Vol. 59, No. 3, July 21, 1972.

Bhargava, P.K., "How to Raise Additional Resources without Adding to Inflation", *Capital*, Vol. 167, No. 4180, September 9, 1971.

——, "Resource Mobilisation in U.P.", *Eastern Economist*, Vol. 73, No. 1, July 6, 1979.

——, "The Indian Tax System : Need for Rationalisation", *Indian Journal of Economics*, Vol. 65, No. 1, July, 1984.

Bhatia, M.L., "The Problem of Tax Evasion in India", *AICC Economic Review*, Vol. 20, No. 11, December 15, 1968.

Bhatia, Shankar Dass, "God Rewarded Me", *The Hindustan Times*, October 12, 1980.

Bhatia, V.P., "Forty New Lakhpatis a Month", *Organiser*, April 11, 1970.

Bhattacharyya, Phani, "Craze for Lotteries", *The Statesman*, January 4, 1970.

Bhatt, V.V., "Taxation and Economic Development", *Economic and Political Weekly*, Vol. VII, No. 26, June 24, 1972.

Biswas, C.R., "Taxation Without Tears", *The Economic Times*, November 1, 1981.

Biswas, S.K., "Lottery Extension of Welfare Plans", *The Times of India*, July 12, 1978.

Borker, V.V., "The Theory of Taxation : From Neutrality to Optimality", *Indian Economic Journal*, Vol. 26, No. 3, January-March 1979.

Chandrasekhar, S., "Inter-State Disparities of Tax Incidence in India", *Economic and Political Weekly*, Vol. III, No. 22, June 1, 1968.

——, "Tax Structure of State Government", *AICC Economic Review*, Vol. XX, No. 11, December 15, 1968.

Char, S.V., "Tapping Tax Potential : Roping in of Rural Rich Vital", *The Economic Times*, April 29, 1981.

Chelliah, Raja J., "Trends in Taxation in Developing Countries", *IMF Staff Papers*, Vol. XVIII, No. 2, 1971.

Chelliah, Raja J. and Narain Sinha, *Measurement of Tax Effort of State Governments 1973-76* (New Delhi, National Institute of Public Finance and Policy, 1983).

Chintamani, R.M., "Legalised Gambling", *Commerce*, February 19, 1972.

Dandekar, V.M., "Government by Gambling", *Economic and Political Weekly*, Vol. V, Nos. 3, 4, 5 (Annual Number), January 1970.

Dhar, Karabi, "Lotteries and Socialism": *Swarajya*, January 17, 1970.

Dhawan, B.D., "Cost of Tax Collection in India : A Comment", *Economic and Political Weekly*, Vol III, No. 16, April 20, 1968.

Dhesi, Autar S., and Ghuman, B.S., "Aspects of Financing State

Plans (With Special Reference to Punjab)," *Margin*, Vol. 16, No. 3, April 1984.

——, "The Responsiveness of State Taxes : A Comparative Study of Punjab and Haryana", *Indian Economic Review*, Vol. 19, No. 2, July-December 1984.

Dikshit, D.V., "Evolution and Growth of State Lotteries", *The Times of India* (Suppl), February 7, 1979.

Doshi, S.N., "Lottery Winners", *The Times of India*, March 7, 1972.

D'Souja, Carol, "Spend a Rupee on Your Dreams", *The Times of India* (Mag.), June 3, 1979.

Dutta, A., "State Lotteries as Revenue Earners : An Analysis", *Yojna*, Vol. XVI, No. 2, February 6, 1972.

Einzig, Paul, "British : Taxation Prospectus", *Eastern Economist*, Vol. 46, No. 3, January 21, 1966.

Faridi, Javed, "The Lure of State Lotteries", *The Hindustan Times*, October 12, 1980.

Gupta, Anand P., "The Budget that can Help : Reforming the Tax Structure", *The Economic Times*, February 18-19, 1981.

Gupta, Anupam, "Tax Revenue in West Bengal : Stagnant Base and Low Elasticity", *The Economic Times*, September 22, 1984.

Gupta, J.R., *Burden of Tax in Punjab* (New Delhi, Concept Publishing Company, 1983).

Gulati, I.S., "Agenda for Tax Base Reform", *Economic and Political Weekly*, Vol. VI, Nos. 42-43, October 16, 1971.

Honavar, R.M., "The Resources Problem in India", *Commerce*, Vol. 142, No. 3636, February 21, 1981.

Institute for Social and Economic Change, Bangalore, *Socio-Economic Impact of Removal of Prohibition, Socio-Economic Impact of State Lotteries and Horse Racing in India*, Mimeographed, February 1976.

Jain, M.M., "Income Elasticity of Indian Tax Structure 1955-56 to 1965-66", *Economic and Political Weekly*, Vol. IV, No. 18, May 3, 1969.

——, "Omtimal Taxation and Efficient Public Production", *Indian Journal of Economics*, Vol. 59, No. 3, January 1979.

Jain, Ram Pyare, "Rationalising the Tax Structure to Promote Economic Growth", *Capital*, Vol. 166, No. 4151, February 18, 1971.

Jha, L.K., "Tax Reform : The Unfinished Task", *The Economic Times*, May 6, 1985.

Jha, Prem Shekar, "The Resource Crunch : Raising Money Through Tax Reform", *The Times of India*, January 21, 1985.

Jhaveri, N.J., "Resource Mobilisation Through Indirect Taxes : Some Aspects of Fifth Plan Strategy" *Economic and Political Weekly*, Vol. IX, No. 37, September 14, 1974.

John, C., "New Levies Unlikely to Cause Setback to the Economy", *Southern Economist*, Vol. 20, No. 22, March 15, 1982.

Kale, S.C., "U.P. Raises Extra Revenue : Avoiding Insolvency", *The Times of India*, November 9, 1974.

Khanna, C.L., "Resource Mobilisation in States", *Mainstream*, Vol. 12, No. 46, July 13, 1974.

Khurana, Iqbal Chand, "Indian Lottery—A Social Commitment", *Indian Express*, July 11, 1985.

Kumara, Sekhar R., "Bribing the People", *Swarajya*, March 28, 1970.

Kusumakar, H., "State Lotteries Lose Appeal but Remain Profitable", *The Times of India*, July 27, 1974.

Lakdawala, D.T., "Is India the Highest Taxed Nation ?" *Journal of Indian Institution of Bankers*, Vol. 36, No. 2, April 1965.

Lotz, Jorgen R. and Morss, Elliot R., "Measuring Tax Effort in Developing Countries", *IMF Staff Papers*, Vol. XIV, No. 3, November 1967.

——, "A Theory of Tax Level Determinants for Developing Countries", *Economic Development and Cultural Change*, Vol. XVIII, No. 3, April 1970.

Maxwell, J., *Fiscal Policy* (New York, Henry Holt and Company, 1955).

Mehta, B.C. and Menaria, Rajendra, "Federal Transfers and Tax Efforts in Indian States", *Rajasthan Economic Journal*, Vol. VI, No. 1, January 1982.

Mehta, Vinod, "Socialist Lotteries", *Economic and Political Weekly*, Vol. VII, No. 24, June 10, 1972.

Mitra, Ashok, "Taxation", *Seminar 57*, May 1964.

Mittal, S.N. "Role of Taxation in Indian Economy", *Southern Economist*, Vol. VIII, No. 22, March 15, 1970.

Mohan, Saroj, "Reform of Tax Structure", *The Economic Times*, April 4, 1981.

Murthy, N. Krishna, "Common Errors in Taxation", *The Economic Times*, June 16, 1984.

Nagaraja, N., "Tax Revenue in a Developing Economy", *AICC Economic Review*, Vol. XVI, Nos. 13-15, January 6, 1965.

Nambiar, K.V. and Rao, M. Govinda, "Tax Performance of States", *Economic and Political Weekly*, Vol. VII, No. 21, May 20, 1972.

Narasimhachar, K.T., "State Lotteries in Tamil Nadu", *Swarajya*, Vol. 19, No. 49, June 7, 1975.

Pai, M.R., "State Lotteries, *Financial Express*, March 31, 1970

Patel, M.L., "Basis for Taxation in the Developing Economy of India", *AICC Economic Review*, Vol. 17, No. 4, August 1, 1965.

Patil, J.F., "Central Taxation I—Level Composition in States", *The Economic Times*, November 16, 1983.

——, "Central Taxation II—Per Capita Revenue from Shared Taxes Received by States", *The Economic Times*, November 17, 1983.

Raghavachari, T.N.S., "The Lottery Craze", *Swarajya*, Vol. 20, No. 8, August 23, 1975.

Rajagopal, V., "Central and State Government and Lotteries", *Swarajya*, May 23, 1970.

Rajagopalachari, C., "Additional Tax Burden", *Swarajya*, Vol. 9, No. 16, October 17, 1964.

——, "State Raffles and Revenue", *Swarajya*, Vol. XIII, No. 9, August 31, 1968.

——, "Lotteries to Square the Budgets", *Swarajya*, Vol. 13, No. 12, September 21, 1968.

——, "Secularism Lotteries and Contraceptives", *Sarvodaya*, Vol. 20, No. 4, October 1970.

Ramakrishna, P., "Role of Agents and Middlemen", *The Economic Times*, November 1, 1981.

Rangachari, A.V., "Economics of State Lotteries", *Southern Economic Review*, Vol. I, No. 4, June 1972.

Ranina, H.P., "Winnings from Races and Lotteries", *Financial Express*, January 7, 1975.

Rao, B. Ramakrishna, "Need for Tax Reform", *Capital*, Vol. 186, No. 4654, April 27, 1981.

Rao, C.H. Hanumantha, "Resource Prospects from the Rural Poor", *Economic and Political Weekly*, Vol. 4, No. 13, March 29, 1969.

Rao, K.B.K., "Income Elasticity of Central and States Taxes", *Margin*, Vol. I, No. 3, April 1969.

——, "Does the Indian Tax Policy Have a Rationale" ? *Margin*, Vol. 4, No. 3, April 1972.

——, "Taxation and Social Justice", *Margin*, Vol. 5, No. 3, April 1973.

Rao, M. Govinda, "Economic and Political Determinants of States' Tax Revenue : A Case Study of Four States", *Economic and Political Weekly*, Vol. XIV, No. 47, November 24, 1979.

Reddy, D. Narasimha and Naidu, K. Muridaraswamy, "State Raffles—An Economic Appraisal", *Southern Economist*, Vol. 8, No. 5, July 1, 1969.

Reddy, K.N., "Inter-State Tax Effort", *Economic and Political Weekly*, Vol. X, No. 50, December 13, 1975.

Rele, Subhash J., "State Lotteries or Private Loot", *The Patriot*, November 22, 1984.

Santhanam, K., 'Parasites All", *Eastern Economist*, Vol. 51, No. 18, November 1, 1968.

Sarang, "Lotteries at Odds", *The Economic Times*, February 12, 1972.

Sauldie, Madan M., "Taxes in Africa", *Eastern Economist*, Vol. 46, No. 8, February 25, 1966.

Sekhar, K. Kumara, "Bribing the People", *Swarajya*, Vol. 14, No. 39, March 28, 1970.

Sen, Pradeep Kumar, "Tax Policy for Economic Growth : Indian Experience", *Southern Economist*, Vol. 16, No. 15, December 1, 1977.

Sen, S.C., "State Lotteries : For Whose Benefit", *The Times of India*, July 25, 1971.

Sharma, J.N., "Measurement of Tax Effort by the States", *Southern Economist*, Vol. 10, No. 12, October 15, 1971.

Shreekant, G. Joag and Mehta, Subhash C., "Mismarketing of Dream", *The Economic Times*, November 1, 1981.

Singh, Rukhan, "Case Study. What is the Response to the Lottery Scheme ?" *The Economic Times*, June 13, 1970.

——, "How to Improve the Lottery Scheme", *The Economic Times*, June 14, 1970.

Smith, Adam, *The Wealth of Nations* (New York, Random House INC., 1937).

Srinivas, P.R., "Unwarranted Taxation", *Swarajya*, Vol. 8, No. 37, March 14, 1964.

Srivastava, R.L., "Taxation in Underdeveloped Countries with Special Reference to India", *AICC Economic Review*, Vol. 16, No. 11, November 10, 1964.

Srivastava, Suresh Chandra, "Is India the Highest Taxed Country in the World ?" *Capital*, Vol. 165, No. 4135, October 22, 1970.

Subrahmanyam, G., "On the Possibility of Conflict in Inter-State Tax Efforts : A General Note", *Margin*, Vol. 15, No. 3, April 1983.

Sury, M.M., "Elasticity of Tax Revenue—Some Measurement Problem", *Indian Economic Journal*, Vol. 26, No. 1, July-September 1978.

Tantia, Rameshwar, "We are the Highest Taxed People in the World", *Organiser*, Vol. 19, No. 42, June 5, 1966.

The Times of India, "Lottery Becomes the Spaniard's Santa", *The Times of India*, January 1, 1984.

Thimmaiah, G., "The Sensitivity of the Taxes of the New Mysore State", *Indian Economic Journal*, Vol. XII, No. 3, January-March 1965.

——, "State Lottery Scheme", *AICC Economic Review*, March 15, 1969.

Varma, C.R. Thiagaraja, "Taxation in Developing Countries", *Eastern Economist*, Vol. 58, No. 7, February 18, 1972.

——, "Taxation in Japan", *Eastern Economist*, Vol. 62, No. 6, February 8, 1974.

Venkateswarm, R.J., "The New Millionaires", *Swarajya*, Vol. 14, No. 50, June 13, 1970.

Reports and Other Official Documents

Government of India, Ministry of Finance, *Report of the Taxation Enquiry Commission*, 1953-54, (New Delhi, 1955), Vol. I.

——, Ministry of Finance, *Report of the Indirect Taxation Enquiry Committee*, (New Delhi, October 1977 and January 1978), Vol. I-II.

——, Ministry of Planning, *Estimates of State Domestic Product 1960-61—1982-83* (New Delhi, January 1984).

Reserve Bank of India, *Report on Currency and Finance*.

——, *Reserve Bank of India Bulletins*.

Government of Punjab, *Statistical Abstracts of Punjab*.

——, *Report of the Taxation Enquiry and Resources Committee Punjab* (1971).

——, Punjab Government Budgets.